WHO DARES, RUNS

FROM FOUR STONE OVERWEIGHT TO RUNNING 32 MARATHONS IN 32 DAYS AROUND IRELAND

Gerry Duffy

Ballpoint Press

To my parents Michael and Dorothy Duffy,
my greatest teachers

Published in 2011 by Ballpoint Press
4 Wyndham Park, Bray, Co Wicklow, Republic of Ireland.
Telephone: 086 8217631

ISBN 978-0-95502-983-7

Book design and production by Úna Design

Printed by GraphyCems Industria Gráfica

© Text copyright Gerry Duffy

Cover photograph by Mark Condren

CONTENTS

ACKNOWLEDGEMENTS

So many to thank and thankfully the opportunity to do so is offered throughout the pages you are about to read. However some need mentioning twice.

To my parents for inspiring me to be a good person and to always be honest to myself and others.

To my girlfriend Jacinta, who spent 32 days and nights as my closest friend during the 32 Marathon challenge and who also helped hugely by way of input and support in the writing of this book.

To my brother Tom, for never being afraid to dispense prudent advice over the years, and to Mary, Katherine and Dorothy my three sisters for their friendship. Also to my extended family of Enda (both of them), John Mac and Orla, my favourite sister-in-law.

To the next generation of Mark, Rebecca, Andrew, Gerry, Lucy and Juliana who inspire me every time I get to spend time in their company.

To Bernard Flynn, a close friend, thank you. You played your part in this story. Bernard also introduced me many years ago to PJ Cunningham who helped me in the editing of this book, while Joe Coyle designed it. To photographers Stuart McChesney and Tony Kinlan, who took many of the pictures in this book, thank you.

To Lisa Gibson for sending me an email from Canada, the contents of which you will soon learn about and to my Uncle Tom who helped instil in me an 'early to rise' discipline which I now live by almost every day.

Finally to Ken Whitelaw for being an incredible friend in the year leading into and for being a partner in what became the adventure of a lifetime. Thirty-two marathons in 32 days.

I hope you enjoy this story.

INTRODUCTION

WITHIN half a second of answering the phone, I recognised the voice. It was unmistakable.

Michael O'Leary, the hugely-successful CEO of Ryanair, one of the world's largest airlines, was on the line.

"So, what do you want with an old fart like me?" he asked. "I can't run for s***."

I had just walked in the door of my house in Mullingar when the phone rang. It was almost 9pm on a Thursday night in October 2009. My sister Dorothy, her boyfriend Enda and my girlfriend Jacinta were chatting away in the kitchen so I immediately diverted into the sitting room, closing the door behind me. This call was important and I needed no distractions.

Eddie O'Leary, Michael's younger brother had given him my number. I explained to Michael all about the 32 Marathon challenge and how a friend of mine Ken Whitelaw and I were going to try to run a marathon in every county in Ireland over 32 consecutive days to raise funds for charities. We wanted Michael to put his name to the event and to run a few miles somewhere en route. If he committed, we would be able to announce his participation, thereby creating more awareness to help us with our goals.

"So how can I help?" he asked.

"Would you come to the press launch?" I ventured, rather hesitantly.

"Sure, if I'm in the country. When is it?"

I gave him the venue and the time and he promised to confirm closer to the date. What a coup that would be, having Michael O'Leary at the launch.

"Anything else you want, now that I'm on?" he asked.

"Eh," I stumbled, not expecting a follow-up question. "Can I put your picture on the website saying you have endorsed the event?"

"Sure," he agreed almost dismissively. "Anything else?"

'S***,' I thought to myself, 'think of something quick.'

"Eh, would you run with us?" I blurted out.

There was a brief silence.

"Blooming hell, what do you want an old fart like me to run with you for. I'm useless!"

2

The reality is he knew I wanted him to run. Eddie had already told him about the event. He was just playing a game with me, I thought. I relaxed a little more and decided if I could bank as big a fish as this, it would provide magnificent publicity for us.

"Ah, c'mon now Mick, don't talk rubbish, I've seen you at our local triathlon here in Mullingar every year, and you know you're in good shape."

"If I said 'yes', how far would I have to run?" he asked.

I detected a tone of mischief. It was obvious he was enjoying the conversation. Hell, it was all duck or no dinner now. I decided to cast for the big fish.

"A marathon."

"Are you flaming mad? Not a chance."

Another silence descended and I started to get nervous again.

"Eh, okay," I said, a little crestfallen that he mightn't be putting on his runners. In desperation, I threw another line. "OK, maybe a few miles in Mullingar then, that way you can be home straight after to put your feet up."

"Tell you what," he replied, "I'll do your marathon if you like."

"Great," I replied, delighted at my ability to sell.

"But over two days."

"Eh, sure". I was confused.

"When is the Westmeath one?" he asked.

"On the last day, bank holiday Monday, the 2nd of August," I informed him off the top of my head.

"And when is the Dublin one?"

"On the second day, in the Phoenix Park, the third of July."

"How about I run 13 miles in Dublin and 13 miles in Mullingar?"

I struggled to contain my excitement. This was even better than I had imagined.

"Yeah, that sounds good. Are you sure?" I asked.

"Absolutely. I'll be in touch."

With that he bade me farewell and the line went dead.

CHAPTER 1

THE 32-MARATHON CHALLENGE

11TH NOVEMBER, 2009
4.30PM

THE medical clinic looked very impressive. As I drove around trying to find my way into its grounds, my eyes peering left and right, I noticed it was located in a hub of futuristic commercial blocks, swanky apartments and manicured flora and fauna.

Twenty minutes later I was lying on a patients examination table.

"So, how many years are you doing these 32 marathons over?" the doctor enquired casually as she began my consultation.

"It's not over a few years," I said.

"Well, how long then?"

"Thirty-two days."

She stared at me from beneath her brown-rimmed glasses.

"Pardon?" she asked in disbelief.

"Thirty-two days," I repeated.

I had already done a medical with my own doctor, 'the full monty' of bloods, ECG and stress. All those readings were fine. I was here to do a VO2 max test to see what kind of aerobic shape my 41-year-old frame was in. The doctor was in her early thirties, I'd say. Smartly dressed, she sported a white mid-length surgical coat over the uniformed short sleeved polo t-shirt that her employer clinic dictated she wear. She stared up from the clipboard in silence, her eyes now riveted to mine and slowly placed the clipboard back on the table.

"Thirty-two days," she enunciated slowly as if trying to take in what I had just said.

"Yes, 32 days," I said, almost apologetically.

"Are you serious?"

"Totally."

"Why?" she asked.

"The challenge," I replied.

"Oh, the challenge," she repeated in a tone that suggested she was trying to come to terms with what I was saying. I saw I had her total, undivided attention.

"Is that possible?" she asked.

At that point I was anxious not to confuse confidence with arrogance. After all, I had never done it before.

"Sure," I reply, adding, "not that it won't be hugely difficult, though." I needed to justify to her where I was coming from. "I have a very strong mind and I have done a few tough endurance events in the past. I firmly believe that we are capable of doing so much more than modern thinking would suggest we are capable of doing."

"Such as what?" she asked.

"Such as running 32 marathons in 32 days."

She looked at me again, only her eyes moving, as she tried to read my face. "You're really serious, aren't you?"

"Absolutely."

CHAPTER 2
THE CHALLENGE REVISITED

THAT night I got home late to Mullingar from the medical clinic. I was exhausted following all the tests they carried out on top of what had been an otherwise hectic day as well. I collapsed into the armchair, still regretting that I hadn't had a bigger window of opportunity to convey to the doctor my full passion for the 32-marathon concept which in many ways had taken over my life.

Resting in the armchair, almost immediately I fluttered between half-consciousness and slumber. Before I knew it, I was back in the surroundings I had left earlier in the day. The clinic had looked like every hospital should with a wide open atrium, smelling not of detergent and antiseptic, but of incense mixed with sunflowers. It had Rachmaninoff warming the air and a receptionist that welcomed me with a smile that any toothpaste manufacturer would proudly pay for to endorse their product.

The doctor greets me again, this time warmly, and directs me to take a chair opposite her desk. She looks me up and down and then with a big smile asks: "Do you really think you can run 32 marathons in 32 days? Can this really be done?"

I smile back at her. It's almost like she is giving me a second chance to deny the madness I had thrown at her earlier. I decide to fill in some of the background on my recent life for her so that she could now judge for herself.

Taking a deep breath, I begin by blurting out: "I have changed my mindset completely over the past 15 years and am now confident I can do something like this."

"This belief," I say, "is not some sort of master plan I devised in the mid-nineties. Rather it is a collection of experiences of normal challenges that I have overcome; the same challenges that most of us face every day."

She nods.

Warming to the subject and her apparent approval of my story so far, I give her instances of things I had already managed to achieve.

"I lost more than four stone in weight, I successfully gave up smoking and in the midst of it all overcame a massive fear of public speaking. Achieving these goals got me to believe that I could accept the challenge of even bigger sporting feats. My philosophy now is simple. If someone else can do it, then so can I. If someone else has never done it, then I can be the first."

To the vague sound of the muffled classical music in the background, I press on, mindful that I should try to put what I hope to do in perspective for her so that it doesn't appear either off the wall or big-headed.

"Ok, so I won't ever fly to the moon wearing a superman cape and I will never be capable of bench-pressing 5,000lbs. Nor will I ever play golf on the European Tour for a living (despite my childhood dreams), but I will continue to strive for challenging goals in my life because I now have the belief that I can overcome whatever I choose to tackle."

The doctor listens intently as I tell her about those who have inspired me - I will introduce you to them all later in these pages. Some of them are people who refused to let themselves be held back because of their physical or medical problems. They have brought home to me how blessed I am to have good health. It makes me realise how lucky I am even to contemplate this ambition to run 32 marathons in 32 days.

Their stories inspired me to push myself continuously out of my own comfort zone. In doing so, I have stretched the boundaries over the past number of years and been fortunate to compete in some arduous endurance events.

What my friend Ken Whitelaw and I are about to undertake, I explain to her, is but a step on a journey of discovery.

I glance up to examine the doctor's face; I can see she is taking it all in.

"Well, you're certainly not my average patient," she says, speaking for the first time since I began my monologue.

"But I am," I interject. "I just changed a few beliefs and a few things, that's all."

"Hmmm," she replies, raising an eyebrow. "If you say so."

I woke up with a shiver. Immediately I realised I had lived out in this dream what I had wanted to say to her earlier in the day. To explain to her, and maybe to myself too, who I had become in recent years.

So there you have me, Gerry Duffy, now in my early forties (at the time of writing), fit and healthy (thankfully) and someone who has learned to grow in his own personal life.

Until my late twenties and beyond, I did not realise that life was about growing. I thought that stopped at 21 or so and that once you reached that age it was about getting through life one day at a time. How wrong and how naive my thinking was.

Thankfully when I was 27 I finally began to take the first steps outside of my own personal 'comfort zones'. Over the past 15 years or so I have significantly improved in many aspects of my life that needed changing. Out of some of these, many other doors have opened for me. It is within these that I have found my own sporting Holy Grail. It is important, I feel, to share the more challenging ones with you, for it is within these experiences that I developed the mindset to believe I could run 32 marathons in 32 days.

In my armchair, I recall a quote I have saved on my computer. It is one attributed to Theodore Roosevelt, the 26th President of the United States. *'Believe you can and you're half way there.'*

CHAPTER 3
THE COMFORT ZONE

MY COMFORT ZONE

I used to have a comfort zone where I knew I wouldn't fail.
The same four walls and busy work were really more like jail.
I longed so much to do the things I'd never done before,
But stayed inside my comfort zone and paced the same old floor.
I said it didn't matter that I wasn't doing much.
I said I didn't care for things like commission cheques and such.
I claimed to be so busy with the things inside the zone,
But deep inside I longed for something special of my own.
I couldn't let my life go by just watching others win.
I held my breath; I stepped outside and let the change begin.
I took a step and with new strength I'd never felt before,
I kissed my comfort zone goodbye and closed and locked the door.
If you're in a comfort zone, afraid to venture out,
Remember that all winners were at one time filled with doubt.
A step or two and words of praise can make your dreams come true.
Reach for your future with a smile; success is there for you.
(Author unknown)

COMFORT Zones follow us in everything we do. It is I believe, where we exist or where we leave, whenever we do or don't do something. If there is one thing I've learned over these past 15 years, it is the importance of leaving my comfort zones.

Maybe the great American writer Norman Mailer put it best when he said: "Every moment of one's existence is growing into more or retreating into less. One is always living a little more or dying a little bit."

When I think back on those endless Saturday and Sundays watching sport as the typical couch potato, I think of all the time I was wasting. The hours I spent 'retreating into less.' Most of us end up staying within our comfort zone unless something happens to jolt us out of the habits of least resistance we dwell in.

Believe it or not, it was a photo I viewed and appeared in, which was the seminal moment for me. Let me share the background to it with you.

Since caddying for my father as a seven-year-old, I had been a golf nut. So when I heard my idol Seve Ballesteros was going to be down in Mount Juliet at the 1995 Irish Open Golf Championship. I got on to my good friend Kate McCann – the Director of Golf there – and asked her to arrange a meeting with the five-time Major winner.

Kate duly delivered and it was a thrill to have my picture taken with him and to talk to him. When they arrived Kate looked every bit the professional businesswoman that she was and Seve, well he looked every bit the professional golfer. He was smartly dressed from head to toe in beige trousers, a crisp yellow polo shirt and an orange sweater draped over his shoulders.

"Ola, Gerardo," said Seve, endearingly substituting the 'G' with a 'H', so it sounded like 'Herardo'.

Given my stage fright, I struggled to offer a verbal reply.

"Kate has told me you would like a photograph, si?"

"Yes," I replied. What a conversationalist I was.

And that was it. Well, almost.

As we posed and Kate was getting ready to snap, I felt Seve clutch my shoulder.

"Ah ya, ya, ya. Look! Look!" he spluttered.

"What the hell have I done?" I thought to myself.

His eyes were transfixed on an approaching figure over Kate's left shoulder and he glared intensely, his face filled with excitement.

"Kate, es Keleeee aqui," he gasped.

"What the hell," I thought to myself because I hadn't a clue what he was on about.

"Kate es Sean Keleeee," he repeated, this time slightly louder.

Soon I realised what the commotion was about. He was staring at Sean Kelly, the former professional cyclist.

"Please," said Seve in his most polite broken English.

"Por favor, please hurry," he encouraged.

Both Kate and I got the message and she snapped the photograph quickly. Ballesteros took off like an Olympic sprinter. I knew he was a very keen cyclist, so I figured he must have been a fan of Kelly. Nice day for both of us, I thought to myself. I hoped Seve had remembered to bring a camera.

Two days later, the pharmacist was locking the door behind me as I stood staring at the newly developed picture. I had been so excited about getting my photo taken with my boyhood hero and I couldn't wait to show my golfing friends.

Seve was instantly recognisable. It was the chap beside him who I didn't recognise. Of course I was looking at myself but I was stunned. No, more than that; I was shocked and disgusted. That was the moment I realised that I was massively overweight as I looked at my belly protruding over my waistband.

How could I hang this picture proudly in my house? There and then, I decided it would have to be confined to a private personal glance every six months or so to remind me of that memorable encounter. This picture, I said to myself, will never see the light of day.

Standing there in the street, I felt embarrassed and ashamed for allowing my body to reach this point. I knew long before this that I had a weight problem. I recognised it in previous few years by way of new clothing requirements. Perhaps I was in denial. I had left school nine years previously a very fit, very active and very normal 12 stone 10 lbs. I got into my car, went home and weighed myself.

From 17 years of age through to my mid-twenties, I had done all the usual things most people of that age do. I had enjoyed my life to the full, shared digs, went to college, got a job and had a relationship with a girl whom I was crazy about. That relationship had lasted almost four years. We had broken up in the early nineties and I took it badly at the time. Looking back, my weight had already crept up to almost 15 stone in 1992. I spent the next few years feeling sorry for myself and as a consequence my weight ballooned even higher. By 1995 I had piled on another 28lbs.

Now as I looked at the photograph I realised that my weight had reached a crisis point. I was in a major comfort zone as far as my weight was concerned. That day the scales tipped at just under 17 stone (238 lbs). That's when it hit me. That was the moment that I knew I had to do something about it.

I was 27 years old.

Now to say that everything after that was easy would be to tell a lie. But it is easier if, as in my case, you feel a sense of outrage at yourself. I vowed there and then that I was going to leave this comfort zone of being overweight that I had existed in for too many years. Little did I know that I was about to start changing my whole mindset.

"Every journey begins with the first step," according to the old Chinese proverb. Well I was about to take that first step, as you will see in the next chapter.

At that time too I had other things that needed changing and soon you will learn about them too. I had no idea of the empowerment I was about to instil into my self-belief nor did I know what places this journey I was about to embark on would bring me to. Yes, there would be times when I hit rocky patches: losing weight, giving up smoking, learning how to overcome an almost pathological fear of speaking in public doesn't just happen with a click of the fingers.

There were setbacks and moments when I felt I would be better off relapsing into my old ways. But something had changed. Something had awakened inside me. And because of that I not only left the zone I was in, but found new ones. And then I left them behind too. The realisation of being able to do this is what I want to share with you most of all. They are important to share because it was the combination of all of them that would lead me to believe that I could run 32 marathons in just 32 days.

There is tremendous empowerment in your life when instead of being on automatic pilot inside your head, you are actually plotting and planning challenges ahead and looking forward to achieving them. I call this active living. I cannot tell you just how much energy that alone gives me in my day. And not just energy. Time too. When I was caught in the trap of 'comfort zone' residence, I never left the compound. I got up, went to work, came home, watched television, over-ate and smoked too much.

Now in this new environment beyond the comfort zone, I was about to start rearranging my schedule. When I did I would find I had four hours extra every day in which to do things. Four hours a day for a twentysomething who hopes to live to 80 and beyond is a significant amount of extra time to find.

I believe there are numerous things which stop us from achieving our goals. The belief that life inside a comfort zone can be so much easier and less stressful. For sure, comfort zones are hard to break out of. It is only in the last 15 years or so that I have grown to believe that I have much more ability than I ever gave myself credit for.

So what I've written in these pages is not just about marathons. It is as much about marathons as Moby Dick is a book only about a whale. Yes, it is about running and about marathons and there is a strong sporting theme throughout. But it is also a book about life, about challenging oneself to change bad habits or increase the good habits to get maximum return. It is about breaking out of comfort zones. It is about doing one's best to see a caterpillar turn into a butterfly by breaking out of a cocoon.

It's the other great Andy Warhol quote that I believe in when he observed: "They say time changes things, but you actually have to change them yourself."

The comfort zone remains one of our greatest enemies when it comes to tapping into our potential. We are addicted to where we think we belong. I found that lighting the candle instead of cursing the dark showed me paths I never thought existed for me.

The catalyst for all of the above was in that photograph. For the record it was six o'clock on Monday the 10th of July, 1995.

That week I started running.

CHAPTER 4
NO CIGARETTES IN TOKYO

THE only exercise I had enjoyed after leaving school was golf. In order to lose weight, I knew I needed to come up with something that would help me shed the excess baggage around my midriff. Running seemed an easy solution. I had watched my dad for years out running but never felt the desire to follow in his footsteps. It didn't appeal to me. Now though, I had a reason to do it. It was not because I was in love with it. I was not a runner. Far from it. Golf was my passion.

On the eve of my first run in 1995 I went to bed early because I wanted to go running at 6.45am. It was a Friday night I recall, and I was sharing digs with a close friend Peter Wallace who at the time had no interest in exercise. He laughed as he watched me unravel the packaging from my new runners.

Although my memory is somewhat hazy, I do remember it was a beautiful July morning. I woke a little after 6.30 and went out and jogged three miles. It probably took me 40 minutes or more. I was a smoker at that time so the truth is my only thought was to get home as quickly as I could so that I could have a cigarette. I felt very good for the rest of the day however. Now that I was exercising, the "feel-good factor" began and some positive endorphins were released.

With my first run behind me I was determined to keep it going. The first week I think I ran three times, probably covering a combined 10 miles. I took to it immediately and became a morning runner, someone who was happiest out among the quiet canal trails and country roads that we are blessed with in abundance in Ireland. A boarding school upbringing that had us rise before dawn as well as an employer who was a very early riser, had instilled in me a discipline that had me out of bed before 6am most mornings.

In those early months of running, I discovered places in Mullingar that I never knew existed, walks and trails of great beauty. Better still, given the early hour, I had my own private wilderness of beauty as my playground.

Weeks and months went by and soon autumn approached. Despite the weather closing in, I continued running about three times every week. With my new found exercise routine, the weight over the next 12 to 18 months would start to come off. I am not saying that it was easy because it wasn't, but I had brought some discipline into my life.

A new eating philosophy emerged where the portions on the plate as well as the menu were significantly altered. I never followed an exact science for the weight loss and I had no inside knowledge of how to lose it. I simply cut down on the obvious things. I went from a full cup of rice to a third when eating a curry. I also introduced my dinner plate to some new items called 'vegetables'. I had previously been tempted by all the usual vices of takeaways and chocolate. Again, portions and frequency were the issue. Takeaways went from three a week down to one, chocolate from seven bars a week to three. Biscuits when combined with a cup of tea went from four down to two.

Four evenings or more a week, I would go for a four-mile walk. This was always after dinner, to work off what I had eaten. The more I walked and ran, the greater the weight loss. The more weight I lost, the more I was determined to keep it off. Within 18 months I was hovering close to the 13st (182lbs) and was deeply proud of this achievement. My waist had dropped by three to four inches and the tight 'XL' sweaters had dropped to a very loose 'Large' fitting.

I must confess that even to this day weight is something I am conscious of. I do have a very large appetite. On quite a few occasions in the early noughties my weight hovered towards the 14 stone mark. Thankfully I have recognised a tipping point which was usually around that mark where an alarm used go off in my head telling me to do something about it. In the past number of years the sporting goals I have set myself have allowed me to eat more than most. I love food and sometimes I love the wrong foods which means I am on constant alert.

As the winter of 1995 approached, the positive endorphins that exercise and running offers the body had really started to kick in and I was feeling great. My once sedentary lifestyle became a hazy memory as my new regime had me up before dawn pounding the roads and trails within a five mile radius of my home.

Cigarettes were next on the hit list.

Ah yes, cigarettes.

I have to say hand on heart I loved or at least thought I loved cigarettes. I had started smoking at 17 and by my mid-twenties I was a 30-a-day man. Like most though, deep down I hated them and I strived continuously to give them up. I had tried on many occasions before but to no avail. At the end of 1995 I mustered up the courage to have yet another try. The prospect filled me with dread, but this time I was more determined than I'd ever been before.

January came and with it an ongoing desire to quit and I did. Amazingly I managed to stay entirely smoke free for the full year of 1996. I did this via the cold turkey method, where I simply confronted my addiction head on, adopting a positive mindset that I could live without them.

For 16 months, I was successful. One night in April 1997 however, I succumbed to temptation once more while enjoying a few beers with friends. I thought I was the big fellow who could have just one. So I did. And then I had a second. And a third. And a fourth... Before the night ended I had smoked 10 or more. The next day I bought a packet. I was a smoker again.

Over the next four years I fought a difficult battle with this addiction yet again but I refused to give up trying to quit. Every few months I would try, usually failing after just a few days or weeks. I am sure many of you out there can empathise with such a tale.

In all, I estimate I would have tried perhaps 50 times to quit. One time my employer even offered me a handsome reward of £250 (around €325) if I stayed smoke-free for three months. With one week remaining I went back on them.

My method of trying to give up normally began on a Sunday; I figured that psychologically I was starting a new week afresh. I usually managed to abstain on Monday and sometimes Tuesday but so many times Wednesday would prove a mountain too great to climb.

It was always a mind game with me. Most people will tell a tale that the smell is the lure, others the bond between cigarette and beverages such as coffee or beer. I had no difficulty with those situations. It always boiled down to a weak mindset... "I'll just have one, and give them up next Sunday instead."

In 1999, I geared myself up again and lasted three full months before once again succumbing to temptation. Finally at the end of 2001 I had had enough and on January 2nd 2002 I convinced myself that I would smoke no more. I am unsure what was different this time. Perhaps it was just an even more determined attitude.

January through March I managed to stave off incredible urges to go back on them. I found it extremely tough, even going so far as to buy a packet on one occasion but not actually opening it.

Six months into my abstention I was in Japan to follow Ireland's involvement in the 2002 World Cup soccer tournament. Late one night on this football odyssey, I was in a karaoke bar in downtown Tokyo sometime after 4am, a tad less than sober. I was with a group of seven friends and we had gone through all the power ballads. Tina, Rod, Elvis and even Patsy Cline had all been impersonated. I perform a mean version of Julio Iglesias (if I say so myself) and after two jugs of the local brew, I even sounded the tiniest bit like him. Okay, that's a lie but after two jugs of beer, I thought I did.

That's when I got the compelling urge... to have a cigarette.

There were three smokers in the group. I leaned out to the closest box to take one having fully convinced myself that I needed it. The box was empty. I tried a second and it too yielded nothing. Finally I got up and went to the far end of the table close to where a female friend Lisa, or Gloria Gaynor as she was pretending to be, was on stage singing 'I will survive' and I found a third box. I opened it, by now desperately seeking some nicotine... but it was empty as well.

Did I recognise on this third occasion that I was not meant to smoke, that this surely must be a sign?

Did I hell? I wanted a cigarette.

Earlier on a visit to the toilet, I had noticed a cigarette machine in the hallway. Undeterred by my failure to track down a ciggie from my friends, I disappeared quietly from the concert and continued on my search.

I studied the machine to figure out its mechanics. I was in Japan after all and it took some concentration. I loaded in some yen as indicated, but nothing happened. I pressed for a refund before reloading and trying an alternative brand. Again, nothing.

Just then I noticed a sign in Japanese hanging out of the side of the machine. Unable to understand it, I asked the cashier for help.

He explained to me in broken English that the machine had broken down earlier that day. A few minutes later the urge had miraculously passed.

That was June 2002 and I am writing this nine years later. That is the closest I have come to succumbing to the temptation in that time.

I guess I had set myself a goal that I was determined to reach. As I said earlier my success on this occasion was the attitude I brought to the table. Never say never though. I always have to be on guard.

Three massive challenges tackled head on. An introduction to exercise, significant weight loss and now a non-smoker. All of these took massive action and determination, nothing more, nothing less.

Other books record the more serious human challenges that people have overcome such as illness, disease, mental disability or of being in a life threatening situation. This book thankfully is not about any of those and I am truly grateful for that. It is about regular things that so many of us face every day in our lives. If you have battled the same addictions and challenges and have tried successfully or even unsuccessfully then I salute you. You are great for doing so, so give yourself a pat on the back.

CHAPTER 5
BIRTH OF AN IDEA

AUGUST 2008

"Thanks so much for the advice. I'll see you around in the next few months, no doubt. By the way I hear you are a bit of a lunatic when it comes to endurance events."

The 29-year-old man left my office "highly motivated" in his own words to do an Ironman Triathlon. He had called in a few hours before to seek advice on attempting his first Ironman. It was my first time we had ever met. We gelled immediately.

As he was leaving, he opened a bag and took out a book.

"Here, have a read of this," he said. "It's just a way of saying thanks for your advice. From what I have heard about your adventures, you will really enjoy it." With that he was gone out the door. More of this mysterious visitor later.

It was a Saturday afternoon in August 2008 not unlike any normal Saturday afternoon. How could I know when I started reading that book where it ultimately would lead me. In the years leading up to this encounter, I had stopped dreaming about things and instead every time I had a really exciting idea, I committed there and then to doing it.

The book was about an ultra distance runner. I went on the internet to research the author in more detail and I learnt about an amazing marathon challenge he had done. Within 24 hours of this visitor walking out the door of my office, I had conceived the idea of running 32 marathons in 32 days. The more I thought about it, the more excited I got.

To undertake such an audacious attempt would require determination, commitment and huge self-belief. To stop you from thinking I was crazy, perhaps I should tell you how I got to the point where I believed without hesitation that I was capable of doing it.

I was always into sport but never in a competitive sense. I was always average at most sports I played. My dad lays claim to my interest in all sports, particularly golf and running. He claims, jokingly, it was the influence of seeing him running while we were growing up that set a good sporting example to myself and my four siblings. I tell him it couldn't have been as I spent my teenage years in a boarding school!

My mum and dad were always a great example to us. Both are now in their early seventies but lead very active lives. My dad was never competitive to a clock but seriously competitive to a challenge. Back in the early 70s he used to confine his running route to our avenue which measured about 300 metres, running up and down continuously to gain fitness. He has an amazing attitude to life and specifically to exercise and has achieved amazing personal goals in his lifetime. This was mostly all done in the 1960s and 1970s when most deemed him a little adventurous. If he wasn't trekking down the Amazon, he was in places as diverse as Pakistan, India, China and Chile. Many of them are regular destinations now, but in the mid-60s they were places most people knew very little about. He was climbing to 17,000 ft on Mount Everest in a pair of golf shoes within 20 years of Hillary and Tenzing having travelled the same route.

Even now he tries to stay as fit as possible. If he arrives into a car park he will park at the furthermost point from his destination. "A 500-metre workout," he calls it. What a great example he continues to set to all our family.

Unfortunately in his exuberance to hold onto his youth, he suffered a dreadful fall on the 11th of March 1994 whilst mountaineering in the Cairn Gorm Mountains in Scotland. Earlier that morning he and his mountaineering team had successfully reached the 4,295 feet summit of Ben Macdui - the second highest mountain in the UK after Ben Nevis. Such was the gravity of the fall he suffered, he devised a method to tell us about it over the space of four phone calls en route from Belfast Airport to Mullingar.

He introduced his injury to us by saying he had hurt his back. "I'm not too bad. Just a bit stiff," he claimed. When he reached Newry a while later, he called again. "Tell your mother I got a serious gash to the head too, but I'm fine, honestly". Half an hour later in Dundalk, we got another call. "Did I tell you the last time that I lost a few teeth, only five or six. But I'm grand. I am on the way home now, I will be there shortly."

Then the final update. "I have two broken ribs as well and I look pretty bad, so don't be shocked when you see me, it's not as bad as it looks". This final call was actually made from outside our front door. He wanted us to be prepared. Good job he did, as he was quite a sight as you can see from the photo in the middle of the book.

The doctors said that he would have severe mobility problems in later life because of the fall. While descending an iceface, he got caught in a 100 mile an hour cross wind. Strapping into the ice for a short rest, he inserted both hand-picks into the iceface as well as both feet. His hands were freezing so he pulled one from the ice-axe to check his circulation. That was not his mistake. His error was in removing his right leg at the same time. The wind immediately whipped him and within seconds, he had slid, tumbled and fallen 600 feet. That happened nearly two decades ago and the doctors were unfortunately correct insofar as they said his range of mobility would be impaired.

His strength of will and mind, however, remains what it was in 1994. He still swims for 30 minutes at 7am three or four mornings a week and still refuses to consider taking a golf trolley let alone a buggy when playing a few holes of golf, preferring instead to sling the clubs over his right shoulder. My dad is 74 and is as passionate about sport and exercise as he was when he was scaling Mount Everest, K2 or Ben Macdui in the 70s, 80s and 90s.

It was my mum and dad who had introduced me to golf. Both were heavily involved in Mullingar Golf Club in the 1970s and 80s. My dad was a former three handicap golfer and he played most weekends when I was growing up. My mum inherited her love of golf from her own father who was one of the founders of our local club in the early 1930s.

I caddied for my dad from an early age. Fifty pence was the going rate for a four-hour expedition of four-and-a-half miles. For this 10-year-old it was like trekking Everest. I lived to go to the golf course with him. Everyone else in the family had leisure pursuits of an equine nature. They got this from mum whose love for horses she passed onto Tom and Mary, my older siblings, as well as Katherine and Dorothy, my two younger sisters.

Dad and I knew horses needed feeding, grooming and riding out. Golf was much less complicated. He loved the fact that I loved caddying and playing and I loved the fact that I could confine myself to this solo pursuit where long silences was a part of the etiquette. To this very shy young boy that was a major attraction.

I played it from the age of seven until my pre-teen year and loved the endless hours on the fairways of Mullingar. It is one of Ireland's finest parkland courses. Indeed, I would argue that there are few courses as naturally beautiful anywhere. It was also home to Ireland's leading strokeplay amateur golf tournament. Each August bank holiday saw the cream of Irish golf talent converge on our course for two days to battle it out for this prestigious trophy. My earliest memories were of seeing Ronan Rafferty, a future European Number 1 golfer, compete as a 17-year-old. In the early 1980s, I was privileged to watch every shot of the highly-talented Louth amateur Declan Brannigan as he went around the course in just 64 shots.

Years later, I watched in awe a number of future greats such as Paul McGinley, Darren Clarke, Robert Allenby and Pádraig Harrington come to Mullingar to compete. The best amateur of the lot that I witnessed was a player from Banbridge, Co Down called Raymie Burns. Mullingar was the leading scratch cup tournament in amateur golf in Ireland attracting the best in the country each August. Burns won it with ease.

I harboured every boyhood dream of turning one's favourite pastime into a future career but boarding school intervened. We did have an abundance of sporting pursuits on our doorstep and I played every one of them including Gaelic football, soccer and pitch and putt. I managed to get my place on the senior hurling team as well, although to this day I am convinced that I only got there because of my great friendship with my school friend Seamus Lynch, whose brother Michael trained the team. It certainly was not because of my prowess with a hurley.

On leaving school, I headed like most of the young population to England in search of work. There were no fairways and greens in the west end of London, so it wasn't until my return home a year later that the golf clubs were dusted off and saw daylight once more. My handicap was 18 at that time but over the next four or five years I improved as a result of being able to play several times a week. By the late 80s I had a single-figure handicap which coincided with a new sales job where golf was encouraged as a way of securing new business.

In the early 90s I lived for golf. I was quiet by nature and golf and its environment meant I could lose myself in this comfort. I harboured boyhood dreams of turning professional. If I had done it, I would have starved for sure. I was never going to be good enough.

I had a passion for golf. It was however, driving me crazy as I knew I had the ability to be better than my swing would allow. So often I would play 9 or 12 holes at level par or better. Then the wheels would come off late into the back nine, usually finishing anywhere between five and nine over par. I had a vision of what I wanted to become and I knew I could get there. Until you put it into action however, a vision is just a vision. What I needed was a plan.

At that time I was reading a lot of golf books such was my interest. I noticed a quote one day from South Africa's Gary Player, the nine-time Major winner. "The more I practise, the luckier I get," he said.

I decided over my 1998/99 New Year's resolution to try to see just how good I could become and enrolled in a series of golf lessons from Gary McNeill, the professional in CityWest golf club. Taking lessons every three weeks for six months, I practised and practised until calluses became a permanent fixture on my hands. I changed my whole mindset and became totally focused on succeeding. I decided I would consider a consistent four handicap, if I could reach that level, as a success. At that time I was a very inconsistent six-handicapper shooting an average of 80 to 81 shots per round. My target was to shoot 76 or below. I also started reading some excellent golf books on the 'mental' side of the game to sharpen up the psychological part of me.

I practised five times a week. Early mornings, late evenings and thousands upon thousands of practice shots later I had lowered my handicap from an inconsistent six to my target of four. It took only six months. I was quite proud of it at the time. I became very consistent for the next 18 months or so and I loved golf again. I even shot a competitive below-par round of 71 shots in the summer of 1999, my one and only time to do so with an official scorecard in my hand. I had six birdies that day and proudly kept the scorecard as a memento.

My playing form in golf often determined my mood. I did not realise it then but this experience in 1999 and 2000 would provide a launch pad into the future. By the early noughties I had grown tired of just talking about doing things. Yes I was a trier, but I had no commitment when it came to finishing things. I had learned a valuable lesson by devoting six months to golf and I had a few years' running in my legs by this time too. I was beginning to see that I got out of something what I put into it. This was brought home to me when in 2001, I devoted less time to practice and my golf game deteriorated once more.

My life in some ways was still like being in a car that had no steering wheel and no accelerator. I had neither real direction nor momentum. On the plus side I was running and I had lost a huge amount of weight. I was endeavouring to give up cigarettes but I was still very lazy in other parts of my life. In a career sense I was still ambitionless and unmotivated. I was stuck in a rut and within a comfort zone. I felt that I had so much to offer myself and the world, and while inside I wanted to do something about it, the truth was I was still mostly in reverse.

Deep down this really got to me and I knew I needed to do something about it. By now I was in my early 30s. I had no major financial concerns and I had no dependants. The devotion I had given to my golf game in '99 had taught me a valuable lesson - it was time to start moving some other personally mountainous challenges. I needed to do something career-wise too. I had worked for the same company for 14 years but had gone as far as I could there and I had become unhappy. It offered a decent salary, a company car and a nice pension but it offered no mental stimulation to me anymore.

I had returned to college a few years previously to get a qualification in Public Relations. This took a lot of effort but it opened my eyes about what life could offer if I made the effort to seize it. I had to make changes and I knew it.

I had had enough of a rudderless life with no destination in sight. I recall having a chat with my older brother, Tom, a person who has always passed on great wisdom whenever I needed it. He could see how unhappy I was and felt it prudent to talk to me about my future.

"Why don't you go working for yourself?" he asked one day.

"What would I do?" I asked him.

At that time Ireland's economy was starting to grow enormously, courtesy of major injection of funds from the European Union and a highly-active property and building industry. Property was the 'in' thing and it was something that interested me. I decided to do a short apprenticeship with a friend who was in that business and enrolled in a two-year, part-time college course to gain the necessary qualifications. Twice weekly for two years, I made the 45-minute journey to Athlone IT to attend lectures. About 20 exams and as many projects later I had the qualifications I needed to begin this new phase of my life.

I handed my notice in to my employer, firmly nailing my colours to the mast. I had worked all that time for an insurance company which specialised in wholesaling travel insurance to the Irish Travel Trade. My boss was actually my Uncle Tom. He was very encouraging to me as he also recognised that it was time for me to move on. Maybe he was glad to be rid of me. I am joking of course, as we enjoyed a very close working relationship.

I told him and my fellow employees that I was going into business on my own and I circled a time-frame on the calendar in my kitchen in February 2003, reaffirming to myself that I would open this new business venture by August. Six months out I worked all hours to ensure I had everything in place. A business plan for the bank, a licence from the courts and a lease on a premises. These were only a few of the hundreds of items I needed to complete. It was a challenging time but I was hugely motivated to succeed.

I had only a small amount of savings which meant I would need a good business plan. I approached my bank manager and tried to exude optimism. I told him about my background, my experience and my confidence in my own ability. I also explained that my family had traded for 40 years in the same street I proposed to open in. I explained how I felt I could establish a successful business quickly. I didn't oversell myself as I didn't want to sound like a know-it-all. I tried to come across as both honest and very enthusiastic.

In my budget projections I had allowed for no income for the first six months as a worst case scenario. I explained it would take me three to four months before agreeing successful sales. With a two- or three-month closing period once a sale was agreed, this meant it could be six months or so before I expected my first pay cheque to drop through the door. I also had done out projected income for the second half of year one. The bank liked what I had presented and I got the thumbs up.

With a bank loan, an overdraft facility and a very generous rent-free period from Tom, I opened the doors of my own auctioneering and estate agency business just four weeks after my original estimation of August 1st, 2003. I was by now well outside of my comfort zone and in truth I was terrified.

Thankfully by the end of year one, working a minimum of 65 hours per week, I had surpassed all targets and was able to employ my first full-time staff member - my sister Dorothy. Year two went even better and by the end of our third year we had four employees and hundreds of clients. I loved every minute of it and the long hours went by in an instant. I was doing it for me, the master of my own destiny.

This time was a big stepping stone in my life. We were steadily increasing the turnover of the company and with it, my personal confidence grew. It was at this time that I started to attend some motivational courses. These courses were as good as the attendee's attitude to them. Like golf, I had finally realised I would only get out of life what I was putting into it. The massive shift to get out of my comfort zone, by choosing self-employment, was just the start. I was determined to inject further new found 'can do' attitudes into my personal life.

CHAPTER 6

A SMALL KEY OPENS BIG DOORS

IN early 2004 my brother Tom and a good friend of his John O'Reilly, two single men at the time, befriended a few ladies whilst on a visit to Dublin.

Sport and charity was the common interest. As it transpired, these ladies were committed members of a triathlon charity event committee. For the previous two years they had organised a triathlon to raise funds for a cancer charity. The lads suggested a change of location for the triathlon and the ladies agreed to move it to Mullingar, thus opening up a whole new marketing opportunity for the event. Tom and John promised a super course and the finest organisation skills in their successful attempt to woo the committee into moving it to the midlands of Ireland.

Tom told me one day about what he was involved in. He was on the organising committee to get people to sign up and take part. He told me there was a team who was short of a swimmer and asked me would I consider making up the numbers. I was cautious and very nervous but agreed to sign up nonetheless.

I must confess that I knew nothing about triathlons at the time. He explained that it involved swimming, cycling and running. Normally the same athlete did the three disciplines themselves but as this was a charity event, relay teams were permitted.

Sure I was fit, indeed I had been running for eight or nine years up to this point, but I was a loner in terms of training and racing and I was anything but competitive. I agreed to take part though and thus my introduction to triathlon was but weeks away. I had been swimming for as long as I could remember but this distance did scare me somewhat. Would I be able to survive a 750-metre swim, I asked myself. I would soon find out. I arrived at race headquarters in the townland of Lilliput, located just outside Mullingar, to be greeted by hundreds of athletes already running around in preparation.

To say I was intimidated would be an understatement. I felt very small which was ironic given our location. It was here at Lilliput according to folklore that Jonathan Swift was inspired to write *Gulliver's Travels*. I felt very insignificant as I surveyed all around me; the white tented village with hundreds of finely tuned athletes clad in lycra. Bikes, water bottles, gels, tubes, wetsuits and organised chaos all around.

The announcer relayed the calendar of the day's activities and suggested where and when marshals, race organisers, stewards and athletes should be. I listened with interest and awe at such organisation.

The surfer's wetsuit which I had borrowed from my sister's boyfriend Enda, would keep me afloat. I had the right gear as wetsuits were compulsory for this immense challenge. I know now however, that the wetsuit I used for my first ever plunge into a triathlon swim was about as practical as Tiger Woods using the cut down 7-iron his dad made for him when he was five years old, in playing the final hole of a major championship. Pulling and manoeuvring the wetsuit around my body took all of 10 minutes. I felt like Michelin man in a babygro.

Suddenly the tannoy indicated just 10 minutes to the start. I felt a massive wave of panic. I ran to the transition area, the place where the bikes and run gear were located. This was where my fellow athletes had started to congregate. I spotted a table with a chap in a yellow organiser's bib and went over to seek more information. There I found John O'Reilly, one of the main organisers. He was hiding underneath a cap to shield him from an unusually hot sun.

"Nervous?" he smirked.

"Bloody right," I replied.

"Can you swim?" he asked half-jokingly.

"Yeah," I said. "But that far? Who knows?"

"Don't worry," he said. "We have lots of boat cover. If you get into difficulty just raise your arm and someone will assist you. Your race number is 309."

He stamped the numbers on my hand. "Oh, by the way, that's one of your team members over there," he said as he pointed to a group of about five people limbering up against a large oak tree. "See the really attractive girl in the red cycle shorts? She's with you."

"Really?" I said, suddenly gaining a greater interest in my new-found love of triathlon.

"Yes," John replied. "Cute, isn't she?"

"Yeah", I said, delaying the pronunciation as a giveaway of my attraction.

"Yeah," he mimicked. "And her husband thinks so too." He burst into hysterical laughter as he also burst any romantic bubble within my now butterfly-filled stomach. "You wouldn't have stood a chance anyway," he continued as he pushed me aside to assist another athlete waiting patiently behind. "I went out with her once... you're not her type."

I waded among my fellow athletes into Lough Ennell. For the first few seconds I felt an autumnal chill from the murky depths but I soon acclimatised. The longer I was in, the more I got used to it. My fellow competitors loosened up by ducking and diving under water and rising out of the depths to stretch their arms. I looked around watching their methods but felt it best to stand quietly and motionless in the middle of the pack afraid to speak a word or to practise.

BANG! The gun went off. Immediately I became engulfed by my fellow competitors and my heart felt like it was trying to extricate itself from my chest. It was a sporting battle unlike any I had ever experienced on the fairways. Heads banged, limbs extended like an octopus in all directions coming in contact with several areas of my body. It would be a fight that the Scottish warrior William Wallace would have been proud were he a triathlete. It was furious.

Several minutes later and just as I was starting to find some room and indeed some momentum I eyed the first of two yellow buoys we would have to navigate around on this triangular shaped course. Just when I thought I was making progress I became entangled once more amidst swinging arms and legs kicking out in all directions. And it was fantastic.

As I passed the second buoy and close to the 500-metre point, I eyed the old stone boathouse, the place of our departure. It was by now only 300 metres from where I was, which meant just about another 300 metres or so to the finish. My stroke technique was probably not the best but it mattered not. I was out competing in an event and I was enjoying the moment. It was a huge adrenalin rush but by now I was tiring rapidly. I had started too fast and I was starting to pay the price. Hardly fatal though as it was a charity event. With 100 metres to go, I found a new surge of energy from somewhere and managed to pass a few of my fellow competitors.

Fifteen minutes after I started, my legs made contact with sand and stones once more and I exited roughly in the middle of the pack. My legs felt like jelly as I climbed the hill to transition, stumbling both with exhaustion and admiration at the sight of my teammate as she extended her arm out to tag me before mounting her bike for the second leg of this epic adventure. My virginity in triathlon was gone forever.

I was hooked.

CHAPTER 7
WHO FEARS TO SPEAK?

According to most studies, people's number one fear is public speaking. Number two is death. Death is number two? Does that sound right? This means to an average person, if you go to a funeral, you're better off in the casket than doing the eulogy.

Jerry Seinfeld, American television actor and comedian

AT that time I felt a massive sense of accomplishment having completed this 750-metre swim. Had I swum across the Irish Sea, I could scarcely have felt more happy with myself.

My only regret was that I had not challenged myself to enter the event as an individual. I vowed to change this however by entering the full event the following year. This did not come to fruition however as I was still in a phase of my life where I was still having to really work to push outside *some* comfort zones. I completed the run leg as part of a team a year later so I was not entirely lazy. Again I felt a wonderful sense of accomplishment and made myself the same promise again for the following year.

By 2005 my new business was taking off and I was seeing the world in a different light. I was very happy working for myself. Some days were very challenging and the lack of a guaranteed wage every Friday did on occasion fill me with fear.

By then I was 37 and had started pursuing several new goals in my life, some big and some small. I was exiting comfort zones on a regular basis, sometimes without even realising it.

That is not to say I stood on the edge of Lough Ennell at the end of my first triathlon swim and screamed "Eureka, I have arrived. I can do anything." Sometimes it is only on reflection perhaps weeks, sometimes months and more often years later when we realise the importance of having done something which at that time seemed relatively innocuous, in this case a 750-metre swim. Now I realise it was so much more and it was about to open up a whole new set of adventures.

I still had personal challenges from a confidence point of view. I was hugely lacking in social confidence and the prospect of speaking in a social situation filled me with dread. Any social setting where I had to communicate with someone made me very uncomfortable. The exception to this was in a business sense when one to one with a client, I was fine. I knew my business, I was a good salesman and I had a great team around me. We prided ourselves on honesty and integrity, something my parents had instilled in me from an early age.

Public speaking was something however that filled me with horrendous fear. In my new business, I knew that the time would eventually come when I would have to stand up in front of an audience and speak publicly. The fear of it was overwhelming. I knew in my new career as an auctioneer that my first auction would not be too far away.

Not long after, it arrived. The farm to be auctioned was on the face of it an easy opener for my auction debut, a modest farmhouse on 15 acres. I had to encourage my client to go down the public auction route rather than the more traditional method of a private treaty sale because I knew in my heart and soul that that was the best route to secure the best price for my client. That is what I was paid to do. The market was very buoyant at that time and it was sure to attract interest. Getting a buyer might be the easy part. Even as I uttered the words 'public auction' from my lips, fear filled my body. The thought of having to actually conduct one really terrified me.

The auction required a lead-in period of six weeks. That led to 42 nights of tossing and turning, sweating and stressing. Earlier I referred to how challenges are different things to different people. Well here was mine, up close and personal. An unbelievably shy person by nature, now whether I liked it or not I would have to get up in public and speak. I was petrified.

My fear was such that I envisaged standing up and opening my mouth only for nothing to come out. How on earth would I survive that? My reputation would be in tatters. What would my client think of me? He had put his faith in me and deep down I was far from convinced I could do it. I went to a close friend, Paddy Dunican, someone who was well-tutored in the public speaking field and asked his advice.

He told me: "Better to be sorry for doing something, than sorry for not doing it."

Paddy promised his assistance and a week before the big day he took me under his wing and we practised every possible eventuality. He taught me posture, hand gestures, protocol and eye contact. What use would all that be however, if I was unable to speak?

Three days before the auction I was a basket case. Something had to be done. I had to come up with a Plan B. I decided to consult the yellow pages to source a 'hypnotist'. Perhaps now you are beginning to get some idea of how big a fear this was for me. I wanted to guarantee success, therefore I was determined to go that extra mile to achieve it.

Two days before the big day, I travelled the 60 miles to the hypnotist's office. I was paranoid about secrecy and felt that by going to a town where nobody knew me I could engage the services of a professional 'under the radar' so to speak. The advert in the yellow pages had caught my eye.

"We can alleviate all fears," it had read.

The hypnotist, a man in his mid-forties, was smartly dressed in a tailored dark suit. The room was modest but boasted two comfy armchairs that both of us availed of. I sat in the black leather chair and blurted out my fear. He listened attentively but gave nothing away in his expression.

Once I had finished he was thoroughly professional and sympathetic to my plight and explained that deep down almost everyone at some time has to confront a fear. He didn't laugh, he didn't judge but thankfully he rationalised things for me. He also taught me a technique which eased my fear by at least one per cent.

He asked me when my event was to happen.

"Next Thursday," I replied.

"Where and at what time," he enquired.

I gave the location of the hotel and the time.

"Ok," he said. "Let's try and rationalise this. Picture yourself walking up the street towards the hotel. Is the street busy?"

"Yes," I replied.

"Full of noise? People? Cars?"

"Yes."

"Ok, now picture yourself walking into the hotel."

"Are you there in your mind?"

"Yes."

By now I had my eyes closed and was in a semi-relaxed state but at all times was fully aware of my surroundings.

"What time is it in your mind?" he asked.

"Two-fifteen," I said. The auction was to begin at 3pm so I had planned to be there with plenty of time to spare.

He made me picture the scene that I expected would unfold two days down the line. This involved imagining myself walking into the room, picturing my audience and the layout of the room. Every detail was explored and rehearsed.

He made me conduct the entire scenario albeit on a much shorter timeline. It involved me speaking in front of my audience which in my dream still seemed challenging but as it was a dream, on this occasion I was successful.

Finally my imaginary auction ended.

"What time is it in your mind now?" he asked.

"Four o'clock."

"Ok," he went on. "Now walk back out the door onto the street."

"Are you there?"

"Yes."

"Ok, is the street still full of noise? People? Cars?"

"Yes."

"There, you see," he said. "No matter what happens to you this week, the world will still go on. At 4pm next Thursday, that street will be full of noise, full of people and full of cars, people all going about their everyday business. For the next few days just picture yourself walking out the door of the hotel at four o'clock. I guarantee you it will arrive and no matter what has happened to you, the world will carry on regardless of what happens to you. You are but one cog in a very big wheel. Every time you feel fear over the next two days just focus in on four o'clock, Thursday."

I walked out of his office marginally less fearful than I had entered. What he said made complete sense. Still, the sweaty palms would not leave.

D-day finally arrived and it came after a night of very little sleep. As early afternoon approached, I felt like I was walking towards the guillotine. I entered the Greville Arms hotel on Mullingar's main street, my palms sweating, my voice shaking and my anxiety now perhaps at its greatest. As I climbed the stairs to the room which I had pre-booked, my heart was pounding.

How many would be there? What if 50 people showed up? How would I speak, let alone perform?

My watch read 2.45 as the first two strangers entered the execution chamber, sorry, auction room. "S***, they're early," I thought to myself. Must be going to be a big turnout. By 3pm the congregation had risen considerably in number to four. The number however, was irrelevant. I was terrified but was now at the point of no return.

I rose, knees trembling, blood pressure at an all-time high, my heart almost exploding. I opened my mouth and silently prayed that my vocal chords would function.

"Good afternoon ladies and gentlemen", I muttered. Just then I realised there were actually no women in my audience of four. Ah well, I don't think my congregation were too worried. With the first hurdle negotiated perhaps I would be able to communicate with my audience after all. I seemed to have managed that much ok, I thought to myself as I introduced the vendor's solicitor and asked him to read out the conditions of the sale. Maybe I can get through this.

As the solicitor rose I sat back down to regroup. I needed to do a self-assessment of how I was doing so I picked up the jug of water. Given how much I had drunk in the previous 15 minutes, it was almost empty. I studied my grip to see if my hand was giving away any obvious signs of nerves. Nothing too obvious, I thought, maybe I will get through this.

I stood once more and thanked the solicitor for his offering and then proceeded to try to sell the farm. Ten minutes later it was obvious that the congregation were not keen to write a cheque that day as they certainly had no interest in bidding for the farm. I thanked them for coming and ushered them towards the exit.

As they left I turned and walked back to my chair. At that moment I was not really concerned about not finding a buyer on this occasion. Many sales happen post-auction and I knew the market was very strong. I was still confident of a sale. A short time after I did indeed sell the farm. But that day as I collected up my paperwork, I experienced a real surge of euphoria; I had overcome a massive obstacle in my life. I spoke in front of my audience, all four of them. I could not have been happier had I been given the farm as a gift. I had done it. I had left my comfort zone and lived to tell the tale.

Wow, what a feeling!

Over the next few days I was on a high. A crowd of four or 54, it didn't matter. I had stood up and been counted by speaking in front of a public audience and survived. As the former Wimbledon tennis champion Arthur Ashe once said: "Success is a journey, not a destination. The doing is often more important than the outcome."

This was a personal achievement of Everestine proportions, comparable in a parallel sense to the 32 Marathon challenge. I was a non-smoker and I was a normal weight at last. I had opened my own business, I was highly active in new sporting pursuits and I had just spoken in public. I was gathering confidence all the time.

What next?

CHAPTER 8

THE MAIDEN VOYAGE

FOLLOWING on from my introduction to triathlon in 2004, over the next few years I made many new friends in the Midland Triathlon Club. People such as Pat Nugent, Anne Coleman, John O'Reilly, Brian and Caroline Boyle and Nicky and Bridget McCabe influenced me without even knowing. Their enthusiasm for sport was infectious. I could see the positivity coursing through them and it was very appealing.

By now, consciously or unconsciously, I had left five comfort zones.

Ironically, it was through leaving another "shyness" comfort zone for only a two minute period one day, that a door opened in my life which was to have a major personal influence.

One day I was waiting for friends David and Amanda Andrews as well as my sister Mary and her husband Enda in a pub in Dublin's Temple Bar. We were going to a show in the nearby Olympia Theatre. I had been in Dublin all day and they were travelling from Mullingar, I was early and they were late.

As I waited, a girl who I guessed was in her late twenties walked in. She was dressed casually in chino trousers and a smart alpine navy sweater. Ordering a coffee, she proceeded to open up a large Dublin tourist map. As the minutes passed, I noticed she was starting to look bewildered and confused. I really wanted to help but I was an incredibly shy person by nature, one who was really lacking in social confidence. Close friends reading this might find that hard to credit, but my confidence in their company was a disguise to how I really felt, especially among people I didn't know.

As time went on, she looked more and more puzzled.

"To hell with it," I said to myself. It was quite obvious she was a tourist and was in need of help.

I forced myself off the bar stool and went over to her.

"Hi, you look lost," was the limit of my introduction.

Lisa Gibson was on a brief 24-hour stopover in Dublin and was looking for Dublin Castle, one of the city's tourist attractions. In our short chat we exchanged emails. Three weeks later, when she was back at her office desk in Toronto, Canada, Lisa sent me an email. It had a four-minute video attachment with it. It was the story of a father and son called Rick and Dick Hoyt. I had never heard of them. Lisa simply wanted to share their amazing story with someone else.

The video was inspirational and I watched it several times over the following few days. Dick Hoyt, a lieutenant colonel in the Air National Guard was Rick's dad. Rick was born in the early 1960s in Boston and shortly after his birth, was diagnosed with cerebral palsy. Many doctors encouraged the Hoyts to institutionalise Rick but they refused. His parents Dick and Judy spent hours each day teaching Rick the alphabet. By the time he was five, they knew Rick was very intelligent. When he was 11, Rick was fitted with a computer which enabled him to communicate. He soon demonstrated full brain activity and would later graduate from Boston University in 1993. Confined to a wheelchair and in spite of the challenges he faced every day, Rick lived a life full of accomplishments and now along with his father competes in gruelling marathon events and long distance triathlons. The video contained footage of them completing an event called an 'Ironman' distance triathlon where Dick literally 'carried' his son through a physical sporting challenge that could last up to 16 hours.

It was spellbinding.

What I viewed in that attachment had a profound effect on me and made me see just how fortunate I was to be blessed with good health. It also made me realise that humans are capable of so much more than we give ourselves credit for. I have watched this video perhaps a thousand times since. I never grow tired of it and of sharing the story behind it.

By pure coincidence about nine months later, I got another email which would have a similar impact on me. This email was from Brian Boyle, a fellow member of the Midland Triathlon Club. The email contained an invite to a talk on an Ironman triathlon, the same distance event that Rick and Dick competed in. I had no real idea what it involved but I was intrigued to learn more. Ironman was known in triathlon terms as the 'ultimate distance triathlon'. Just getting to the start line took competitors massive commitment and determination.

What did it involve?

A swim of 2.4 miles (3.8km) followed by a 112-mile (180km) cycle, finished off by running a full marathon of 26.2 (42.2km) miles. Long distances for each discipline. The cut-off for competitors is 16 hours.

I was captivated by the challenge and hung on every word of the speakers. As I listened, I pledged to myself that one day I would get to the start line of one of these amazing events. I was thoroughly respectful of what was involved not just to complete such a distance but to do the necessary training to prepare for it. I knew I had some apprenticeships to serve first before I could tackle such a challenge. In the back of my mind I reasoned that it would take 18 months before I would try and attempt it. Now I had to put a strategy in place to help me get there.

Over that winter I hatched a plan to spend the following year getting experience at different distance triathlons including several sprint and Olympic distances. The 'sprint' distance I had done already. An 'Olympic' distance involved swimming 1500 metres, then cycling 40km finishing off with a run of 10km or 6.25 miles. This was double a sprint distance but was just a quarter or thereabouts of the Ironman Distance. Over that winter I took to the discipline of training with military focus. I learned so much; from proper swim technique, fixing punctures, to cleaning chains and I became an expert at one particular aspect of cycling - falling off. If falling off your bike was an Olympic sport, I would have made the Irish team for sure.

Bike shoes had advanced significantly in the preceding years and I splashed out on a pair of clip-in shoes. These meant you were literally clipped into the pedals, something that took getting used to. It took me quite a while to master it.

I enrolled in early morning swimming sessions and started to compete in 5km running road races in my local area. What I needed to gather was knowledge and experience. The year 2007 was spent travelling the length and breadth of the country competing in many triathlons. Dorothy my youngest sister made this journey with me and we had a ball, making many new friends along the way. So much was learned that would prove invaluable a year on.

With the 2008 Ironman in mind, I decided in the summer of '07 to enter my first ever marathon. I figured it would give me an excellent foundation not just in terms of effort but also experience. A year from then, I hoped to do an event where a marathon would be but one of three elements. I had never even run a marathon on its own for heaven's sake. It was time to change that.

The original marathon event was instituted in commemoration of the fabled run of the Greek soldier Pheidippides a messenger from the Battle of Marathon (the namesake of the race) to Athens. The marathon was one of the original standardised Olympic Events in 1896, though the distance did not become standardised until 1921. The standard distance is now 26 miles and 385 yards.

It is not for the faint-hearted and requires participants to undergo a minimum of four months training to get to the start line. After that, success requires a combination of fitness and a very strong will to succeed. I had always been captivated by the idea of running a marathon and it was a lifetime ambition yet to be fulfilled. Each year at the end of October, I had always regretted not entering the Dublin City Marathon. The year 2007 would be different.

Now I was a man filled with determination and a 'can do' attitude.

That summer I had achieved a very good standard of fitness competing in triathlons. Over the months of July, August and September, I switched my focus and started training vigorously for my debut marathon event. Each week I stretched out the mileage, always hitting my goal of a long run as well. As the weeks climbed, I hit the 20-mile mark for the first time ever. The next week I ran 22. It was tough but I managed it. At 20 miles, I developed a sore pain in my left hip. I slowed but kept going. By 21 miles it was gone, never to reappear.

On reflection, I think it was almost like I had broken through a barrier. This was the first time I had ever run such a distance.

Perhaps my hip was just saying: "Eh, what the hell are you doing to me, I've never done this before."

Despite running further distances since on many occasions, the pain I felt for that 10 minutes or so has never returned.

By early October I was only weeks away from joining 10,000 other hardy souls at the start line of my first ever marathon. Bank Holiday Monday arrived and together with the support of Dorothy and her boyfriend Enda Munnelly, we made the journey to Dublin. We travelled in Enda's camper van parking it on St Stephen's Green.

The city looked gorgeous and the beauty of the Georgian buildings was striking as the autumnal colours enveloped them. There is something very special about Dublin and indeed the Dublin City Marathon. I have always maintained that if you take the gridlock out of our capital city, it is a truly special place. Around 9am on a bank holiday morning is a great time to see this thousand-year-old urban environment.

It was eerily quiet as we left the sanctuary of the camper van and made our way towards race headquarters. As we closed in on this arena, more and more people were gathering. Each street or side street we passed brought more athletes into our group. By the time we turned onto Merrion Square there were hundreds of fellow runners all heading to the same rendezvous point. All looked pensive and nervous. I took solace from this because I felt exactly the same.

Fitzwilliam Square dates back to c.1798. It was just a short walk from St Stephen's Green and on that day it would be the starting point for the race. Many moons ago as a student, I had lived among these gorgeous Georgian buildings. Almost 200 years after the Viscount Robert Fitzwilliam had laid out this beautiful enclosure, I had rented a top floor, four storeys over basement apartment at £25 (€38) per week. It was in the late 1980s. Those were days filled with not a care in the world. As I made my way to the start I gazed up through the morning sun which was peeking through the clouds. As I did so, I picked out the apartment I once occupied. For a few brief moments I reminisced over those times two decades previous. I thought of the friends whose company I kept, my employment at that time and I recalled briefly how simple life seemed.

As I walked past my former home, I found myself suddenly at the start line. In my enthusiasm to be early, I was. Yes there were other athletes all around but I was in the front row, with the ticker tape pressing against my chest. With hindsight it was great as I had an opportunity to see the final marathon preparations amid a flurry of organisation, just metres in front of where I was standing.

I glanced at my watch. It was only 8am, an hour before the 28th staging of the Dublin City Marathon. I was so filled with excitement for my maiden voyage I didn't care. I looked a sight in a black binliner but it would keep me warm for the next 60 minutes or so. I watched with respect and admiration as the wheelchair competitors commenced battle shortly before 9am followed by the male and female elite competitors a few minutes later. Then it was our turn. The last few minutes were as long as a prison sentence as we all waited impatiently to start.

At 9:05am the gun went off and so did the muscle fibres, 20,000 feet pressing forward, some fast, some not so fast but all with one common goal, the challenge of completing 26.2 miles.

We descended the first 500 metres from Fitzwilliam Square crossing over Baggot St and down towards Merrion Square. A few years older than Fitzwilliam Square, Merrion Square's beautiful buildings contain many which are of historic importance to Ireland. Once home to such well known figures of Irish society as Oscar Wilde and W B Yeats, the square is overlooked by Leinster House, the Natural History Museum and The National Gallery.

My target was 3 hours 30 minutes, and it was, I felt, a goal well within my grasp. I had planned to run an average of eight-minute miles, which would pace me for such a time. My pre-race strategy was to take things gently for the first mile or so, anything remotely close to that pace would do just fine. As I turned the corner onto Pearse Street, about four minutes into the race, I spotted Dor and Enda, her boyfriend of five years. They could not pick me out from the multitude so I gave them a yell to let them observe my early progress.

"Go on ya good thing," Dor screamed, her hands cupped around her mouth for maximum volume. Enda stood there leaning against his mountain bike taking in the sight of thousands of athletes negotiating the early stages of the race.

The first mile was completed as we entered Westmoreland Street for O'Connell St. I glanced at my watch and realised my pace of eight minute miles was exceeded by 90 seconds. In my naivety I thought this was fine, that I could bank this precious minute and a half to be shaved off my ultimate target. Miles two to five also felt great as I knocked out the same split times of roughly six and a half minute miles. I was enjoying every yard of the experience.

It was liberating being able to run down the centre of main roads and streets such as Westmoreland St, O'Connell St and the North Circular Road. These were more familiar to me from behind the wheel of my car, usually stuck in traffic jams.

By 10.30 I was still feeling comfortable having completed 10 miles or so. It was a pleasant morning with temperatures in the early teens. The tens of thousands of spectators who were lining the best vantage points made it feel like we were in the centre of the boxing ring in Madison Square Garden, New York and boy did it feel good to be on the inside of these ropes.

Up until the 11-mile point I was fine. We had taken in some lovely sights, the highlight of which was the greenery of the Phoenix Park, Europe's largest walled park. It was at this point, however, that the first warning signs appeared. It started as an ache but as I climbed into the early double mileage figures of 12 and 13 miles, the pain intensified.

It wasn't immediate but it was noticeable. Each mile spread more discomfort into the fibres of my muscles. By mile 15 I was very uncomfortable and by mile 17 my body's energy was sinking like the Titanic. Indeed by 18 miles it had turned into an epidemic with every limb screaming at me to stop with every laboured stride I took. My early pace was coming back to haunt me.

As I approached Milltown Road, I glanced at my watch. Were I to keep a similar pace to the finish I would complete the race in about

3.10.00 – way ahead of expectations. This was the error I had made. Sure, I got to this point of the race well ahead of my scheduled time but therein lay the problem. I had used up far too much of my reserves, and my body was starting to insist on retribution. I was about to hit 'the wall'.

Within seconds I had veered, careered, smashed, call it what you like, but I had definitely hit the wall and very hard at that. My ability to put one leg past the other was rapidly becoming hard to do. A run became a jog and the jog got slower and slower and slower. My body was engulfed in pain. My ears were receiving sounds from an out-of-tune violin quartet injecting Beethoven's 5th symphony into each eardrum.

A thought entered my brain. It whispered. "Walk away, Gerry, and the pain goes." It was only a thought though and it was trespassing. It was never a plan. There was no way I would quit.

As we climbed the hill close to Foster Avenue, I came to a complete stop. I was in agony. Tears of pain ran down my cheeks. I felt like an idiot. I stood at the side, just inches from the encouraging spectators. I was in no mood though to embrace their encouragement. In fact it irritated me. I felt like giving up, but I knew I wouldn't. I would reach Merrion Square and that finish line, even if I had to crawl.

I recall an inner thought. "Just finish this and you need never do it again." But it disappeared quickly. I knew that it was just a thought and that the passage of time would erase such negativity. I was stronger than any of that now. No matter what pain arrived I would finish.

I was by now 39 and no longer someone who wilted at the first sign of difficulty. I had stood up and overcome a number of major challenges. I am not saying that these thoughts came flooding into my brain at Foster Avenue. Did they hell? They were a million marathons from my mind.

What they had done though in the preceding years was instil into my formerly fragile belief system a confidence or thought process that I could achieve challenging goals. I would finish no matter what. Just at that moment I was unsure how.

As I stood immersed in self-pity, I felt an arm come around my shoulder. By now a steady trickle of tears was making its way down my cheeks. I felt embarrassed and had my head bent over, shielding this visual sign of my condition. I needed to know however who my guardian was, so I raised my head feeling its weight like never before. I was met by the sight of an elderly man perhaps in his late seventies. A man whose face offered sympathy, empathy and encouragement all together.

"Don't worry. They're all feeling it," he offered.

I had neither the energy nor the will to respond verbally. Even if I had I could scarcely have mouthed a response as I had nothing left in the tank.

"Just put one foot in front of the other," he continued, "and I promise you that you will reach the finish."

They say good things come in small parcels. In its simplicity, his advice was brilliant. That elderly man made me realise that I was not alone, that all the humans in this race were feeling it to some degree, and that this was called a marathon for a reason.

"Just put one foot in front of the other and I promise you that you will reach the finish."

How appropriate were his words of wisdom for any normal challenge we face in life? When we are faced with any struggle or challenge, surely all the advice from the experts or the text books could have one common requirement... "Just put one foot in front of the other..."

I wonder do we give due credit to the power of positive words when we are immersed in a difficult situations? Not just in a sporting context. It can apply to any situation or circumstance we may find ourselves in. It might be to a child needing encouragement to learn to ride a bike or to add two and two. It might be when someone has a difficult medical challenge to overcome or it may be needed to help a friend who has just started a healthy eating regime. A word of encouragement, a simple utterance of 'yes you can' may reignite perhaps a lost feeling of self-belief and can be immensely powerful. This was most certainly what happened to me here.

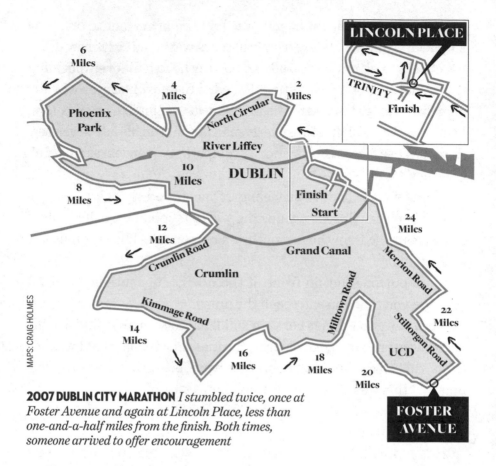

MAPS: CRAIG HOLMES

2007 DUBLIN CITY MARATHON *I stumbled twice, once at Foster Avenue and again at Lincoln Place, less than one-and-a-half miles from the finish. Both times, someone arrived to offer encouragement*

He was my guardian angel. How could I not take his advice? He was rooting for me as he was for everyone. I stood tall once more and jolted my brain back to positivity.

"Come on, Gerry," I quietly muttered. "You can and you will get there."

Slowly I ticked off each step and in turn each mile marker through a mixture of running, jogging, shuffling, waddling and walking. Thankfully I never had to crawl. Each metre negotiated brought me one step closer.

"Just put one foot in front of the other and I promise you that you will reach the finish."

Four miles from home, as I inched my way across the Stillorgan dual carriageway at the UCD flyover, I halted once more. My body was in uncharted waters and was engulfed in pain. I walked for a few hundred metres and was passed by scores of runners, but I didn't care.

Twenty three miles was reached and about 11 or 12 minutes later 24. I was getting there with little enjoyment, but I was getting there.

I struggled ever closer and soon the 25 miles sign came into view. As I approached Lincoln Place, I could see the finish line across in Merrion Square 200 metres to my left. I could also see a multitude of runners arms aloft in celebration as they reached their holy grail. The only problem was I had to turn right and do another mile and a half before I would reach that destination. For now it was just an unwelcome mirage.

As I turned the corner at Lincoln Place onto Tara Street my legs gave way and my body headed to the ground. Out of nowhere I felt an arm grab me and keep me from buckling. No, it wasn't the elderly man. That would be too much to expect. This was real life. It was Enda who amazingly just happened to be standing at the precise spot where I needed another guardian angel to appear. His timing could not have been better. Had I fallen, I might not have been able to re-ignite my muscles to finish.

"Come on, you're almost there," he said encouragingly.

I could not reply, but it did allow me to move forward once more. I was now going purely on passion for completing the day's challenge. I was discovering a strength which I didn't realise I possessed.

By now I was on Pearse Street for the second time that day. We had passed it many hours before in mile one. This time however, we were to turn left onto College Green and then to Nassau St, with the finish line agonisingly close. It was a little after 12.30 and Nassau street was thronged with spectators, thousands and thousands of them yelling, shouting, encouraging every athlete as they arrived within 500 metres of the finish line.

I heard and then spotted Dor in the crowd screaming her support. I gave her a look she later claimed scared her. She said it transmitted pain. I don't remember, I was in too much pain.

She was running behind the crowds that lined the finishing chute, giving a running commentary to my dad in Portugal via her mobile phone.

Then I stopped.

F***!

I couldn't move.

Just 100 metres from home. Thousands watching and screaming..

F***! F***!

My body was shutting down. How embarrassing.

S***!

Crouched over in pain I gave myself a serious talking to.

'Come on you idiot.' I thought to myself.

I could see the finish line, I could see the clock.

"Come on," I screamed loudly, not caring now who heard.

I shuffled forward once more, 90 metres, 50 metres, 30 metres and then finally I crossed the line. What did I do when I finished? Did I hold my arms aloft in triumph? Are you kidding me? I could not have raised my arms if I had been told at that precise second that I had won the lottery. I had nothing, and I mean nothing, left. I cried and I threw up. That's what I did. Wiping the evidence from my lips, I gulped water with exuberance from a bottle placed in my hand, washing it down my throat to clear it of any lingering taste.

Moments later, I rose to my feet once more and realised that major stiffness had engulfed every muscle. On checking my watch it read 3.31.41, within two minutes of my goal but the reality is that I had made a massive error. I had trained for 3:30, but I crossed the half way point in 1:34:44, way faster than I should have. The marathon, I had learned, only starts when you hit the 20-mile mark. That is when I paid the price for being naive. You cannot bluff your way to a faster time than you have trained for. It cost me dearly in terms of pain that day. The good news was that it would prove a huge learning curve, one I would draw from in the future.

This wasn't a failure on my part. Far from it. It was a wonderful learning curve, an 'apprenticeship'. I knew I would grow immeasurably from it. It would deeply empower me in other areas of my brain. It meant that much. Michael Jordan, the US basketball star once famously said:

"I've missed more than 9,000 shots in my career. I've lost almost 300

games. On 26 occasions I've been trusted to take the game-winning shot and missed. I've failed over and over and over again in my life and that is why I succeed."

I felt like that even though the walk back to the car was agonising and was taken at a snail's pace, the 700-metre journey taking a full hour to complete. That night the feeling of accomplishment continued to course through my veins. It was several days though before I had recovered totally.

I had completed my first marathon. My running CV now had some text on its pages and I felt a part of something great. I also had some street credibility when it came to telling people I would soon be training for an Ironman triathlon.

That was next.

CHAPTER 9
FINDING AN IRON WILL

THURSDAY 26TH NOVEMBER, 2009
6.30PM

THE interviewer seems intrigued by our challenge.

"I'm tempted to ask, are ye mad? How on earth do you train for 32 marathons?" Matt Cooper of Today FM asks.

Cooper is sitting opposite Ken Whitelaw and I, manoeuvring himself back and forth on an office swivel chair. The studio is nightclub dark with television screens all around. The backroom team sits in the production studio peering into the small darkened studio that is the engine room for The Last Word on Today FM, one of Ireland's most popular drive time radio shows.

As we explained to Matt and to the hundreds of thousands of listeners about the apprenticeships we had served, my mind wandered momentarily back to June 2008 and the Promenade Des Anglaise in Nice, on the French Riviera and to the start of Ironman France.

It was on that day that I realised how much I was really capable of achieving. It was not just about the race itself. It was about so much more. As the official Ironman.com website says: 'The Ironman promises to be a transformational experience for any athlete. Life-changing is how most might describe it. While many of the changes are of a physical nature, a mental transformation also occurs. Athletes develop a stronger will, a sharper focus and greater confidence. The words 'can't' and 'quit' vanish from their vocabulary, and their definition of a goal is not a desire but destiny.'

Through completing this event my confidence in every aspect of my life soared to a higher plateau. This would be a major catalyst in leading me to the point where I could publicly commit to running 32 marathons. You will recall earlier I mentioned how I had served many apprenticeships to get me to the start line of running for 32 consecutive days around Ireland. I had dropped two sizes around my midriff. Other boxes now ticked included shooting a subpar round of golf, I was by now a long-term smoke-free zone and I had overcome a massive public speaking challenge. In addition I now had triathlon experience and I had finally run a full marathon.

Next on the list was a 2.4 mile swim followed by a 112-mile cycle and rounded off with a marathon distance run of 26.2 miles.

An Ironman triathlon.

CHAPTER 10
A NICE LEARNING CURVE

I STARTED training for my debut Ironman event in January of 2008. I had researched it thoroughly reading any race reports I could find of people who had completed the feat. I was captivated and inspired by all the stories I read. I knew it would take dedicated training over a six month period and I vowed quietly to reach the start line of Ironman France on 22nd June 2008 in top condition.

Having Ironman ambitions had bitten me well and truly early in the spring of 2008. I was ever mindful though of another challenge I was facing, that of a decline in the turnover of my company. It was not just us and our small property agency. Around this time a rolling stone of economic distress was gathering early momentum. Consumer confidence was ever so slightly starting to show signs of an about-turn. Interest rates had crept back up, our phones were getting quieter and appointments were not as frequent. Email enquiries were less in number and all of a sudden we had only the odd bid on properties here and there. A tap was slowly being turned off. Soon it would be wrenched tight. Like many, I just didn't realise how serious it would soon become. Who did?

Dorothy and I had no idea of the avalanche of economic woes that were about to be unleashed both nationally and on other shores. We worked together every day in the property business and we were very close. While we were doing all this training, I was also very conscious that the economy was changing colour. I started to make cutbacks in the winter months of 2007 and some more in early 2008. By doing so I thought we would not have to sell as many properties to survive.

I had heard that the easiest 10 per cent growth you could make in a company was to cut your overheads by a similar margin. I decided to put this to the test. Over the spring months in 2008 we scrutinised everything and moved the business from a main street retail office to a quieter location, off the main thoroughfare. "Cut your cloth according to your measure" were words of wisdom that seemed appropriate. This was only the beginning.

Being proactive in trying to secure our business future helped my head to remain very clear and very positive. By this time I was training vigorously; it was unlike anything I had done before. Sure I had trained for the three disciplines of triathlon and competed in many shorter distance races. The Ironman training however required a massive step up in terms of commitment and effort. Dorothy had also decided to register and she was a great student over the next six months, applying herself to every goal in terms of our training schedule.

The leap in training had been immediate. I consulted heavily with Brian Boyle and John O'Reilly, friends who had completed an Ironman themselves. I was eager to learn from their experience and to study their training schedule.

In the first week in January 2008, we began a 24-week training programme that pushed our bodies to limits never before experienced. Straight away we were into 12 hours or more of weekly training. Each seven-day block saw a minimum of eight or nine workouts. In January, short swims were hour-long sessions in the pool and this was just the beginning. Within a few months, one hour would edge towards two.

We confined our swimming to Tuesday and Thursday mornings at 7am in the local pool. A regular session was often in excess of 120 lengths before breakfast. As time has passed, the mental challenge that this presented has dissipated but I recall always being in a great mood on finishing each session.

I found the cycling the hardest to train for. Cycling at this level was something I came to late in life. I was like any young kid growing up spending hours on my shiny BMX bike. But cycling was then sent to quarantine for over 20 years re-emerging in the early noughties. By then I had swapped my 1970s BMX for a more modern Trek 1200 and I did enjoy the level of fitness it started to provide.

My early triathlon days had consisted of races where the cycle element never exceeded 25 miles lasting about 80 or 90 minutes. Now I had to train for a cycle that would potentially take seven hours or more. In late 2007 I had completed a cycle for charity from Mullingar to Galway and back over two days. This involved a journey of approximately 90 miles in each direction and I found that I was well up for such a distance. Thus I knew my legs had a good benchmark from which to launch into 2008.

Early in our new found training regime, I would cycle three times a week, two short spins of perhaps 40 miles each with one long cycle pencilled in for Saturday or Sunday. In January this long cycle would be about 60 miles. Early into the programme these workouts really tired me out. On Saturday lunchtimes, I would return home after a 50- or 60-mile cycle often collapsing on the couch for 20 minutes to recharge. Little did I know however that by April I would return from cycles of 100 miles or more, full of energy.

February, March and April were spent steadily raising the distances. Sixty-minute swims were stretched by about 10 per cent each week as were the other two disciplines. Seventy, 80- and 90-mile cycles became routine. I know these distances sound daunting as they were to me not long before. Now however with many years of a good exercise routine behind me, a positive mental attitude and a goal in front of me, I hardly noticed. I was loving every minute of it and each week I felt I was breaking through to higher and higher levels of fitness.

The particular Ironman race we had entered was rated among the top three most difficult of the 20 or more Ironman races spread across the globe. Rated only behind Lanzarote and Hawaii in terms of challenge, Ironman France could boast the Alps for negotiation on the bike leg. Many of the Cols (climbs) that we would have to overcome were regularly used in stages of the famous Tour de France cycle race.

Some quick internet searching showed us the level of difficulty we would have to train for. The route profile looked very intimidating and the many race reports I had studied were all in agreement that the cycling would be the most challenging part of the day. Over 5,000 feet of climbing on 112 miles (180km) of terrain would have to be completed. Then there were the descents too which would prove to be very hard, requiring a lot of focus and concentration. Doing 50 miles an hour downhill with only a helmet for protection can be scary to say the least and this was something we would have to train for as we had no experience of it.

The closest training ground we could find local to the midlands was just outside Tullamore in Offaly. Four hundred million years in the moulding, the Slieve Blooms are known in the midlands as the ultimate cycling workout, with three climbs offering up to 10 per cent gradients of ascent. In the winter of 2007 and spring of 2008, 'The Cut' climb just outside Clonaslee and my bike became intimately acquainted.

The 'Glendine' is the most difficult with the aptly named 'Wolftrap' a close second in terms of gradient. 'The Cut' climb is probably the least challenging of the three but it offered five kilometres or so of nonstop uphill gradient. This, I felt, would offer excellent training for the challenge that lay ahead. It offered no respite from the time you turned the corner out of the small village of Clonaslee. The legs were worked constantly until the summit was reached, just what we needed.

For someone whose only previous climbing experience was as a five year old getting into a bunk bed, I grew to love the early Saturday starts to Tullamore. We would climb the five kilometres or so over and over again taking anything from 22 to 28 minutes to negotiate its ascent, before descending in less than 10 minutes to where we had started. The descents were scary as the road had many pot holes. To hit one at speed would not have had a pleasant outcome so we had to really concentrate at every metre. Throw in an Irish winter and a wind chill factor well below zero, mixed on many occasions with sleet and driving rain, and you have a good idea of what was involved.

On reaching the bottom, the massive drop in body temperature was a shock to the system. We often had four layers of clothing on to warm our torsos. Although we arrived at the top sweating heavily from our efforts, the about-turn and a 10-minute descent would plummet the body temperature into reverse. By the time we reached the bottom again our teeth would be chattering with the cold.

The Cut climb had an average gradient of four per cent which meant you were climbing approximately four metres for every 100 metres progressed. For every three climbs of The Cut we did, we would throw in one climb of The Wolftrap. This was a longer climb of about eight kilometres and it presented a much steeper ascent with an average gradient of eight per cent.

Ninety per cent of the Wolftrap was negotiated by being out of the saddle where every ounce of energy was needed just to ensure you turned the pedals. The driving wind, rain and sleet certainly ensured we were getting stronger mentally as well. I tried to adopt a mindset of realising how fortunate I was to have the health to be there doing it. Sure, I got cold, wet, and was exhausted on many of these Saturday mornings but ask my cycling companions Doug Bates, Caroline Boyle, Philip Wade and Paul O'Brien how we felt. We loved every metre. You think Dorothy and I were mad for doing it? We had a goal a few months ahead, whereas the rest of our friends were doing it for fun!

At 31, in 2006 Dorothy had returned to active sporting pursuits having avoided them since her early twenties. Her background was in fitness having qualified in sports and leisure. In addition she had for many years worked as a swim instructor and lifeguard.

By late April, Dor and I had completed over half a dozen 80-mile-plus bike rides. The bike was the part I found the most challenging. It took the longest time out of our training schedules with a typical cycle in May taking up to six hours of time in the saddle. Swims were a couple of hours and a long run up to three hours, but we had to double that duration for the bike.

Running was a welcome respite from the arduous bike training. It was just us and the terrain beneath. I would typically run a half marathon before breakfast at least twice a week. I never actually found that part of the jigsaw hard as I had by this stage been running for about 13 years. I loved running, particularly in the early mornings and would encourage anyone to run at dawn at least once just once to see nature at that early hour. The untaxed pleasure of seeing the sun rise always set me up for the day with a very positive mental attitude and ready for whatever that day had in store.

We reached our peak in terms of training in April and early May. Dorothy and I booked a last-minute flight to Nice and spent a May weekend surveying the course completing a short swim, a short run and a longer than planned bike ride. The cycle route we rehearsed on was the exact course we would have to negotiate on race day. By the time we finished however, we had cycled over 125 miles having lost our way on a few occasions. Our planned eight-hour leisurely cycle took 10 hours to complete.

We arrived back at our hotel exhausted having spent the majority of that time in almost 80 degrees Fahrenheit. The acclimatisation would do us no harm however as it was only a light tanning compared to what we would face six weeks later. By early June our training programme came to an end. We had hit every number we had asked of ourselves and we were cautiously confident of achieving our goal.

Three weeks from race day we started to taper to allow our bodies to rest in advance of the main event. That period was a drag as the days seemed like weeks and the hours like days. Finally race week arrived and we started to pack in earnest.

In the spring and early summer of 2008, business had failed to improve. Ever conscious of not being away from the office for too long, I had booked just the minimum period away. My finances were tightening. This would be my main holiday for the year and yes, I did look on it as a holiday. This kind of challenge really got my adrenalin juices flowing. I did not view it as hardship, I saw it as something I was privileged to have the health to do. It would be a short privilege though. Out Thursday and back Tuesday. Short, but oh so sweet.

CHAPTER 11
THE FRENCH CONNECTION

THURSDAY 18TH JUNE, 2008

WE had booked a very early morning flight, so we were up by 2.30am. In the taxi were my parents, Dorothy, Enda and myself. Our entourage was bigger than this but the rest were making their own way to the airport.

There we met up with fellow Ironman virgins Joe Holton, Pat O'Hara and Malcolm Craig. A number of our friends added their support by booking their summer holiday to coincide with the race. At the check-in desk we met up with two friends who had completed an Ironman themselves, Sonia O'Mahony and Brian Boyle. These were accompanied by Brian's wife Caroline, and Sonia's husband, Lenny. Also there were their children Hannah Boyle and Eabha O'Mahony as well as two other friends, Yvonne Kane and Marie Louise Johnson. In tow also was my brother Tom's wife Orla, who hails from Lancaster, Pennsylvania.

Arriving in Nice we loaded into a city bus for the short journey to the city centre. Naturally we got lost, but eventually we managed to locate our accommodation and finally get a chance to relax. In the afternoon we went down to the Race Headquarters to register. Thursday evening was spent generally chilling out and an early night was the order of the day.

FRIDAY 19TH JUNE

We woke a little after 7.30am and decided to go for a quick swim in the Mediterranean sea, a short five-minute walk from our apartment. A few butterflies started to flutter at this stage. I spotted Jan Sibbersen in the area cordoned off for the athletes. Jan was the world record holder for the swim leg of the Ironman, his time being 42 minutes and 17 seconds for the 3.8km distance.

In the afternoon we decided to do a reconnaissance of the bike course. Joe Holton, a friend from home, was also competing in his first Ironman event. He hadn't had the chance to see the course before, so off we set. Joe, Enda, Yvonne, my dad, Dor and myself, all packed into a lovely comfortable hired car, or so we thought.

As I mentioned earlier, Dor and I had come out a month previously and cycled the bike course, but this was Joe's first opportunity to see it. In a car in the heat of the afternoon it looked unbelievably tough.

Joe's mood worsened as the afternoon progressed, so I tried to reassure him that it was well within his ability to do it. Given the severity of the climbs and the heavy weight of five of us on the vehicle, even the car struggled to get up the hills. I could see his demeanour change over those few hours.

What I had forgotten was that we had done it in a relaxed state taking 10 hours on a pleasant May day, unlike the fire and furnace that Sunday would bring. It was by now late June and the temperature had risen significantly too. Thursday had been extremely tiring and today was just as bad. Three-and-a-half hours after we started we arrived back at the apartment car sick, overheated, disillusioned and a little downhearted.

SATURDAY 21ST JUNE

Saturday was largely uneventful. Joe's demeanour had perked up again and we went for a quick two-mile run along the promenade at about 7:30am. During the morning we checked and rechecked our gear. We all asked each other the most stupid of questions about gear, chaffing, bars, hats, stuff we knew all the answers too. It was just nerves, I guess.

As part of the logistics of the event all competitors were required to leave their bike into transition on the afternoon before the race. On arrival we had to queue for about 30 minutes before entering the transition area. While waiting, Enda went for a quick spin to check my bike, leaving me with his Specialised Stump Jumper FRS mountain bike. Picture the scene. I was in a queue with over 2,000 perfectly toned, highly primed and motivated athletes. I am standing there surrounded by Cervelos, Ridleys and Specialised ROAD bikes and he left me holding his 'mountain bike'. People were staring. One guy even came over and took a photograph. Did they really think I was going to try and cycle 112 miles (180km) on a mountain bike?

I did say the day was largely uneventful, that is until we got a shock over dinner, when to our surprise a group of unannounced friends from Ireland appeared into the restaurant in the form of Philip Wade, Doug Bates and Paul O'Brien. They had decided just the evening before to fly out to join us. We were thrilled to see them of course. It gave us a huge lift.

LA DIMANCHE
SUNDAY 22 JUNE 2008 (RACE DAY)

We had retired at about 9pm the night before. I had managed to get a fantastic night's sleep dozing off at about 10.30pm and not waking until 3.45am. This was a bonus as I had allowed for only getting about two or three hours sleep at most. I woke up feeling great and roused the three sleeping beauties, Dor, Enda and Joe.

It's amazing what goes through your head at times like this. It was still pitch dark outside with late night revellers still roaming the streets. Silly questions and doubts re-entered my brain. I devoured a large bowl of muesli with a banana blended in, followed by bread and tea. Leaving the sanctuary of the apartment at 4.50am, we headed into the unknown.

As we walked along the promenade en route to the start line, an irony unfolded in front of us. In the real world it was a normal Saturday night. We passed by hundreds of young people still sitting on the beach, drinking beer, smoking cigarettes and some with guitars still in hand. Some were sober, some not. Just a few hundred yards away was the other extreme as over 2,000 very fit people were gathering to embark on what would be for most of them the pinnacle of their sporting lives.

On entering transition, I pumped the tyres and was particularly careful to leave plenty of air capacity. This would allow them to expand in the midday heat. A quick loo stop and before we knew it, we were being summoned to the start line. I spotted Doug, Yvonne, Phil and Paul as well as Siobhan Topp, another friend who was in Nice on holidays with her husband Roland, all encouraging supporters. I bade them farewell and on I went.

By 6.15am we stood on the shoreline and stared out into the Mediterranean Sea. The words of General Patton, the former US Army General and 1912 Olympian, would have summed up what lay ahead for the next many hours in Nice. He once said:

"Now if you are going to win any battle you have to do one thing. You have to make the mind run the body. Never let the body tell the mind what to do. The body will always give up. It is always tired morning, noon and night. But the body is never tired if the mind is not tired. When you were younger, the mind could make you dance all night, and the body was never tired. You've always got to make the mind take over and keep going."

Although I had been feeling nervous all morning, I must confess that once the ocean was in front of me, I experienced a sense of calm. A helicopter circled overhead, hundreds of encouraging spectators balanced on every free inch of viewable platform. The race referee paraded on a jet ski and told us by way of hand signals how long was left - three minutes, two, one, 30 seconds, and then...

TROIS! DEUX! UN! ALLEZ!

THE RACE
6:31AM

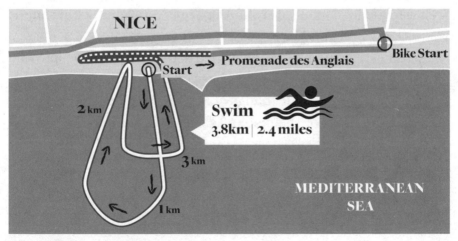

LA NAGER / THE SWIM
(2.4 MILES/3.8KM)

The klaxon went off and 2,277 athletes headed to the blue sea, limbs exploding into action and all disappearing into our marine exam paper.

Battle had commenced. We had an ocean in front of us but everyone seemed content to merge together like a shoal of piranha at a feeding frenzy. Arms and legs flung in every direction. It was a frantic scuffle. Oxygen was a scarcity and space nonexistent for the first 500 metres or more. Such was the struggle on some strokes, I had to deny myself even the luxury of a breath. My race strategy and carefully rehearsed swim technique sank to the ocean floor. This was all about survival.

Where was the beautiful stroke I had carved out, over months of carefully considered training. Where was the masterful breathing technique I had practised, the extended follow-through to gain maximum distance. F*** that! Brute force was the only thing that would get me through this.

"Don't worry, it won't last," I thought to myself. I was wrong.

Nothing prepared me for this. I wrestled, jostled, belted, fisted, punched and dragged with the best of them and lost. What the hell? Just as I was getting used to it I exited the water having completed the first of a two-looped course. With 2,400 metres done, I had 1,400 to go. Back in for one more spin in the washing machine. Soon it would be over.

I exited finally after one hour and six minutes, bang-on target and feeling fantastic. I glanced around for a quick spotting of Caroline as well as Paul, Phil and Marie Louise.

Entering transition I was astounded at the number of people who had finished ahead of me. It was so busy I couldn't find a vacant chair in which to sit for a quick change of clothes. So I changed standing up. Socks on, shoes on, helmet and gloves, wetsuit into the bag and off I went to find my bike.

C. 7:45AM
LA BICYCLETTE / THE BIKE
(112 MILES/180KM)

I started the 200-metre jog to find my bike among the thousands of other steeds. Grabbing it swiftly, I headed out, mounting at the designated area. Just then I heard something fall to the ground. It was my sunglasses. I had left them perched on the handlebars

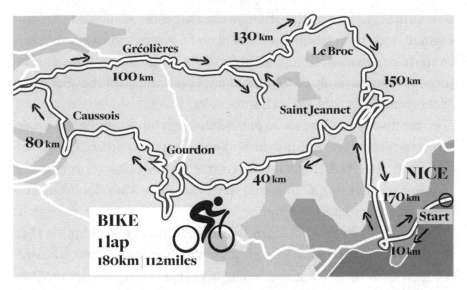

before the race. Thank heavens this happened. If I hadn't heard them this would have been a problem as I would have struggled enormously in the sun for the following 10 or 11 hours.

The first 20 kilometres of the cycle was very flat, largely uneventful and all about settling into a nice rhythm. A condition of the race is that for the bike leg all competitors must wear their race number on their back. This displays both your number and your name. At the five kilometre point I noticed the name Laurent pass me by. This was none other than Laurent Jalabert, the famous French professional cyclist. On retiring from professional cycling he had turned to Ironman competition for his sporting pleasure. At least I beat him on the swim, I thought to myself.

As he passed I unravelled the first of the many energy bars I would eat that day. During training I had come to really like them. However the first of these on this day did not overly agree with my stomach. Perhaps it was too early in the morning. It was still short of eight o'clock in the morning.

At the end of the first 20k there was a very nasty 500m climb. We had been well warned about it but it was much more difficult than in training largely because it was a very narrow climb, barely five metres wide. Given that it was full of cyclists, most of whom were wobbling from side to side, navigation was very difficult. I struggled to stay upright and pushed the lowest gear ratio available to ensure I did. It took every ounce of strength to get me through this but thankfully it was over as quickly as it had started. My heart rate jumped from probably 140 to 180 beats per minute in the space of a few seconds but that would do no harm.

Over the next 40k or so we passed through the stunning mountain villages of Gattiere, Saint Jannet, Vence, Torrettes Sur Loupe, Bar Sur Loupe and into Chataneuf De Grasse. At this point we were about to enter what they call in boxing parlance 'The Main Event of The Evening' of the bike discipline.

The main 'climb' was 21km in total distance. It had an average gradient of 4.2 per cent, meaning for the duration we would climb 4.2 metres for every hundred metres we cycled. It was broken into four stages of 6km, 3km, 4km and then an arduous eight kilometres of a steep ascent. The final 6.5km of climbing had a gradient of 6.5 per cent to really test us. The first stage had seemed relatively okay when we had tested it in May. Not today.

The temperature, like the gradient, had started to climb... 28, 29, 30 and finally reaching 34 degrees Celsius. It was getting very hot.

Just after Bar sur Loupe, I spotted Doug, Phil, Marie Louise and Paul and it was great to see them. I gave Paul a big high five as I passed. Whilst I really felt like I was working, I still felt great at this point. I had met them just as we started the second stage of the climb, a nasty 3km stretch with a gradient of seven degrees. The sun was creating a cauldron of heat all around us. I was surrounded by slowing cyclists but nobody said anything. It would have been foolish to do so as it would waste energy that needed to be stored away for the afternoon and evening onslaught still to come.

This part of the course was stunning. We didn't get to see much of it but I knew it was there and appreciated the fleeting glances I got of it. Into Gourdon and a final left hand turn to begin the 8km climb to Col De Lecre, our highest point. This was relentless and exhausting. I happily let a number of riders pass me and in turn passed a few myself. Those winter Saturday mornings spent down in Co. Offaly climbing The Cut over and over again were paying off.

The climb was made all the harder because you could see a mile in front of you for a lot of the time. I thought of Dor and Joe still having to do it, assuming they were behind me which I wasn't actually sure of. At the top of Col De L'Ecre and with a high degree of climb behind me, I felt a real sense of achievement. This was our highest point. There was still 9km of climbing to do later but it would not be quite as severe. "These mountains are not getting the better of me," I thought to myself.

Soon after we began a blissful 12km of downhill which was utter heaven given the brutality we had experienced for the previous two hours or so.

The next 30km were uneventful and offered a beautiful landscape. I was conscious of not losing concentration for a split second given the hair-raising descents we were now having to navigate.

Nutrition is a key component in ensuring success in an Ironman event. This was a potentially 12-to-15-hour event after all. I was managing the nutrition poorly. A pre-race strategy full of military precision and good intentions went out the window. I had ignored my 20-minute eating rule a few times and I was taking on board a large volume of liquid, close to 1000ml between each aid station.

Later I found out that I was taking on too much water and not enough energy drink. I also should have been replacing lost salt from my body. The sheer volume of water I was drinking, whilst helping to rehydrate me, was also excreting all the salt from my pores. This was shortly going to start affecting my performance.

Soon after, we arrived into a village called Coursegoules where we had a quick out and back 10 kilometre loop. It gave me a good idea of how many cyclists were ahead of me. I couldn't believe so many were ahead but I was comforted on the return 5km by how many more were behind.

At 120km into the bike leg, I encountered pain, real pain, for the first time. It came in the form of massive cramping from my calf muscles on both legs. During training I had never ever experienced cramping and I was shocked that this was happening now. I searched my brain for a reason as well as a solution, but nothing came back.

I stood up on the bike and freewheeled, stretching as best I could while doing 25 miles per hour on this section but the pain continued. Such was my immediate shock that I thought about possibly not finishing. I recall however not being panicked about this. If it was a physical rather than a mental reason for a DNF (did not finish) then I could cope with that.

After a quick yet severe 2km climb back into Coursegoules and a gentle descent shortly after, we arrived into a forested enclosure. The Forest stretch is a seven-kilometre climb up to Cote De Saint Pons with an average gradient of about 4 degrees. It is what a friend of mine calls "The Doctor". It is here, according to the Ironman France veteran, that you get to find out what kind of condition you are in at this point of the race. If you have gone too hard then you will suffer greatly as it offers no respite, except for some shelter from the fast approaching midday sun. I recall during this climb giving it another name, "open heart surgery".

I had a very nasty lapse in concentration here and momentarily lost sight of the road in front of me. When I looked up I was heading for the edge. This would not have been too bad except that a 100 ft drop awaited me if I hadn't raised my head. I gave myself quite a talking to.

A short time later, I noticed a banner with the wording in English, that a supporter had left on the roadside to cheer someone on. It read: "Remember pain is temporary but success is forever." I took great heart from this and would use its motivational message many times over the next four or five hours.

At the top of this climb the hard work for the cycle was almost over. I still had a hefty 60km still to go, but the only pain left was the heavy pain of concentration. The remainder was a series of descents meandering continuously around very nasty bends that required the utmost respect. To lose concentration would not have a pleasant outcome.

One section in particular had a 35 kilometre descent. It sounds great, but in reality I didn't feel confident going at a speed my bike could simply because there were too many dangerous bends to navigate. I descended as fast as felt comfortable, passing and being passed constantly by the same five or six riders. I cannot remember going faster than 52 kph purely because of the severity of these descents and bends. It was more important to finish the 180km cycle than have a nasty fall at high speed trying to pick up a minute or two on my fellow competitors.

Back down on the flat I felt a lot safer that the dangerous work was now behind me. As I neared the end of the cycle, the cramps continued and I stretched as much as I could. With 20 kilometres to go and a nice flat road ahead, I began to stretch out my calf muscles as often as possible, and freewheeled by rising out of the saddle every half a kilometre or so.

As we hit the 160km point my feet started to hurt like hell and I looked forward greatly to being able to take my cycling shoes off. They had been on my feet for over six hours at this point. I surmised that the heat of the midday sun and a tight shoe fitting was to blame. Looking back, a half shoe size larger than normal would have been a better strategy, it was hitting 34 degrees Celsius which was just over 93 degrees Fahrenheit and my feet were obviously expanding in the heat.

This final stretch took an eternity. I glanced at my watch. We had entered the water just after 6.30am and it was now approaching 2pm. I had been working for almost seven and a half hours to this point and my only thoughts were of the bliss I had to look forward to in dismounting my bike so that I could begin to run 'a marathon'. Such were the mind games in this event.

As we re-entered Nice, I came in sight of the run route. I was astonished at the number of athletes already running and distinctly remember a feeling of negativity entering my mind. They had one or possibly two loops of the four loop course already completed and here was I still on my bike.

As I dismounted I heard a familiar cheer from the crowd. I turned around to see my father yelling encouragement in my direction. At the same time, my legs touched the ground for the first time in six hours and twenty minutes. It was at this time that I had my second trial of the day, one I thought momentarily I would not recover from. As I dismounted, my legs completely seized up. The bike fell over and in my mind I screamed in pain. I was stuck rigid to the ground, my legs frozen solid and riddled with cramps. My mind raced.

My dad screamed encouragement from the barriers. Just then a fellow cyclist fell to the ground beside me and it was obvious he was suffering a similar physical challenge to me. I actually gained some encouragement from this. At least I was still standing. I walked two or maybe three steps and just then I received the most enthusiastic yell of "Come on Gerry" from a complete stranger in the crowd (my name was on my race number). I cannot describe what this did but it focused my mind back 100 per cent to the job in hand. You will recall my earlier observation of the power of a few simple words of encouragement in any challenging time we are experiencing.

With my bike in tow, I walked slowly into transition, monitoring every step my body was taking for signs of recovery.

"Ok, at least I can move again", I thought to myself.

"Now for the marathon."

Passing the bike to a female volunteer I started to gently jog towards the transition tent. As I entered the tent, I knew somehow I was fine again and my mind turned totally positive once more. I opened my run bag and took out the running attire required for the 26.2 miles that awaited.

It was at this point that I made my second big error of the day. The first had been to take on too much water on the bike. The second was to ignore the two sachets of salt replacement in my run bag. My logic was that I had not practised taking salt tablets in training. They had only been recommended to me the week before. I had packed them but now when the requirement was so obviously there, I ignored them. What an idiot.

C 14:20HRS
LA COURIR/THE RUN
(26.2 MILES/42.195KM)

The marathon ran along the famous Promenade Des Anglaise. The

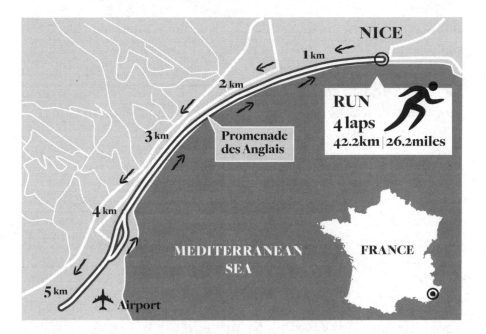

out and back course of four laps where each lap measured 10.5 km was broken into halves of 5.25 km. The first thing I noticed was that I immediately started to pass out scores of runners. I was now onto my favourite discipline. For months, I had thought methodically about my pace for this first loop and had planned a 26-27 minute turnaround for the first 5.25 km. I turned in 25:30 but already I began to slow down and to suffer heavily. It happened that quickly. My stomach was experiencing turmoil as it was full of energy bars, energy drinks, bananas and an energy gel which I had taken on the bike.

At the turnaround point of the first lap the energy drained from my body like a running tap. At that moment, I had no idea why it was happening. Immediately I went from a brisk running pace to a walk. Never once in training had I practised walking and I was shocked that my body seemed to accept such a fate so easily. It had never entered my mind that it might be a requirement on race day. I looked all around and saw a huge number of my fellow competitors had adopted a similar strategy. "What the hell was happening?"

I had only completed six kilometres or so of the 42 but I knew from here on I would have to adopt a run, walk, run strategy. I was still many hours from finishing and this was not something that I had planned for. I had no idea how to react. I took refuge momentarily behind a nearby tree, out of view of the spectators. I didn't have an incredible urge to go to the toilet it just felt like something to do to stimulate some other brain activity from the onslaught of pain that the rest of my body was experiencing.

I started walking in kilometre six and did so for about 300-400 metres before jogging again at a very slow pace. My one-loop split I recall was 1:03 which meant the second 5.25 km took me over 37 minutes, a full 12 minutes slower than the outer. This was a lot slower than I had planned. My stomach was extremely sick at this point and the thoughts of consuming a gel, a bar or anything revolted me.

I soldiered on through the second lap of four but I was physically a wreck by now. A 1:03hrs first lap turned into a 1:09hrs second. This was only going one way I thought. By now I was walking as much as I was running but was quite happy just to do so. I never considered that I wouldn't finish, I had long accepted that I would have to mix this strategy but my hoped for 11 hours 30 minutes finishing time was now gone out the door. By now I was over 10 hours into the race. The cut off was 16 hours so I still had six hours or more to finish the remaining 13 miles.

My body was devoid of any energy, surviving now on a mixture of adrenalin and stubbornness. I knew however I would crawl if I had to. The heat had engulfed this Irishman who was not at all used to such temperatures. I was properly attired, had gallons of sun screen rubbed in and I even ignored the opportunity to get a water shower from the volunteers for fear of getting blisters. I could do no more to protect myself from the rays.

Lap three was sheer brutality. My stomach churned, I wanted to throw up so much as I felt this might offer some relief. I picked up a slice of something resembling bread from a feed station but it was hard and I threw it away just as quickly, choosing a small piece of banana instead. My pace was deteriorating with each lap but I scarcely cared. All I wanted to do was finish.

By now I had worked out where each of our invaluable supporters had positioned themselves on the course. It was great having them at different places. I was unable to muster a smile as each cheer greeted me but I was so grateful for their support and did acknowledge with a wave each and every time I saw them. They were magnificent one and all and I know they all suffered in the heat given their stationary positions in 93 degrees Fahrenheit of heat.

Lap three was a similar strategy to the two previous laps. It was on this lap that I first spotted Joe Holton. He caught up with me as I was shuffling along on one of my many walks. His mood was sombre and it was very apparent that he was equally as drained as I was. I was taken aback to see that he had one less wristband on than I had, indicating that I was a lap ahead of him. At the end of each run lap, athletes had been given a coloured wristband to denote the number of laps they had completed. Lap ones reward was a red wristband and blue was given for number two. I noticed Joe had only a red one which meant I was about six miles ahead of him at that time. He told me that he had experienced a very hard time on the bike. I empathised . Over the next hour or so, I passed him and he passed me continuously.

Enda had long before told me that Dor was safely in from the bike and it was around now that I spotted her for the first time. My sister was one tough lady. Here she was the other side of the run loop with a big wave, a big cheer and a smile as wide as your arm for me. I waved, but simply did not have the energy to mouth a response. The five metres that separated us would have required too much energy for me at that time to shout anything meaningful.

With the third band which was white in colour, safely around my wrist, I commenced the last lap with a walk of 100 metres. A white band was akin to gold in colour as it indicated we had only one more lap to go. By now the legs were almost gone, the body was a wreck, but the heart and mind were both 100 per cent. Looking back I am amazed at how mentally alert I was for the entire day.

The final lap was as tough as the three before. Between two aid stations, I actually set myself a mini-goal of trying to run continuously to the next feed station, a distance of perhaps 600 metres. I recall saying to myself that to accomplish this would be as great as finishing the Ironman itself. I focused on this for about two minutes but it soon became clear that I would have to walk again. No matter, at least I was a little bit closer to finishing.

Enda appeared on his mountain bike at the final turn for home and offered huge encouragement. I asked him to stay close by for the last five kilometres but I asked him not to speak as I was incapable of carrying on any conversation. He could see the physical wreck I was and for some strange reason that was important to me. At the turn I met Malcolm Craig, a friend from Sligo who was also about to finish his first Ironman challenge. I greeted him briefly before he headed off into the distance eventually finishing three minutes ahead of me.

The last five kilometres took an eternity but I scarcely minded as I knew I was nearly home. Enda was there all the way on the bike, on the phone, on the camcorder. He was very encouraging and I will never forget his support over that final three miles.

Approaching the finish line my eyes didn't well up, I didn't get emotional, I didn't get flashbacks to all the training or efforts over the past six months. I was just so glad to finish. For the last 100 metres down the finishing chute the crowds were great and I savoured the moment, and even managed to high five a band of complete strangers, all family on this day nonetheless.

Over the line 12 hours 18 minutes and 16 seconds after starting, I was presented with my medal. I had other priorities though at that moment. I immediately spotted two large black bins and headed straight for them to throw up. That was all I could think about.

POST RACE

I was directed towards the athletes area behind the finish line, passing the medical tent as I did so. It wasn't a pretty sight. Some had had a much harder day than I. I lay on the grass for 20 minutes. There was an eerie silence here. No mad chatter, no cheers of congratulations. I guess it was because in this area, there were only competitors, no family or friends. We were all simply too exhausted.

A 15-minute post race massage turned into in excess of an hour as I had cramp in every inch of my legs. The masseur looked on in utter astonishment at my lack of ability to bend my legs even the tiniest amount. He tried everything and I must admit I felt at least 50 per cent better upon leaving.

When I was finished I apologised for taking up so much of his time and headed out to hopefully catch Dor finishing. I met Joe parked on a bench. The poor guy looked drained, but thankfully soon after he was back to his normal jovial self.

When I got back out I met friends and family including Dave and Amanda Andrews and Orla my sister-in-law at the finish line. They told me Dor had about 20 minutes left to go. I went out to cheer her on and shortly after spotted her with Enda in tow on his bike, shouting and roaring encouragement in her direction. To my astonishment I was able to run again and I did so for about 500 metres and together we cheered her towards the finish line. She was savouring every moment and had a fantastic smile on her face whilst crossing the line. She finished in a magnificent 14:30:50.

Malcolm had earlier finished in 12:15:01, Joe in 13:44:01 and Pat O'Hara, a fellow Mullingar man, in 14:06:22, all previously Ironman virgins but now champions one and all. A quick trip to a local restaurant was made where we met up with our family and supporters. Then we headed back to the finish line to watch the remaining athletes crossing the line. These were the most amazing of athletes having been out for almost 16 hours without rest. They crossed the line with as much enthusiasm as the winner of the race.

That night I felt completely drained so Marie Louise, a friend who was also a medical doctor, gave me some IV fluids which helped me recover. I lay on the bed as she administered this medicine and the next thing I knew it was 8am the following morning.

Over the next few days I reflected on our achievements. On paper it seemed almost impossible but all of us had applied ourselves to the task of completing this amazing event. I guess we were the lucky ones as we were blessed with the good health to be able to do it. Back home over dinner my dad summed up its magnitude.

'You rise at 4am, enter the ocean at 6.30am in jelly fish-infested waters, negotiate strong currents not to mention 2,200 bodies all around you. You then face 5,000 feet of ascents through the early Alpine peaks, climbing, climbing, and climbing all the time. Then, taking all your courage you descend from whence you came. Not to mention the heated cauldron of a French summer. Then when you complete this 183.8 km distance... eight or nine hours of hellish punishment... All you have to look forward to... is a bloody MARATHON.'

CHAPTER 12
IF LIFE DEALS YOU LEMONS, MAKE LEMONADE

THE Ironman Challenge and the distances it presents can be very daunting when put on paper. They are however, more than achievable. Perhaps there is a comparable route to success in any challenge we face. If we focus on overcoming a challenge and go about it the right way, we can almost always find a way to get there.

The percentage of athletes who finish an Ironman is exceptionally high. An unexpected race day injury or mechanical failure on the bike explains the majority of the remainder. And yes, the vast majority of the participants are normal people just like you and me. There are elite athletes taking part but they number perhaps only 20 or 30 in each race. A total of 2,277 competitors started Ironman France in 2008 and 86 per cent finished.

Have you ever taken a look at your diary of six months ago. Check out some of the challenges that you faced around that time. What happened to them? Maybe you were nervous about a speech you had to deliver or were facing some sort of major crisis at work. Perhaps you were about to sit an exam and you still had to cram in some last-minute study. Maybe it was all three. Whatever the challenges that you faced six months ago, you have probably by now overcome them all. How did you do it? You simply found a way. The speech has been successfully delivered, the work issue dealt with and the positive exam results have arrived.

One day early in March 2006 I was having a very frustrating day at work. At that time, business was extremely good. That however, brought its own challenges. Every day of self-employment up to that time was action-packed, where every minute of every working day was consumed by labour. There was always a job to be done.

Working for myself had really opened my eyes. I was the managing director and I was the chief negotiator. My responsibilities did not stop there however. We were a very small company which meant I was also the head salesman, the accountant (a poor one), the purchaser of goods, the website supervisor, the advertising executive and the toilet cleaner. Dorothy was the office manager and in charge of administration. She was streets ahead of me in that department. We were a small company, a very small company and had only two additional members of staff. The first was Christopher Taaffe, a recently graduated property degree student who had come first in his year, and the second was a man who had graced the hallowed turf of Croke Park quite a few years before. That was Robbie O'Malley, the former Meath footballer and Ireland captain in the Compromise Rules games against Australia. I met Robbie through Bernard Flynn. Both Bernard and Robbie were twice All Ireland football medal winners and All Stars. Bernard had lived in Mullingar for over 20 years and we became close friends in that time.

Just like the three previous years, in 2006 every working day was filled from 8am till 8pm and beyond. We never had a minute. On this bright Tuesday spring morning, I was having a very busy but typical day. March was always a good month for business, perhaps the peak of the year's trading. I had worked 13 hours the day before and I had a diary full of appointments ahead of me. I had viewings to be conducted, a couple of valuations to send to various institutions and a tricky commercial lease to be scrutinised for a client by lunchtime. I was really feeling the pressure and I knew the remainder of my week would be just as hectic. My diary was full from early morning till late at night for the following week. My phone was buzzing non-stop on the table and the office phone displayed three flashing red lights, an indication of additional demands.

As all this happening, Bernard walked in.

I held my hands up to my head in frustration.

"I can't take this anymore," I said to him.

It was a cry to share a problem. Self-employment had no safety net. Everything ultimately can rest on your shoulders. I was stressed.

I showed him my diary. It was two A4 pages in size, showing that day and the next. The white background of each page was barely visible, camouflaged by the blue ink from my pen. Writing filled 95 per cent of the available space, filled with appointments and tasks yet to be completed.

"Look," I said to him, pointing at the diary and pushing it across the desk for him to see.

"I can't cope. It just never stops. I can't handle it."

He looked through the pages and then in the following three seconds, Bernard taught me one of the greatest business and indeed life lessons I have ever learned.

"Close your eyes," he ordered.

I did as he asked. Then I heard a movement of pages.

"Now open them," he directed.

As I did so, he was pushing the diary back to my side of the desk.

"It could be worse," he continued.

He had moved the diary three months forward. Before me were two completely blank pages.

"It could be like that," he said.

His theory hit me as hard as an express train. I was immediately jolted from this self-indulgency. He was so right. I needed to realise just how lucky I was to have such a thriving business, such a busy life. His theory was that I had clients to meet and business to transact. I should recognise this positive, and simply reorganise myself. Be happy that I was so busy and then formulate a better way of planning my work. It was a lesson that I have never forgotten.

I believe now that we should always try and find a positive out of everything we might perceive as a negative. If it's raining outside I try to remind myself that we need it for the grass to grow and that life cannot exist without it. If it's a work issue then I try and devise a plan of action to accomplish whatever it is that needs doing. I try to remind myself to give thanks for the fact that I have a job to do. On the occasions I have had exam stress to deal with, I tried to project myself to a time when I would be earning income from work related to the qualification I was studying for and in the process encouraging myself that all the long hours of study will have been worth it.

It is as easy to see a positive as it is to see a negative in so many of life's experiences. I know this might sound a little unreasonable to expect in certain situations. If you told me that I had accidentally deleted the book I have written to this point, I would probably take a year to find a positive and have lost all my hair in the process. But within reason there are hundreds of everyday things that frustrate us all the time, where this simple redirection of attitude can help.

Many other people are faced with enormous life challenges where deriving anything positive from their circumstance can be very difficult. I am fortunate and eternally grateful that I have never had to deal with anything of such magnitude.

CHAPTER 13

IRONING OUT MY TROUBLES, ON THE DOUBLE

BY early July 2008, I was rested from my first Ironman endeavours. Given that these events are so popular, our triathlon club decided to hold a meeting to find out if anyone had any interest in signing up to do another one the following year. Ironman races tended to fill out as soon as they are announced so now was the time to make such a decision. Eight or nine people turned up at the meeting. Over the course of the discussions someone mentioned that they had read earlier that day on the internet that Ironman UK still had a few 'charity slots' left for their race in 2008 which was only three weeks away.

They say that impulsive decisions are not good. Well, before I had left the table I had gone online and registered. Crazy but true. The group could not understand my madness. I had only finished my first Ironman three weeks before. Conventional wisdom tells you that for non-elite athletes, one Ironman Triathlon a year is all that is recommended. There was no going back however as I had paid the fee to guarantee entry. I was committed.

The next morning, I felt I should have been committed.

What had I done? I felt an idiot. By lunch time I had decided I was withdrawing but by mid-afternoon I was full steam ahead for it again. That day was a roller coaster of confused thoughts. I knew I was fit enough physically. I had come back down from the euphoria of Nice. This race demands not just physical attributes but also strong mental ones as well. Just three weeks before I had completed the full distance. The training was in the legs. I figured that with sufficient mental preparation, I would be able to do another. It seemed a shame not to take advantage of such an opportunity, so I decided to go ahead.

Three weeks after registering, unbelievably I was at the start line of yet another Ironman distance triathlon. The venue was a small hamlet called Sherbourne in the county of Dorset, in South West England. Beside me were 1,500 other brave souls including three fellow Midland Triathlon club members, Doug Bates, Nicky McCabe and

Mary Daly, all with the common goal and belief that they could complete an Ironman Triathlon.

The contrast in surroundings and climate from Nice could not have been more stark. Gone was the balmy Mediterranean waters, replaced with an autumnal-chilled lake. The warm summers morning of southern France exchanged for a delayed 6am start to allow the fog and mist to clear. The temperature too had dropped by about 16 degrees celsius from my maiden Ironman.

Shortly before seven am the gun went off and with it another 12 hours or so of sweat and effort commenced. I felt two inches taller entering the water as I already had an Ironman medal adorning my wall. The swim was a lot less frantic than France but in the water there was still a lot of jostling. I exited three minutes faster than I had before, the watch showing 1:03:54 as I rose from the depths.

Unlike France which had one loop of 180 km, this bike route was a three-loop circuit of 60km each. The weather was cool and blustery which made the cycle quite challenging. The 180km of distance to be covered might have had something to do with it as well. Each loop had one very long climb to be negotiated but it had a very fast descent, where my speed at one point hit 74km per hour. Very hairy.

Surprisingly I was over 10 minutes slower on the bike that I had been in Nice, finishing the cycle in 6hrs and 33 minutes. I put this down to post-Nice fatigue. The course whilst challenging, was not as difficult as in France but the windy conditions presented a completely different exam paper.

As I began the run, I felt great. I knew that I could do it and I felt blessed to be able to compete again in such an event so soon after my debut. People train for years for one and years again to get a second opportunity. I knew the season ahead would be a long one and that these two events would fill my head with wonderful memories to tide me over the approaching winter months.

The run was on a variety of terrain including grass, gravel, tarmac, mud and also included the main street of this picturesque Dorset town. It seemed every local was out to cheer us on. The atmosphere as we turned into town was electric. Four loops had to be negotiated on this course and given the narrow routing the course was very busy and full of tiring athletes. Once again my dad was in tow and we had many more friends over from Ireland to lend their support.

As I came to the point where I realised I had but one mile to go, I knew the opportunity to run under 12 hours was there for the taking. I picked up the pace with ease, which in itself amazed me. Here I was over 11-and-a-half hours after starting, and still I was feeling strong.

Crossing the line was a defining moment. As I savoured an 11:52:53 finishing time I studied my body and its condition. Physically I felt unbelievably strong. My marathon time was only 4:08 over 30 minutes faster than France. Gone were the exhaustive feelings of Nice. I felt fantastic, even telling myself that I had the energy to do it all over again. I felt very strong mentally too. Endorphins of positivity coursed through every cell of my body. I was greeted shortly after by my family, who were amazed by how fresh I looked. I returned home now with two Ironman medals on my CV and I craved more challenges. It was a massive leap of faith for me within my own self-belief system.

A few weeks after returning my mind was already in overdrive.

I wanted more.

CHAPTER 14
DRAWING INSPIRATION FROM HIGH ACHIEVERS

BY the mid-noughties and beyond I had started to get a surge of confidence in my own self-worth and personal ability. Most of this was through personal growth by way of exiting the comfort zones I have outlined thus far.

I now also understood that we could learn so much from each other. For almost everything we might want to achieve, usually there is someone we can find who has already done it. Why try and reinvent the wheel when we don't need too? If it is something new and unique, perhaps we can use our own self-confidence to lead the way.

A great case in point of the former was the story of Michael O'Leary's tip received from his boss Tony Ryan, the owner of Ryanair. At a time when Ryanair was going through huge turmoil, Ryan suggested to O'Leary that he go to America and study a man called Herb Kelleher who was profitably running South West Airlines, one of the largest airlines in the United States. O'Leary returned convinced that Ryanair could in fact be turned around if they applied the same 'no frills' principle which Kelleher was successfully doing in America. The rest, as they say, is history. Ryanair is now one of the world's largest and most profitable airlines.

For my own inspiration I have studied many people. I also began to attend seminars on motivation and self-belief. I wanted to improve so many more aspects of my life. 'Why settle for being any less than the best you can be,' is a quote I had read somewhere. I felt the need to raise my own standards in business, academically and in sporting pursuits.

In the mid-noughties I became a really big fan of the teachings of Anthony Robbins, the American self-help and peak-performance coach. I attended a number of his four-day "Unleash the Power Within" seminars. This event was a real eye-opener to me, highlighting just what we can achieve once a positive mindset is adopted. The seminar placed heavy emphasis on the implementation of a healthy fitness and nutrition regime to assist us in achieving success in anything we wish to do.

I also admire and have been influenced by high achievers such as the aforementioned Michael O'Leary of Ryanair. Another person I have studied and learned from is the successful Irish businessman Bill Cullen of *The Apprentice* fame.

I once attended a business seminar given by an American businessman Keith Cunningham. Cunningham had earned millions, lost millions and made them back again. I am not excessively motivated by money. Rather it was the philosophy of what he learned from his errors which motivated me. Cunningham dusted himself off when others might have given up and made a successful career once more.

For raw inspiration, I look no further than my own parents, who are two very wonderful people that have influenced me in many ways. My older brother Tom has continually tried to raise his own standards in all aspects of his life and his example has influenced me greatly.

I once stumbled across another inspirational video on You Tube similar to the 'Rick and Dick Hoyt' story. It narrated a tale of a young Australian called Nick Vujicic. Nick's story, like the Hoyts, was compelling. At 17 he started his own organisation called 'Life without Limbs,' a non-profit organisation focusing on disability, hope and finding meaning in life. His reason for doing so was that he was born without arms or legs, yet he lived a life without limits. What an incredible challenge to be thrown in life. Despite his challenges, he enjoys a life full of activity, where he plays football, golf and swims, refusing to let his disability hold him back in any way. He now travels the world holding motivational seminars and inspiring people young and old as he does so. How lucky was I? I had two arms and two legs. It reminded me of how fortunate I was to have my health, a gift we should never take for granted. I always try now to adopt an 'attitude of gratitude' for what I have.

They say a healthy body is a healthy mind. I am absolutely convinced that this philosophy works for me. Another personal discipline which has worked wonders for me for many years is the "early to bed, early to rise" routine. From it I get so much. I cannot overstress the importance of such a discipline to me personally. It is part of who I am. An early start allows me to fill so much more into every day. I owe this discipline to three different parties.

Firstly, boarding school had initially taught me the discipline of rising early. Secondly, I worked under my Uncle Tom for 14 years and he instilled in me the importance of starting the day early. He was at his desk shortly after 5am every morning. What a great example he was to me. I was two hours behind him arriving into work but I had to travel 50 miles to get there, so I too was up at the crack of dawn.

Thirdly, and long before 2008, perhaps 10 years before, I had recognised a trait in many of the successful people whom I admired. I had read numerous autobiographies and studied many techniques and consistencies into how highly successful people achieved what they did.

It seemed to me that the more they did, the more they could do. They had conditioned their minds and bodies to stretch beyond what conventional wisdom might dictate are normal practices and indeed regular working hours. I noticed many similarities and traits in these people; they seemed to be full of energy, always positive, always wanting to do more and in turn achieving so much.

To me it appeared that the people I admired realised the importance of 'time management'. One of the many consistencies appeared to be that 'early to bed, early to rise' philosophy. All of us are given the same 24 hours every day. These people however, seemed to have realised that it is very easy to steal a march on 'normal' waking hours. They used their time so much more productively than I was doing. I also realised that this early rising philosophy was one of the keys to how they were able to have so much energy.

During that unproductive phase in my mid-twenties, I also used to lounge around on the sofa watching worthless television before retiring around midnight. I am unable to recall anything good, bad or indifferent that I watched in those hours from 10pm till midnight during those years. I saw though, that if I could change this routine I could steal and insert an additional four hours a day into my life. Two hours from 10pm until midnight when I would recharge my body by sleeping rather than passive TV watching and another two hours between 6am and 8am when I would either 'work out' or 'work at' my office desk.

Successful business leaders such as Bill Cullen had incorporated this routine in their lives from an early age. Naturally a strong work ethic was also key. They had more though. They were at their desks and could work without distraction from 6am until 9am whereupon they joined up with the 'normal' day when phones and office staff would become active. It wasn't rocket science. It was actually very simple. I decided to join that early set.

Almost instantly I found that by retiring to bed earlier ensured I had the energy to rise much earlier, usually at 6am. I was now playing the game of these successful people by using their secret weapon.

In truth many of those successful people would consider me a late riser. A lot of them including my close friend Jim Hickey, a Peak Performance Life Coach, rise at 5am and before. Most of them have far greater responsibilities and commitments than I. I continue to be inspired by how they fill so much into their busy lives.

Normally I rise at 6am, even earlier on occasions. This is not as challenging as it might sound. It simply requires the correct mindset. After that, it is a matter of turning it into a routine, which in reality takes only a few weeks.

Normally I would now start my day with a workout and get to my desk at a time when there are few distractions. I have been going for early morning workouts since 1995. It hasn't and doesn't always suit but usually I manage to complete a run, a swim or a cycle at least five mornings a week. By 8am most mornings, I am well set up for the day ahead and am usually buzzing with enthusiasm, ready to tackle whatever challenges lie in wait.

CHAPTER 15
RUNNING THE COUNTRY

AUGUST 2008

One day Dorothy told me that a friend of hers was coming in to seek advice on Ironman triathlons. He had signed up for one the following summer in Austria, but wanted to talk to someone who had done one. Dorothy and I had also registered for the same event a year in advance, because Ironman races fill out very quickly.

Into the office one Saturday morning walked Ken Whitelaw. I knew his family but had never actually met Ken before. He entered rather shyly but I took to him immediately. He appeared quiet and unassuming.

Ken was 29 at the time, had dark hair, was about 5'11" and was smartly dressed. He carried himself very well and asked all the right questions. I asked about his experience and he told me he had been running competitively from an early age but had just one marathon to his name. A mark of his modesty was that I had to drag the finishing time out of him. The first time I asked he avoided answering, but this made me even more inquisitive. It turns out it was a highly impressive 2:54:31 which placed him in 31st position out of approximately 4,000 runners in the 2006 Edinburgh marathon.

Our chat went on for a few hours and I was happy to answer any questions he had. It was only a very short time since I had asked the same questions from people who had accomplished this goal themselves and I felt pleased that Ken had come to Dorothy and I for advice. As he was leaving he opened a bag and took out a book, placing it in front of me.

He had heard I enjoyed challenging events and thought I might fancy this read. The book *Ultramarathon Man* was about an ultra distance runner called Dean Karnazes. I had never heard of him before but I was unable to put it down once I had started reading it. That afternoon and that book would change my life dramatically again.

I was enthralled from the first page. The book was about a guy who had run colossal distances despite the fact that conventional wisdom suggested that such feats were impossible. From 50 miles to 100 miles, he knew no boundaries. Karnazes, I later found out, had in 2006 completed 50 marathons in as many days. I was in awe of his achievement and the more I read, the more my mind started to formulate a future for me. "I'm going to do something similar in Ireland," I decided. An idea to run a marathon in 32 counties in 32 days was born.

It was that quick.

Was I apprehensive, scared and in awe of such a challenge when I considered it? Absolutely. But I reasoned that if someone else could do what appeared to be insane distances then so could I. There had to be a way.

Soon after, I started to develop the idea more and more in my head. Given that Ireland was such a small country, such a challenge would be sure to attract media attention. Why not take advantage of that attention to raise awareness and funds for charity. Sometime before I had attended a motivational seminar where Anthony Robbins had explained that there are different standards in life. Everything we do, we do to a standard, whether it is bad, good, very good or excellent. He went on to explain that there is a standard beyond 'excellent' and that this is something we should strive to achieve with anything we are passionate about. That standard is 'outstanding.' If I was going to put myself out there and announce that I was going to run 32 marathons in just 32 days, then why not make it an 'outstanding' event, one that would have more than just the goal of running the marathons themselves.

I rang my 'go to' man in these circumstances, Bernard Flynn. He was somebody whom I greatly admired not just as one of the best GAA corner forwards of all time but because he was a tireless worker and charity fundraiser.

I should have known he would become even more animated that I was. I explained I wanted to do it to push my body to a level above what I had achieved before. Together over a few discussions we hatched the idea of encouraging runners to join me along the way. Bernard had for many years organised an annual fundraising golf event for Irish Autism Action, a very worthwhile charity whose headquarters were in my hometown.

Years before I had a very minor involvement in helping Bernard with one of these events. When I had signed up for Ironman France, it was Irish Autism Action as well as another small charity called TEAM (Temporary Emergency Accommodation Mullingar) in my hometown that I had fundraised for.

Through this introduction, my eyes were opened a little into the world that is autism. Autism is very prevalent in Ireland as well as in other countries. I felt that we might in some small way highlight this condition and the challenges that children with autism and their families face every single day.

By the time we had finished talking, we had created in our minds a unique event that would involve hundreds of runners and a few celebrities to encourage people to sign up and run with me. By getting hundreds of people to run, we dreamed of raising huge funds for the charity. Our vision was becoming clear.

Over the next few weeks my mind continued to throw up ideas, angles, issues and logistics of what this challenge would entail. The more we thought about it, the more bells and whistles we added on. We came up with the idea of having 32 runners every day, over 1,000 participants. Each runner would be asked to raise funds for the charity.

There was another issue for consideration - fitness. At that time, I wasn't near fit enough. One of the lessons I had learned over the previous 15 years was that if I wanted to achieve something, I needed to plan. First, I needed to know my outcome, then I simply had to plot a course to get me there. No matter what I wanted to accomplish, whether it was an educational qualification, opening a business or completing an Ironman Triathlon, I now realised that I could do it but only through proper thinking and hard work. Only then would I have the best chance of passing the exam, successfully running the business or completing the challenge.

By now I had a marathon on my CV with a second one just a few months away. I also had completed two Ironman triathlons as well.

These experiences allowed me to believe I could achieve anything I set my mind to. The long periods of intense training made me realise how capable I was of focusing on a goal - and then achieving it.

I understood too that I needed more experience. It would have to be something more challenging than an Ironman. I was after all over 40 years of age, apparently well past my sporting prime. I needed to undertake something tougher, something longer than anything I had done before to prove to myself that I could take on a challenge of running 32 consecutive marathons. If the 32 marathons would require a 10 on the fitness ladder, I had only reached a 5. I needed to find an event that would move me further up the ladder.

I had one more apprenticeship to serve.

CHAPTER 16
'YOU'RE STONE RAVING MAD'

AS always, Dorothy was the first person in my family I confided in. We had similar mindsets and both of us were by now hooked on endurance sporting challenges. By the time this book was written, she would have a third Ironman medal on her sporting CV. An impressive tally.

Through completing these gruelling events she too had developed a 'can do' attitude to many other aspects in her life. Five years previously when she was 29, one day I called Dorothy from the car. I was unable to carry out a property appointment, so I asked her to close the office for an hour and to go to meet the client on my behalf.

She was in her own words 'terrified'. At that time, in certain aspects of her life she was short on confidence in her own ability. This was one such example. In the office environment she was fine but going out to meet someone at a property on a one-to-one basis was, according to Dorothy, a fear similar to my public speaking fear.

It took me all of 20 minutes to persuade her to carry out my request. I wouldn't have insisted but I suggested to her that she could do it. She had seen how I had confronted my own fear a few years earlier by speaking in public. Now I suggested to her that it might be 'her turn'. To her credit she did go and confront her fear. And guess what? She survived.

"Better to be sorry for doing something than sorry for not doing it," she quipped later that evening. Now where had I heard that before? She was buzzing from the high of confronting and surviving the demolition of this fear. Not only had she done it, she had sold the house as well.

Isn't it the case that the thought of doing something is very often far more stressful than the reality? The harder part can sometimes be changing your mindset or your limiting belief. Once your decision is made, the resulting action can actually sometimes be the easier element. These changes can present us with a whole new world of opportunities. I am not just talking about big life changing decisions we decide to take or not as the case may be. Sometimes exiting the tiniest of comfort zones can reap huge rewards.

Fast forward five years and as evidence of her new-found confidence in her own ability, in 2010 Dorothy would open a brand new business of her own, a running and triathlon sports store called 'Tri and Run' in Mullingar.

Perhaps that appointment five years before was a first step for her. Dorothy herself has since acknowledged that exiting comfort zones can reap huge rewards.

"You're mad," Dorothy said.

I knew she was not being serious as she had a smile on her face as she spoke.

"You're stone raving mad," she repeated.

I had just revealed to her the latest challenge I had concocted in my head.

"So it is 4.8 miles of swimming, 224 miles of cycling and 52.4 miles of running?" she repeated back to me after I had told her.

I nodded.

"Non-stop?"

"Yes," I replied.

"You are completely insane," she stressed.

But she knew from my demeanour that the next course on my sporting menu was indeed a *double* Ironman.

It was hard to argue with her. The magnitude of the distances even got to me a little when I analysed them, but I knew it was an apprenticeship that would stand me in great stead for my ultimate goal of running 32 marathons in 32 days. If I could accomplish something as exceptional as a 'Double Ironman', then I felt I could tell people I was going to attempt to run 32 marathons and they might just take me seriously.

My logic in entering this event was as much for the mental challenge as the physical. I had yet to formulate a training plan for the physical element. However there is only so much physical training you can do. I knew that this would mentally challenge me to the limit. The mental component alone would be a good enough reason to sit this exam paper.

The first event of its kind in the UK had been held just a few months before in August 2008. What's more, some people had finished it. The more I researched it, the more excited I became. An insane idea to many, but perfect for what I needed to do it for.

Another comfort zone to exit.

The night before I told Dorothy, I had gone online and registered.

"Congratulations. You have been accepted for the Double Ironman UK 2009. We look forward to seeing you on race day."

This was the same guy who in 2004 had completed one leg of a sprint triathlon, a swim of 750 metres and thought at the end of it he was greater than Michael Phelps.

A Double Ironman. Was I crazy?

What had I done?

CHAPTER 17
LONG DISTANCE INFORMATION

"GERRY, you should stop running and concentrate on cycling," the surgeon said to me as I was being wheeled into the operating theatre, just before Christmas 2008. He had a smile on his face as he spoke because he knew he was talking to someone who had no intention of following that piece of advice.

This was my second knee operation for a cartilage problem. The first was three years previously and that had been a success. Now because of my own stupidity, I was back again. This time I needed an arthroscopy which meant inserting a camera into my right knee to repair some more cartilage damage.

It was completely my own fault that I was back again in the same operating theatre. In October, 2008 I had decided to compete in the Dublin City Marathon to round off what had been a truly memorable year for me. Like the year before, the weather was kind to us on the October bank holiday Monday morning. Dublin is known as the 'friendly' marathon and the tens of thousands of spectators who lined the route at every vantage point certainly enhanced the experience. I felt proud to be Irish as I was cheered at every corner as were the other 11,000 runners, many of whom had travelled from foreign parts to be here.

My target time was to break three and a half hours by about five minutes which I did comfortably finishing in 3:22:04. I was determined to learn from my maiden experience so I paced myself as if it was a military manoeuvre. It paid off as I was comfortable throughout. Once again, the weather was very favourable. With a mile to go I felt great. I had vowed never to go off too fast like I had a year earlier. Fool me once etc.

As I entered Pearse St for the second time, I felt fantastic and decided to push the last mile. Only in the days following did I realise the damage I had done. In that final mile, I aggravated the cartilage in my right knee, the same knee that had previously given me trouble a few years before.

I had been greedy in pushing myself on that Monday when I should have been grateful for everything that 2008 had given me. I had an abundance of wonderful memories but foolishly tried to go perhaps 60 seconds faster than I would have. That time was meaningless in the overall context of what I had achieved but a competitive streak came out when it was not needed. I crossed the line successfully but it was with complications.

Later that winter, I realised I would have to go under the surgeon's knife again, for the second time in three years. December 22nd was the day and six weeks abstention from running was the penance I would have to serve.

That Christmas I was miserable. I was told to rest as much as possible and was on crutches for a few days but it was purely precautionary. I was not in pain but I was nervous about whether the operation would be a success. Sometimes we only really appreciate things when they are taken from us. I was a bad patient as I wondered how long it would be before I could start training again. I spent the holidays preparing my training schedule for the months ahead, provisionally pencilling in some runs for late January. The reality, though, would turn out to be very different.

Early into the New Year I started swimming and cycling. The surgeon had told me not to run until the end of the month and I was determined to take that part of his advice. I longed to run, but patience would take precedence.

As I explained earlier, in 2007 and 2008 we had started to see a sharp downturn in turnover in the business. By 2009 we were really feeling the pinch. In the preceding few months, Robbie had left to set up his own business in Bettystown, Co Meath and Christopher had handed in his notice to spend a year in Australia. Now it was just Dorothy and I. The truth is we were really starting to struggle. We didn't have any deep pockets to dig into to ensure survival. We had not been in business long enough. In fact I was still paying off the original start-up business loan from 2003.

As a consequence of the massive drop in income, Dorothy sourced another job. Despite cutting back and working harder than ever before, the business was just not there. The American businessman Keith Cunningham had outlined at one of the business seminars I had attended that the number one reason for business failure is "the lack of a second idea".

I didn't have one. A cardinal error. I had no back-up plan. I knew I needed to find other sources of income so I started to put together a Plan B. A return to a hobby last visited in my early twenties was just months away. That would provide some much needed and immediate income. More of what that entailed shortly.

By late January, I still did not feel confident enough to run. I felt it was still a risk so I waited into February. By mid-February I decided to test it. A short distance into that first run I felt pain. Back to the bike and the pool I went, deciding that I would build up endurance in these two disciplines and await the day when I could return to running once more.

By March I was getting very frustrated. Near the end of the month I tested it again and this time thankfully it felt good. I was 10 weeks into my training programme for the Double Ironman. My philosophy for this training was to add approximately 25 per cent to my workload that had enabled success in my two Ironman races to date. By then long swims were already up to two hours and bike rides of four hours plus on weekends, were a regular occurrence. This was still way short of peak training but the workload at such an early stage was vital if I was to be successful in August.

By now Ken Whitelaw and I had become friends. We soldiered on many long cycles together. He was three months into his training programme for his upcoming maiden Ironman in Austria. I can recall after one long bike ride of four hours in February how he questioned his ability to complete an Ironman. His rationale was that this particular cycle had shattered him. How could he be certain he could do 30 miles more as well as a 2.4 mile swim and a full marathon?

I told him that this was a normal reaction as it was the first time he had done it. He was simply stepping outside of his comfort zone. I reassured him that he had the ability and to just hang in there.

Ken was always flexible and obliging about times for cycles and was great company on the many hours we shared on the roads. We gelled extremely well and had much in common, I found out he had worked in Bank of Ireland in Dublin for the previous three years. A business degree graduate, he had returned to work in Mullingar shortly after qualifying. Having worked at home for three years he felt it was the right time to move back to Dublin to pursue a career in banking. He had an easy-going attitude and, like me, always seemed keen to learn new things and was constantly researching new ideas.

As part of our training we decided to do a half-Ironman practice race and would use the experience to review where we stood. We held this on Good Friday. I was back running for three weeks or so by then and was starting to feel really good again. In this training exercise, I ran a 1:25:00 half marathon which I was extremely pleased with, feeling strong throughout. My joy however, was short-lived as a week later I felt a pain once again in my right knee which meant another enforced four week rest.

May arrived and still no running. By mid-May I was tearing my hair out and was starting to worry that I might not run again for the rest of the year. I sought help from a friend, Noeleen Bourke, a chartered physiotherapist. I had met Noeleen through my membership of the Midland Triathlon Club. Within a day I had an appointment with her and she diagnosed that I had a "palellofermoral dysfunction" which was a muscle imbalance around the knee cap. I had neglected to attend physio after December's operation and thus this had occurred unknowns to me. After a few sessions she recommended I test it. I was hesitant but Noeleen told me to put my faith in her, her only request being that I test it on a flat surface. I decided to undertake the run at 6am on my local golf course.

I stepped from the car the next morning nervous but thoroughly excited. How would it react? Noeleen had told me to start slowly, a light jog and then after a kilometre or so to up the intensity a little. Four kilometres later, I returned to the car overjoyed. I had felt no pain whatsoever. My knee had passed the test.

The timing could not have been better. I entered an Olympic-distance triathlon the following weekend. Before the test, I decided I would compete regardless of whether I could do the run or not. If I was still unable to run, the swim and the cycle would be great training. Now, though, I knew I would be fine.

Saturday was a blistering hot day. Athy in County Kildare was the venue and TriAthy the event. An Olympic distance triathlon consisting of a 1.5km swim, a 40 km cycle and a 10km run. TriAthy was a brilliant race that was by then in its fourth year. It attracted the cream of Irish triathletes as well as regular participants just like me who understood that just by being out there competing we were winning. I spent the entire day quietly thanking the man above for restoring my health to allow me to run again. A placing of 58th out of 814 competitors with a sub 40 minutes 10km run gave me a great injection of confidence.

Training for the Double Ironman had opened my eyes.

In 2007, I had completed in six or seven triathlons and the Dublin City Marathon. That marathon goal involved rising to two hours of run training and once or twice beyond. In 2008 a new year and a new goal meant I had to focus on achieving longer distances that required longer training hours.

In 2008, swim sessions peaked at 90 minutes with cycling workouts hitting six hours. Simply by shifting my brain to the goal I had committed to for that season, these durations of effort were no more difficult than training for the marathon. This was the same principle that I would use as part of my training for 2009.

In 2009, long swims stretched to two hours or more. I swam on at least two occasions per week when I was at my training peak. Given my injury issues, long runs were not as long as I would have wished for. I was doing very little running from January to late May so I would have to rely heavily on the endurance I had gained over those months on the bike. I have heard it said that running does not get you bike-fit but that cycling can help with running. Well I was about to put this to the test. My run preparation for the 'Double' had consisted of seven or eight 10-mile runs, a half-marathon and an 18-miler in April together with a full marathon in Ironman Austria as part of my plan. Not ideal, but given my injury challenges it was all I would manage.

My cycling regime was a different story. This is where I elevated my fitness to a previously unreached level. Cycling is non-weight bearing so I could cycle to my heart's content. I was aware that I had to train twice as hard on the bike given the fact that I was doing so little running. With hindsight, this was actually a good thing. Over the first six months of 2009 I lived in the saddle. A friend Joe Duffy had told me years before that cycling training is all about getting miles into the legs. Every opportunity to cycle one mile or a hundred miles had to be taken.

In those spring months I did a large volume, peaking one day with a cycle where I left my house at midday and didn't return until 9pm.

That particular day I learned an awful lot about myself. I believe it is on days such as these that we actually achieve our goals. This was the day that my training peaked, a day when I reached a cycling milestone that I had prepared myself for when I had sat down and plotted my training programme five months before. On that day I cycled 150 miles, navigating my way through five different counties along the way. Back in January I had written 150 miles down as a distance I wanted to be able to reach in one single bike ride. Writing it down on a sheet of paper was easy. This was the day I actually did it.

Muhammed Ali was once quoted as saying. "The fight is won or lost far away from witnesses - behind the lines, in the gym, and out there on the road, long before I dance under those lights."

I knew that if I wanted to achieve my goal I had to be prepared for such a day, a day where I would push myself way beyond what was comfortable. On such days I was preparing for my fight, I was behind the lines and I was out on the road, metaphorically and literally.

When we see success in others in anything, we only see the day of glory. We are not privy to the blood, sweat and tears that has gone into achieving it. That day is one I will always remember. The reason? It was the enormity of the cycle and the fact that I was so mentally strong for the duration. I had nobody for company but myself. It had sunshine and it had showers. It had hailstones and it had heavy rain. I loved it all. If I could survive this, I could survive anything I thought.

It is amazing to think that just a few short years before in 2004, I had felt that just completing the swim leg of 750 metres distance was a huge accomplishment. I still rank that swim five years before as possibly the most challenging of all the events I had done. That day offered the key to the door. I didn't realise it at the time but it really was the catalyst to all these other opportunities. That debut triathlon event five years before was a day I got out of a comfort zone, an action that would subsequently open so many other doors.

As part of my Double Ironman training I had entered a full Ironman distance event in Austria in early July, the same one Ken was training for. Dorothy, as well as friends Brian Ivory and Seamus Bracken had also entered. Ironman Austria was held in the southern town of Klagenfurt and a carnival atmosphere greeted us on arrival. I had long pencilled this weekend as the final part of my Double Ironman training programme. The event in Klagenfurt was brilliant. During the weekend I heard many Irish accents, all of whom had made their own sacrifices to get to the start line.

I have a motto that I try to live by - every day is a 'school day'. Every day of my life I try to learn something that will make me a better person in a multitude of different ways. Sunday in Austria would definitely be a 'school day'.

The swim went great. I emerged in 1:04:16 which was very consistent with my previous two Ironman events. The cycle went well, too well as it turned out. On reflection I pushed too hard. My bike time was 5hrs 45mins which was over 40 minutes faster than my debut in 2008. Yes, it was faster but it is difficult to compare routes. As it turned out I had pushed fractionally too hard, a factor that would only be evident three miles into the marathon.

As I climbed the Rupertiburg, an infamous hill at 686 metres and just 40km from the end of the bike leg, I heard a familiar voice from over my left shoulder. "I was wondering when I would catch you." It was Ken.

I had the experience but Ken, who was 11 years younger, had youth and more talent. It was only a matter of time before he caught me. We chatted for a few brief moments before he took off. He completed the bike four minutes faster than I but had a brief rest in the transition area, allowing me emerge into the run a few minutes before him. We only realised this three miles into the marathon when once again he appeared over my shoulder.

"Fancy meeting you again," he joked.

This time there was no further banter as it was obvious he was on a much faster pace. I had nothing only admiration for the way he had dedicated himself to rigorous training over the preceding six months.

My earlier push on the cycle would mean a challenging marathon lay ahead. I had used up a little too much energy. It was early afternoon and the temperature, just like in Nice the year before, was uncomfortable. Miles three to 10 were a mixture of the run, walk, run strategy I had learned in Nice. Once more I felt awful, my body vacuumed of all energy.

Soldiering on despite my distress, I eventually managed to break into a run again. My exhaustion was a combination of pushing too hard on the bike and perhaps getting my nutrition slightly wrong again. I had been careful about drinking sufficient levels of energy drink, unlike in Nice, but I had ignored the opportunity to use a special needs bag which you are allowed place en route. Many athletes put something nutritious here such as a sandwich. I did not feel the necessity. Maybe with hindsight, I should have.

I managed to continue a run/jog strategy for the remaining 16 or so miles, crossing the line in 11:42:28, my fastest to date . Ken finished in 10:46:20 and Dorothy in 13:22:50. At the finish line I fell down in a heap as a wave of nausea came over me. A medical aid rushed to my side and immediately elevated my legs to get blood flowing to the top half of my body. Ten minutes later I got up, convincing her I was fine. Thirty seconds later I was back on the floor again as the sickness returned. A doctor was called and he recommended a visit to the medical tent to get an IV drip. Who was I to argue? Thirty minutes later, I picked myself off the medical stretcher. I was unbelievably stiff after the previous 12 hours of effort and I walked at a snail's pace to the post race food area.

This was a day when old lessons were relearned. Food, salt, water, pace. The Ironman challenge demands that you get so many things spot-on come race day. When would I ever learn? I ingrained this into my head once more. Food, salt, water, pace. Food, salt, water, pace. My biggest test of the year and my toughest physical sporting challenge of my entire life was just four weeks away.

Despite my Austrian experience, I felt deep down I had the training done. By the time I competed in Klagenfurt, I had ticked all the training boxes and more. I had swum thousands and thousands of lengths in my local pool during spring and early summer. I had ridden so many three and four hour cycles. In addition I completed six cycles of six hours each, two cycles of seven hours each, one of eight and one bike ride of a colossal nine hours.

On the flight home from Austria, I reflected on where I was now, relative to my main goal for the year. I knew that I was more prepared than I was giving myself credit for. Austria was another tough day at the office but I had to overcome the days' challenges. These would only make me stronger.

The fact that I was still able to run and jog most of the marathon meant the legs had got a good workout. Over the next four weeks I tapered as best I could. I always find taper periods difficult as it is a time when your body is in great condition but you need to be patient. You need this time to build up stores of energy. I felt like a sprinter in the starting blocks.

Within a few more weeks I would be back at the airport, bound for Birmingham.

I was about to exit yet another comfort zone.

CHAPTER 18
DOING THE DOUBLE

DOROTHY'S boyfriend Enda Munnelly was a bike mechanic genius. There is very little he didn't know about them. On top of that he was a very meticulous individual and I knew he would prepare my bike with military precision. Doug Bates, a very close friend, had soldiered with me on many training sessions. He also knew a lot about the Ironman triathlon. He had shown a display of courage at Ironman UK 2008 that left me speechless. His knee gave in one mile into the marathon. Many would have retired, lamenting their luck. Not Doug. He walked the last 25 miles in just over six-and-a-half hours. It was a display of fortitude that I sometimes think back on whenever I'm facing a tough challenge.

Jarlath Mahon, another close pal, was someone whom I regularly sought advice from on a variety of topics. In addition, Ken Whitelaw and Dorothy were aboard the plane. All five would be my crew for my Double Ironman attempt in the centre of England.

The race organisers had encouraged us to bring a minimum of two people for crew support. I gave mine plenty of consideration. All of them brought something to the table that would complete the jigsaw to ensure success for my greatest sporting challenge to date. Everyone except Jarlath boarded the early morning flight. A prior arranged work commitment meant he would follow the next morning.

Given the short commute, we decided to arrive just one day in advance. A town called Lichfield, home to a well known Air Force base, just outside Birmingham was our destination. Having gathered our bags and my bike we jumped into the estate car we had hired for our short 30 minute journey. Not content with driving up the A38 North of Birmingham, we decided to check out lots of other roads as well. We arrived two hours later, a little after 4pm.

We checked into the hotel, a typical motorway accommodation house of three floors. As we unpacked I started to think of the weekend ahead. This race was about to challenge my body to complete amazing distances. As race day approached, butterflies were starting to flutter in my stomach. I was very apprehensive. After unpacking, we headed over to the race registration facility, a short 200 metre distance from our hotel. There we met up with the two race organisers and signed in.

During sign-in we were told of a compulsory race briefing that would take place later that evening. Now I started to get really nervous. I went for a short stroll outside to clear my head. Over the following 10 minutes or so I paced up and down the car park scanning my brain for positive thoughts, but the walk offered little compensation.

At seven o'clock we climbed the stairs to the first floor of the leisure centre where the weekend's itinerary would be explained. This was a lot more detailed than I had expected but in hindsight I should not have been surprised.

I felt like I was among a very special group of just 54 people whom I felt shared a similar ambition to do extreme sporting challenges. Steve Haywood and Eddie Ette, the race organisers, tried to settle a lot of nerves at this point. I don't usually suffer from pre-race nerves but this was definitely different. This event had consumed a huge amount of my thinking time in the preceding 12 months. I had lived and breathed it over six-and-a-half months of training. Still, however, I really doubted my ability to finish even this late on. I was very confident of the swim and to some degree of the 224-mile cycle. But when combined with a 52-mile run to finish it was definitely a journey into the unknown.

The organisers offered calmness and assurance during the 45-minute race briefing and they passed on some very insightful tips. They encouraged a regular and disciplined nutrition strategy, the importance of rest periods as well as the benefits of getting physio massage, which would be readily available. They spoke about the experiences of the athletes who had successfully completed the challenge a year before and how it was definitely achievable.

Shortly after 8pm we went to a nearby restaurant for some pre-race nourishment. By 9.30 I was ready for bed.

A little after 10pm, I closed my eyes.

5.00AM
1 AUGUST 2009

I woke up full of apprehension but managed a breakfast consisting of two bowls of muesli and two croissants. We loaded up the car and headed down to race headquarters, a short two mile journey.

Race HQ was located in a school yard with a hard surface football pitch acting as the bike transition area, all of which was conveniently adjacent to a public swimming pool complex.

We arrived at the leisure complex a little after 7.15am. The field of 54 athletes had been split into three waves of 18 competitors. The swim would be completed in a 25-metre swimming pool and I had been drawn in the middle wave commencing at 09.30am. Wave one had started at 6am so the first 18 athletes were already past the 3km mark of the 7.6km swim distance when I arrived.

As I entered the pool area I felt a sense of calmness come over me. I recalled a race report from a year previous where the athlete had said something similar and now I understood why. I had done plenty of training, I had completed a full Ironman race four weeks previously. I was confident of the first two disciplines and what the hell, I would walk the entire 52 miles if I had to. As I sat and watched, confidence started to filter into my body cells. By 8.30am, the negative thoughts had left. Something told me all would be well.

There was a great atmosphere poolside. They had music playing over the loudspeakers with a lovely beat which certainly helped to create a feeling of solidarity among the athletes, crews, marshals and supporters. I spotted one of the race organisers Steve poolside where he was reassuring, encouraging and running errands for swimmers, helping them cool down if they overheated in the wetsuits, which many of them did.

I had decided many months before not to wear a wetsuit. The organisers had discouraged us from wearing one. This was an event with a 35-hour cut-off. If not wearing a wetsuit would add 15 minutes to my finishing time, it would be no big deal. I lost count of the number of times I saw someone having to be cooled down with cold water being poured down the back of the wetsuits following overheating, so I felt confident I had made the correct decision. This event for me was all about finishing. Nothing more, nothing less.

SWIM 4.8 MILES (7.6KM)
Course Description: 304 lengths of a 25-metre pool

At 9.25am we were called to our swim lanes. I felt very excited. I had thought about it for 12 months and finally the time to experience it was here. I introduced myself to my fellow lane swimmers, one an Englishman and the other from Northern Ireland. The English athlete, Drew, expressed a desire to go first and Robert Davidson wanted to go last. That left me in the middle but I didn't care.

At exactly 9.30am the gun went off and with it an explosion of arms and legs in unified propulsion, all with a goal of swimming the required distance of 4.8 miles. After just four lengths it was obvious I was holding Robert up so I let him pass. I had decided a strategy of counting my own lengths in bunches of 40 to mentally get me to the finish. At the end of each 40, I planned to have a quick drink. The swim felt like a tasty appetiser before a main course. I knew a tough challenge lay ahead over the next 35 hours or so. I simply adopted a mindset that the swim was there to be enjoyed, a chance to warm up my body before the main event.

After the first 40 lengths, I stopped momentarily to sip some water. As I did, I noticed Jarlath taking a seat at the side of the pool. He had just flown in from Dublin and he gave me a wave. Beside him were the rest of my crew, all part of the team who would never be too far away for the next day and a half or so.

In my swim training sessions I regularly had to jolt myself into focusing, so as not to lose concentration. To do so would have meant I would lose count of the lengths I was swimming. It was the same now on race day but concentrating for more than two hours of swimming is hard. As a consequence, my mind wandered on a few occasions. Everything from the falling turnover of my business back home to knowing I would never have the body to audition for Baywatch were thrown around in my brain as the lengths ticked by.

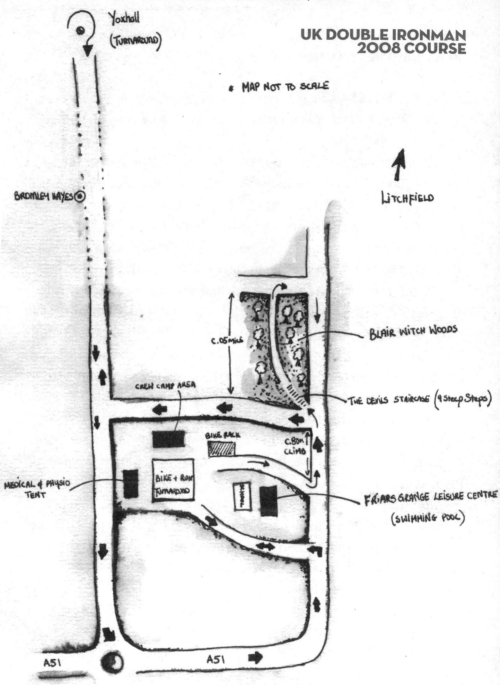

Map: Kathleen Ivory

Every 40 lengths I stopped and took a sip of either water or an energy drink. Perhaps I did not need so much as my decision not to wear a wetsuit meant I wasn't going to get dehydrated. Robert exited in about 2 hours 20 minutes and Drew was just two lengths ahead of me at the end. I had obviously miscounted somewhere along the way as I thought I had four more remaining when it was actually only two. It took me 32 seconds over two-and-a-half hours which was bang on schedule. I had paced myself comfortably, which I knew was critical this early into the event.

"Pace, pace, pace," I reminded myself. Remember Austria.

On finishing the swim, I jogged briskly to the changing rooms, before sitting down and chatting briefly with the male members of the crew, Jarlath, Enda, Ken and Doug. They had prepared a ham and cheese sandwich, a tip I had read in a 2008 race report. Two and a half hours of exercise had already used up about 1500 calories of energy. I needed to replace it.

BIKE 224 MILES (360KM)

Course Description: An out and back course of seven miles in each direction, one gentle 500m hill helping on the way out and downwind, with the reverse on the way back. This meant on average that most laps for me took 23/24 minutes out and 28/30 minutes coming back.

Sixteen laps of 14 miles. Yikes!!

Two hundred and twenty-four miles or three hundred and sixty kilometres. Dress it up whatever way you like. It's a long way. It is the equivalent of cycling from Belfast to Limerick, or from Glasgow to a few miles north of London.

I mounted the bike a little after midday targeting an average pace of 16 miles per hour. That might seem quite slow. It wasn't. It was all I would be able to manage, given the 4.8-mile swim just completed and the small matter of 52 miles to be run once I finished the bike.

I completed the first lap of 14 miles in 48 minutes. I knew this was too fast but I was conscious of it and I had plenty of time to get the pacing right. Those in wave one were rather unfortunate as it had bucketed down while I was doing the swim. By the time I had started cycling, the rain had stopped but it would soon be back. After the first lap I stopped for five minutes to have a proper meal of potatoes and beans, which went down easily. By the beginning of lap 4 (42 miles) the clouds darkened once more and the rain started to come down in sheets.

Early on I had cause for amusement. Doug had given me a serious ticking off after lap three for being a few minutes ahead of schedule. After this scolding, I was genuinely in fear of returning under less than 52 minutes from the next lap. As I turned the last corner heading into the transition after lap four I glanced at my watch, noticed it read 50 minutes and thought "s***, he's gonna kill me". I slowed to a snail's pace for fear of another reprimand and hid just out of view at the entrance. The clock read 52 minutes and 14 seconds as I appeared back before Doug, the headmaster!

My plan was to stop again after this lap, and every three laps thereafter, which I did, even coming into the tent and sitting down for a few minutes on the first of these.

By 56 miles the rain was bucketing down. It made cycling conditions very tricky. Although only early August, by 6pm it had become very dark and we were ordered to put on high visibility clothing and lights. Enda had prepared the lighting requirements with precision. It was a great comfort to know that he was in charge of this. By now I had been on the bike for almost six hours but had negotiated only 90 miles of the 224. The weather was awful for all of Saturday afternoon and early evening. Despite the rain though, I was still enjoying every moment.

After lap seven or 98 miles I stopped again for another baked potato and some beans. I also seized the opportunity to get a quick rub down with the event physiotherapist. I immediately felt its benefits. My lower limb muscles were showing early signs of fatigue so I felt it a good race strategy to stop briefly. I did so again after 154 miles as I was starting to feel some cramping once more.

A strange thing happened as I was on the return leg of lap 11 out of 16. It was now close to midnight. As I progressed, I noticed a cyclist approaching in the opposite direction. As he came more into view, I saw two youths were spraying him with a jet powerwasher. This was not some form of courteous assistance to cool the athlete from a searing hot sun. Rather it was two hooligans up to dangerous mischief. As I passed, the cyclist was remounting his bike and was yelling at them. Later I heard that the same hooligans had actually knocked this athlete to the ground and kicked him heavily while he was defenceless. Wasn't this event hard enough? By the time I finished the next lap we got word that the same two youths had been given a nice warm bed in the local police station.

Laps 11 and 12 were ticked off and the 168-mile point (270km) reached. By now it was after one o'clock in the morning. I had been on the go since 9.30am the day before. Given the torrential rain we had experienced for many hours, I had earlier changed my clothing for a second time and put extra lights on the bike. I am unable to recall very much about what I was thinking about during this time of the evening. For so many hours I had been busy just concentrating on all the different challenges that we were faced with.

For starters there was the uniqueness of the event and the event location to stimulate my brain, there was the physical challenge of cycling this enormous distance, there were the road conditions, the constant traffic and the sight of my fellow athletes every few minutes or so. There was a rendezvous with the crew at the end of each lap and the nutrition that had to be managed. Maybe I was just too busy to think about anything else. As the night unfolded though and as the uniqueness became the norm I had more time to think.

By 1.30am, the only sign of life came from two sources; the street lamps in the small villages which we passed through on a regular basis and the sight of double headlights from my fellow cyclists. Indeed the lights took on a strange appearance as most, including me, had a light emanating from their helmets as well as one from the front of the bike. It really was quite surreal. By this stage the busy open roads had quietened. It was the dead of night and the temperature had dropped considerably. At 1.45am, I was still in a great place mentally. That, however, was about to change.

LAP 13

I don't know quite what happened. Perhaps it was because I had been cycling for almost 13 hours. It was very cold and I had been soaked through time and time again, and a fog by now had also descended. It was a very lonely environment. The once noisy Saturday night villages that earlier had been full of revelry and atmosphere were now quieter than a cemetery. It was almost 2am, about 15 hours since I had first entered the pool and I still had another 56 miles (90km) to cycle. I had been feeling so good up to this point but somewhere on the darkest part of this lap my mood changed and my inner self-belief evaporated. It happened in an instant.

What the f***!

Negative thoughts came from nowhere and invaded me like an infestation. Immediately I started to doubt my ability to finish the race. With hindsight it was not unreasonable of my brain to demand such a turnaround. After all, this was a tough event. When I began to look for solutions, pessimism consumed me.

As I entered the school yard, another 14-mile lap completed, I was mentally and physically at my lowest point ever in an event. I tried to convince myself that I could finish the bike leg, that I was almost there. The other side of my brain was reminding me that I still had 42 miles left to cycle. Once there, I would then have to run the equivalent distance from Mullingar to Dublin, not one but two full marathons.

I had planned to rest for a few minutes at the end of this lap and as I got off my bike, Dorothy was there to greet me. I was really low, my confidence and my ambition gone. I threw the bike at her and collapsed on a bench.

Post-race, Dorothy shared with me her thoughts as I sat there.

"I was unbelievably worried for two reasons," she told me. "The first was that you looked totally and utterly exhausted, the worst I had ever seen. The second was because I knew how stubborn you could be and I thought you might push yourself beyond what was safe."

Enda saw it differently. He thought it was "just a hiccup". Interesting how two people can view the same event so very differently.

On seeing my plight, another athlete's crew member came over to me. As she approached, I did not offer any welcoming signals. I was engulfed in self-pity and was in no humour for chat. She sat beside me and did not speak for a minute or more. As her silence tactics continued, my inquisitiveness grew. She just sat there offering support simply by casting a casual glance of empathy every few seconds. In the end, it was I who spoke first.

"Hi," I mumbled.

She did not reply, rather she put her arm around my shoulder.

A few seconds later, she spoke.

"My husband did this event last year," she said.

"Oh," I replied, as it was obvious some words of wisdom were imminent and I felt it mannerly to engage her.

"He's out there now again," she said. "He started in the first wave, three and a half hours before you but is now behind you in race classification. He got knocked off his bike a few hours ago by two hooligans who sprayed him with a power hose. Not only that, but when he was down, they kicked him all over. He is a fighter though and so are you."

I was starting to feel guilty about my indulgent self-pity.

"Look," she continued.

"I have watched you come in here for the past 12 hours and you have struck me as one of the strongest athletes out here. You would not be human if you did not have a weak moment sometime during a race of this enormity. Stick with it and I guarantee that when the sun rises in about three hours you will feel so much better."

Those words hit me like a ton of bricks. I thought back to the advice that the hypnotist had given me five years before, that no matter what challenge you face, the world will always continue about its business and just to power through whatever obstacles are put in front of you.

I got up and I could immediately feel my physical and mental state change. I grabbed some pasta and chicken and washed it down with a can of Red Bull. My crew came out in the car to visit me on the bike course about nine miles later and I sang James Brown's 'I Feel Good' to them.

My lady friend had reminded me that no matter what you are facing there is always somebody going through a more challenging time. Gone were my feelings of self pity. I was back in the moment, my head clear once more and the road ahead even though it was pitch dark was completely clear. I had trained for a year for this. Nothing was going to stop me from finishing it.

Laps 14 and 15 came and the fog became thicker. The temperature dropped even lower again. It was now after 3am so I guess that was to be expected. I managed to keep warm thanks to my crew. Even the pre-race favourite had dropped out by now, citing hypothermia as the reason.

The last lap offered a huge feeling of relief that this was the last time I would have to navigate the junctions, the villages and every twist and turn of the 14-mile routing, within which I had lived for almost 17 hours. I felt obliged to stop for a second or two at each junction to thank the marshals. Those people were heroes. They had given their entire weekend to help us achieve our goals. One guy marshalled at the furthest point for nine straight hours and then came back to marshal on the run course.

Sixteen hours and 42 minutes after starting the 224-mile (360km) cycle, I dismounted and turned my attention towards the run.

RUN 52.4 MILES (84KM)
Course Description: 42 laps of a 1.25-mile circuit

AROUND 5AM
SUNDAY 2ND AUGUST, 2009
By now, the sun was awakening from its night-time slumber just like the lady said it would. A beautiful Sunday morning would soon appear. I had been on the go for 19-and-a-half hours to this point but there was still the matter of two marathons to be run.

As I left the transition tent I was greeted by Steve Haywood, the race organiser. Steve was an athlete of some note. In 1992 he ran a sub-four-minute mile, finishing in a time of 3 mins 59.2 seconds.

"Just go over that timing mat there Gerry and run for 52.4 miles and I will see you when you're finished," he said laughing. But he was serious too.

It was a 42-lap circuit so we actually kept coming back to the same point. That might sound strange but it made complete sense as it meant we got a positive bit of energy from the organisers, the DJ's music, my support crew and the spectators at 11–15 minute intervals. It also meant it was easy for the crew to keep an eye on my food and drinks intake.

Now here is the amazing thing. I felt fantastic, I really did. My strategy in advance of race day was to stop after each 10-kilometre mark and rest for a minute or so but I was not expecting to feel such strength at that stage. So after the first mile or so, I was confident of running non-stop for the first half marathon or so. The first lap of 1.25 miles was completed in about 11 minutes.

The run commenced in the school yard before meandering out onto a main road. Once there, we had to run up a short but severe 80-metre climb. One time might be fine, but we had to climb it 42 times. When we arrived at the summit we had to negotiate nine steep steps locally nicknamed 'The Devil's Staircase' into a woodland known as 'Blair Witch Woods'. The trail we ran on in the woods went on for about a half a mile before returning to the road once more. From there we had about half a mile on a mixture of road, footpath and grass before descending the 80-metre climb and arriving back to the playground to start all over again.

At the end of the first lap I got an intense craving for a sandwich. By now, Dor, Enda and Jarlath had gone back to the tent for some much-needed sleep, leaving Ken and Doug on duty. I spotted them at the turnaround point and yelled at Ken about my urgent need for food. He ran off in the direction of the tent. I had a decision to make. Stop and rest or do another lap and meet him on my return. I decided to keep going. Eleven minutes later, I was back and gratefully accepted a chicken sandwich from him. It went down a treat as I ate it slowly over the following two laps.

At this point I started to get a feeling that I would indeed finish this event. I had completed the swim and the bike. Now I was safely on my feet covering my favourite discipline. The low point I experienced on the bike on lap 13 was also now well behind me. Laps three to 10 or approximately the first 12 or so miles went great, bringing me towards the first half-marathon milestone. I was grabbing a mouthful of water or Red Bull, a few jelly beans and some pieces of chocolate from Ken and Jarlath at the end of each lap.

Twenty miles came and went and Ken started to run a few laps with me. Soon I passed the 26 mile mark, the first marathon completed. Ken informed me that my first marathon had taken me 4hrs 34 mins. My watch showed 4hrs 8mins so I was confused. I later found out that the official time included a 26 minutes transition period from bike to run when I had stopped for some physio and a change of clothing and footwear, so in reality my feeling that I was faster was actually correct.

At this point while I felt very strong, I was certain that I would at some point hit another low or perhaps even the dreaded wall, that so many runners hit during the marathon. The prospect of this didn't scare me at all. If it happened, the walk would probably bring a welcome relief and so I felt I had nothing to lose by gambling to continue to run. Ken did six or seven laps with me and he was great at going ahead to prepare drinks and food so that I would not have to stop. He also continuously checked the recorder's hut to see how many more laps I had to run as I kept losing count.

By now Dor, Jarlath and Enda had returned from a brief rest. Dorothy then joined me for a few laps and I laughed to myself because when I asked her to run with me, she couldn't say no despite the fact that she was wearing a pair of jeans. I really enjoyed her being there.

Later Jarlath and Enda came out on the course as well. Jarlath Mahon was someone I had known for about 10 years. About six years my junior, he was a former GAA player who had turned to triathlon when he realised he couldn't keep up with player 10 years younger than him on a football pitch.

Running now beside me was great as he balanced his running with carrying a camcorder to film my progress. Doug Bates I had met through triathlons and he would have loved to have run but couldn't.

He had come straight from the operating theatre of a hospital to meet us at Dublin Airport. Sporting a pair of crutches from a knee injury and just over not one but two full anaesthetics in the previous three days, he still offered huge vocal encouragement at the end of each lap.

I had started this event at 9.30am the previous day. By now I had swam 4.8 miles (7.6 km) and cycled 224 miles (360 km). A little after midday on Sunday I passed the 39-mile mark for the run, one and a half marathons completed, I had less than 13 miles to the finish line. I was nearly there.

At the 35-mile mark, I had started to feel pain slowly seeping into my muscles and so by mile 40, I was really feeling the demands of such amazing distances. I guess you would not be human if you did not feel some major discomfort.

A portion of the run was adjacent to a busy road. I wondered what the Sunday morning drivers were thinking of these zombie-like characters that must have looked an unusual sight on their footpaths. A line of humans writhing in pain as they moved slowly up and down the pathway. All of us by this time were in some level of discomfort. If I resembled anything like my fellow competitors, with distorted body parts and sombre expressions, then I was a sight myself. I was sure I was.

By now, it was approaching midday Sunday. As I reached mile 47, I was really hurting. Pain was emanating from every pore and I was unable to speak. Enda and Jarlath who were running in support alongside me didn't mind as they saw my visual signals giving clear evidence of my discomfort.

Lap 38 came and went. Now I had just five miles remaining (miles 47.5-52.4) The body was really starting to creak but I knew, barring disaster, I would make it. To keep my mind occupied and focused, I started to work out roughly what time I could finish in. If I kept running I realised I would almost certainly break 29 hours, well ahead of my pre-race expectation.

It was a bad idea to work this out because I suddenly became consumed by a desire to break this 29-hour barrier, yet I hardly needed this pressure. Jarlath ran three straight laps with me. I couldn't speak but he knew that was no slight on him. Finally I came to the last lap. I thought this one would be easy but it was definitely the hardest of the lot. With the pain I was in, it was a case of so near but yet so far. That might sound strange but I read later in other post-race reports that all the athletes felt the same. This lap took an eternity.

The final 1.25 miles was run in reverse of the other 41. The logic was that you could receive words of congratulations from your fellow competitors as you met them en route. Positive words from them came in abundance.

The final metres and the final minutes ticked by agonisingly slowly. Eventually, I reached the exit of 'Blair Witch Woods' with only the 'Devil's Staircase' to be negotiated. If I thought going up those nine steps 41 times had been challenging, going down just once was excruciating. My body was very sore and each downward stretch was like Shylock extracting his pound of flesh from each of my calves and quads. I got down, though, and have since watched footage of it with much hilarity.

Finally I reached the transition area for the last time. Steve, the race organiser, was announcing my imminent arrival over the speakers and I received huge cheers from the wonderful supporters. I high-fived and applauded as many as I could. I was so grateful to them, particularly a complete stranger in a black t-shirt at the entrance who had shouted my name 84 times in and out, for nine solid hours.

I had 50 metres to go and I could see all my crew waiting for me at the finish line. I don't tend to get emotional at these times and this was no different but I was relieved to have completed this mammoth task. Over the line, I embraced them all. They had played a vital role in helping me achieve my goal.

POST RACE

My official finishing time was 28:41:11, placing me in 14th place. Forty-five out of the 54 who started the race completed the challenge. I was over the moon as my one and only objective in starting was to finish.

My two swim-lane partners enjoyed mixed fortunes. Robert Davidson from Northern Ireland who exited ahead of me in the swim heroically finished in 33:10:54, despite enduring a very hard time on the bike. Drew, the English guy, unfortunately did not finish. I never found out the reason but the records indicate he did not complete the bike leg.

Within a few seconds of finishing, I was panned out on the ground, feet up in the air to stave off an inevitable sickness which I always seemed to get after long distance races. I stayed there for about five minutes before heading into the transition tent for one last bout of physio.

I had completed my interim examination paper for the 32 Marathon Challenge. Twelve months previously, I had set this event as a stepping stone to convince myself that I could run 32 consecutive marathons.

At the airport the next morning, I sent a text to Kevin Whelan, the CEO of Irish Autism Action. It was a text of massive personal significance.

"Kevin, we are good to go."

CHAPTER 19

A RUNNING MATE

11TH NOVEMBER 2009
5.40PM

Still in my beloved armchair it is now almost midnight as I continue to reminisce on the day's events. The American doctor led me into the testing room where I was greeted by one of her male colleagues. He immediately hooked me up to a range of wires and scientific devices. As he placed an oxygen mask over my mouth, she smiled and waved a brief farewell.

"Let's see how this Vo2 max tests you," were her final words as she closed the door behind her.

Ninety minutes later, I am seated outside her office. I am told the results have been relayed back to her. I am summoned from the waiting area. For once I could not wait for the results. I knew I was in good shape as I had only finished the event in England a few months before.

I watched the doctor as she studied the page. I could tell by her eyes dilation that she was impressed.

"You're in great shape," she said.

"Thanks," I replied. "So I'm not totally mad?"

"Oh you're mad alright. Doing 32 marathons... in 32 days. You're definitely mad."

As I left, Ken went in for his results.

He too was in superb physical condition, after his Ironman Austria exploits. Ken was a keen member of Mullingar Harriers growing up and he spent much of his 20s in non-competitive sporting arenas, while allowing his social skills to shine at the same time. It was his late 20s before he returned to competitive sports action.

I was impressed by Ken the first time I met him. I found we shared many ambitions. Ken had given me a loan of the book about Dean Karnazes, the ultra-distance runner. That was the seed for the 32 Marathon Challenge. Ken had only agreed to come on board the challenge a few months before. During our time spent training for

Ironman Austria, he and I had gelled very well. He was always going to finish ahead of me in Austria but I didn't care. He was a young man who was in his sporting prime. On the plane home I asked him if he would do me a big favour and become a crew member for my Double Ironman attempt. Thankfully he agreed. I knew that he would bring a huge amount to the table.

In late August, with the dust settled on a memorable sporting year, I started to tell a few people about my idea of running 32 consecutive marathons. One of the first people I told was Ken. I trusted him completely to keep it under wraps. As I outlined my ambition to run 32 marathons in 32 days his face lit up with excitement. While explaining it to him I had an idea. Before voicing it though, I went home to think it through.

I was nervous not just of the challenge but also of the responsibility and the heavy burden of duties that the event would require. The event was still only in my head but I had highly ambitious plans for it. It was something I had thought about in minute detail. I wanted it to be an outstanding event, one to be proud of. To achieve the vision I had would involve a massive workload. Having someone to share that load was an attractive concept. Firstly, I had to identify someone to whom the challenge might appeal. Secondly, and as part of my brief in asking someone, I would need to explain about the workload it would involve.

I weighed up the possibility of asking Ken. Now that he had one Ironman under his belt, he wanted to challenge his body further. He was supremely fit and entering his prime as a long distance athlete. I decided he was an ideal candidate, so I picked up the phone and asked him.

I recognised that he was someone I could work with. I knew he would not commit lightly, that he would be a tireless worker and would apply himself to reaching peak physical condition. I felt that he would like to be asked. I was right.

He didn't commit straight away. I asked him on a Friday evening over a long phone call and I suggested he spend the weekend thinking it over. He left me in suspense until the following Tuesday but I respected him all the more for that. After some personal think-time and consultation with his family, he agreed to join me.

This event would involve a massive workload to get 1,000 people to run with us. Who they would be, I had no idea. I simply had an end result in my head. The devil was in the detail but a strategy had yet to be created for that.

I waited in the reception area for Ken to reappear from the doctor's office, where he was getting his V02 results. Moments later, he appeared.

"What did you get?" he asked, a smile beaming on his face as he approached me.

I gave him my result.

"Ha, I beat you," he said.

"Why, what did you get?" I asked.

His score was three points higher than mine.

"Apparently I am in the elite athlete category," he uttered proudly.

I knew for sure I had chosen the right partner.

CHAPTER 20
PLANNING FOR THE LONG RUN

'It is not enough to take steps which may someday lead to a goal; each step must be itself a goal and a step likewise.'

Johann Wolfgang von Goethe

THEY say one marathon is hard. If you had told me after my first one in 2007 that just a few short years later I could contemplate taking on 32 marathons in just 32 days, I would have had you locked up.

I got different reactions from my family when I told them of my plans. I broke the news to my parents over a few days. It was a strategy on my part. I needed their support but I was nervous about how they would react. I felt confident in my ability to do it having completed the Double Ironman but I wanted to respect any concerns they might have had.

On day one I told them I was going to do a long run every day for a month of about four or five hours a day. This did not overly concern them. The next day I told them it involved a full marathon every day. This time they really stood up and took notice. My mum was fine with it however. I was relieved. My dad had been very nervous of the Double Ironman attempt. By now though, he realised that I did not do things foolishly and that I was not considering these challenges naively. We chatted about it and I alleviated any unease he had. Their endorsement was vitally important to me.

Dorothy was fine as I knew she would be. She had by now completed two Ironman distance races herself and she had seen the 'Double' attempt up close. Tom was also fine with it. Finally, I went to tell my other sisters, Mary and Katherine. Both expressed concerns. In particular Mary questioned my sanity but after a day or two, she came around and was indeed one of the first to sign up to run with us.

In addition to running 838 miles over 32 days we had identified two other goals as part of this challenge, as I identified earlier. We wanted to devise a strategy to raise funds and awareness for our chosen charities by mobilising over 1,000 runners to share our journey.

Why not use the event as a platform to assist charities that were in need of funds. The concept of getting people to run with us in their chosen county would serve a dual purpose. By asking these runners to raise funds it would help us reach our financial goal for the charities and also help create an 'event' within an event. It would also provide Ken and I with company as we travelled the country. It would be a win-win scenario.

The only drawback was the workload increased a thousand fold. By setting these additional goals, it brought a whole new dimension to the organisation. If it were simply Ken and I running we could go quietly around the country with a GPS watch starting wherever and whenever we wished each day. Inviting members of the public to participate would be a different ballgame.

It would involve a huge amount of additional man hours and hundreds of meetings. For starters, we had no idea where we would find these 1,000 runners from. We needed to plan a public relations initiative and set-up a website for publicity and registration. To attract media attention we contacted a number of celebrities to get them to support the event either by endorsing it or to involve them as race starters or in some cases to actually run with us.

Our ambition in terms of numbers was to find 1,024 runners. This figure was the equivalent of 32 runners in each county. In reality we did not mind if this meant five runners in a county one day, 25 on the next and 50 on another day. Once it averaged out at 32 a day we would have ticked that box.

We would have a big media launch to ensure there was an awareness in every county. We would need it as we were going to try to persuade complete strangers to log onto our website, register, pay a deposit, commit to training for six odd months and to fundraise. A tall order to say the least.

On top of that, we had to find 32 suitable and safe routes. We had to find local route co-ordinators to help us source these routes and assist us with local expertise and local knowledge. We had to map the routes, find accommodation, prepare safety statements and encourage sponsors to come on board.

Over 1,000 runners was a big responsibility and opened up an enormous logistical challenge. The good thing is we were up for it. The workload we knew would be challenging, the rewards however would be great. By getting outside our comfort zones of a quiet, low key but hugely physical challenge, we were going instead to create an event that hopefully people would be proud to be a part of, proud to fundraise for and proud to run in.

We decided that Irish Autism Action (IAA) would be the principle charity. Many people have asked us why we chose them as neither Ken nor I had a direct link with autism.

Through my previous contact with Irish Autism Action, I had seen close up the invaluable work that they do. I also knew they were not state-funded and were desperately in need of funds. Like all charities, they had seen a significant decrease in fundraising activity because of the economic downturn.

SO WHAT IS AUTISM?

Autism is a developmental disorder that affects the normal development of the brain in areas of social interaction and communication and is marked by severe difficulties in communicating and forming relationships with people, in developing language, interacting with people and following simple instructions. Autism is a hidden disability because people who are on the spectrum show no significant physical difference to their peers, but it is their behaviours that mark them out as different.

The three main areas of difficulties for people with autism are social communication, interaction and imagination. The first signs of autism usually appear as developmental delays before the age of three years. Autism is described as a 'spectrum' disorder'. This means that the symptoms and characteristics of autism can present themselves in a wide variety of combinations and can range from mild to severe. One in 166 people have autism which is a staggering statistic.

Reference: Irish Autism Action

In 2008, I had observed some of the work they were involved in through direct support of 13 schools nationwide and through the setting up of a diagnostic centre in Dublin. I really felt strongly that if Ken and I were going to do this event, the media attention that it would generate should be used for a common good and what better angle than raising funds and awareness for charity. Our decision to choose them was further cemented in the summer of 2009. One morning I walked into a local hotel and noticed Kevin Whelan, the CEO of the charity, finishing a meeting with two people I knew.

John and Dorothy Hanlon were old friends, whom I had not seen in quite a few years. Like myself, John had just turned 40 the previous year. I was unaware that by now, he and Dorothy had three beautiful children. John and I had shared digs in Dublin many years before around the time when Stephen Roche was winning the Tour De France in '87, Ray Houghton was putting the ball in the England net in '88 and you could rent a room in Fitzwilliam Square for £25 a week.

As soon as I saw them I put two and two together. John told me their youngest, Thomas, had been diagnosed with autism when he was two. They were keen to praise the wonderful care, advice and support that the IAA had provided them with. They explained how Thomas had only moved up nine places in three years from number 35 to number 26 on the list to get into Saplings, the specialist autism school in Mullingar. I went home immediately and rewrote the few words I had planned to say at the upcoming launch. What a legacy the 32 Marathon Challenge could leave behind, I thought to myself, if we could help move young Thomas further up that list.

In addition to Irish Autism Action in the south, Autism Northern Ireland would be the designated charity in the North. Everyone agreed that all of the money raised there should and would be used for autism projects in the communities in which it was raised.

In addition Ken and I made the decision that a small percentage of the proceeds should go to a cancer charity. All of us know somebody either directly or indirectly who has been affected by this disease so we wanted to do something to help in this regard also. We chose the Irish Cancer Society.

CHAPTER 21
LAUNCHING THE 32 MARATHON CHALLENGE

IF we were to raise awareness about the event and to encourage hundreds of people to join us we knew we had to have a launch, so we did. In fact we had three.

The first two which we decided to hold in Dublin and Mullingar would be in the same week. The first one in Dublin would hopefully result in national media coverage and the second was to be a local launch in our hometown. It was on that night that we would hope to begin encouraging people to formally register to be part of the 32 Marathon Challenge. A third launch in Belfast was scheduled for January.

In advance of these launches we built a website with the domain name www.32marathons.com. It was an obvious address to direct people for further information. Included on the website was a registration facility. It also outlined in detail the many celebrities and well known faces we were persuading to endorse our event.

They say you are never more than six degrees of separation from meeting anyone in the world. Thankfully in Ireland it is probably even less. Before long we had secured the endorsement of such well-known faces as GAA legends Darragh Ó Sé and Henry Shefflin, Charmaine Kenny, the 2009 Rose of Tralee and Johnny Donnelly ex-drummer with The Sawdoctors, a renowned marathon runner himself. Furthermore, we managed to get former 1984 Olympic marathon silver medallist John Treacy on board. Another who would lend her support at our Belfast launch was Dame Mary Peters, the 1972 Olympic Gold Medallist (pentathlon).

The website and the domain were critically important. It meant that whenever we did a radio or newspaper interview we could direct people to it.

We put a huge amount of information, training tips, fundraising ideas, route maps et cetera there for people to download. We provided some information on the designated charities, provided local autism contacts and a list of the individual dates for the 32 days.

Another well-known sports star and an Irishman who had a running CV like few others on the globe was soon identified as someone we would try to get in contact with and an endorsement from. If we could get to speak to him, he could offer us advice and knowledge to help us with our challenge. A contact who knew him was approached and within two days a meeting was arranged.

"There he is," exclaimed Niall, our contact, pointing out to the disguised motorcyclist, his identity hidden by the helmet shielding his face. We were in a restaurant in Smithfield just off the North Quays and were seated in the window seat with a clear view of the streetscape outside. Seated beside me was Bernard Flynn.

"Are you serious?" I asked Niall. "You're messing" That couldn't be him. On a motorbike?"

I had expected this man to arrive in a Mercedes, a BMW Coupe or similar type mode of transport, not a Suzuki motorbike. The 5' 10" frame of the sports legend we were about to meet dismounted and immediately spotted Niall who was waving furiously in his direction.

The biker motioned towards us, still disguised underneath his helmet and jokingly pressed his head against the glass, giving us a big thumb- up at the same time. Just then he raised the helmet from his head to display a cheeky grin. It was indeed the man we had hoped to meet. An entrance perhaps befitting a man who at the core of it all was one of the lads.

It was Eamonn Coghlan, the 1983 world 5,000 metre champion and known to many as the 'Chairman of the Boards' (the US indoor circuit). We had arranged this meeting with two goals in mind. Firstly to ask his advice on a range of topics from athletics contacts and protocol to training plans. We also wanted his guidance on organising a marathon in the Phoenix Park, our proposed location in Dublin.

We hoped to get 30 minutes of his time. He gave us an hour. His advice, enthusiasm and offers of access to a range of contacts proved invaluable. In the middle of our discussion he asked the waiter for a pen and paper. I wasn't sure why but it soon became obvious. With pen in hand, Eamonn started to write down a list of things that he was going to do for us. It was more than we could possibly have hoped for.

I had in fact been quite nervous in advance of this meeting but I walked away feeling 10 feet tall that this sporting hero of mine appreciated the challenge we were attempting to take on, not just by running 838 miles, but also by the scale of the event we were trying to organise. We rose from the table and I put out my hand to shake Eamonn's, thanking him profusely.

He held my hand momentarily refusing me leave to take it away.

"I'll run with you in the Phoenix Park marathon if you like," he suggested. In my eagerness to jot down as much of the advice as possible, I had forgotten to ask him. Now here was Eamonn offering to run with us without having to be asked. An amazing guy. Needless to say, we took him up on his offer.

A sad note to finish this chapter. In the autumn of 2009, I had been introduced to a man called Niall McCrudden. Within days of meeting Niall, he rang me to say he wanted to be the first sponsor to sign up to help with our challenge. He owned an internet company called sunglass.ie.

It was Niall who set up the introduction with Eamonn. Within four months of this meeting, sadly Niall would die prematurely. I will always remember him fondly and will never forget his offer of sponsorship. We hadn't even asked him.

CHAPTER 22
RUNNING ON AIR

KEN and I paced up and down Grafton Street in Dublin for what seemed like hours.

Our Dublin press launch was on a Wednesday morning. We got a smack of Murphy's Law on that occasion as we were the victim of a more newsworthy story. Understandably the media invited to our chosen venue had, at the last minute, gone to the northside of Dublin as a roof had blown off an apartment block earlier that morning. Thankfully nobody was hurt, but it left our launch a little quiet.

We camped out in the hotel lobby to review strategy and talk tactics. A few phone calls were made and the day was saved when we got word that Matt Cooper from Today FM was interested in having us as studio guests on his drivetime show, *The Last Word*. The only problem was it would be a live interview and it was to be later the same day. Talk about being thrown in at the deep end.

Queue major stress in the heads of two lonely marathon runners. You will recall from an earlier chapter my fear of public speaking. Well Ken wasn't much better. I could immediately feel my heart racing - and this was four hours before we were due to go on air. Neither of us had any background in talking to the media and the prospect filled us with fear.

We knew we had to do it as it was a stepping-stone in helping us achieve our goals. The exposure to the huge listenership offered a welcome public relations opportunity. We were scheduled to go on just after the six o'clock news, the time of peak listenership. The thought of it was terrifying but somehow we managed to keep our sanity as our slot grew ever closer. I made the mistake of telling Dorothy about it, not thinking she would text and email half the country to tell them to tune in. At about four o'clock the texts of good luck started to arrive. This only made us feel more nervous knowing that people I knew would be listening.

My mind went back to the hotel auction five years before. That day I had an audience of four. Today it would be up to 50,000 times that number. At 5.30 a friend from Kerry sent Ken a text to tell him that Matt Cooper had already told his audience of our upcoming interview. Bloody hell, this was real.

We arrived at the studio shortly before six o'clock. I was not in a good place mentally. We entered the reception area of the thoroughly modern and highly impressive Today FM studios. In the open office plan area there were about 20 desks and perhaps five people still working. I spotted a guy in his mid-30s in the distance and tried to figure out where I knew him from. He too looked back with a similar gaze but a second later both of us were otherwise distracted, his back to his computer and mine in search of the nearest bathroom. I was nervous.

Cooper's voice from his live show filled the air all around. I was absolutely terrified at this point and looked at Ken and Kevin Whelan, the CEO of the charity, for comfort. Finally the producer arrived to escort us to the studio. Just as we were about to enter, Kevin turned to me with a cheeky grin, "Don't worry Gerry, there are only about 200,000 people about to listen to your every word. You will be grand". Believe it or not, his words did actually settle a few nerves.

We entered the studio, a room not much bigger than the average bedroom. Cooper was seated in front of a large red microphone introducing an upcoming ad break to his listeners. There seated close by was my old friend from the reception area. He turned to me, offered his hand and whispered,

"Hi Gerry, welcome. Michael, Michael McMullen. Remember me?"

Once I heard his voice, I knew who he was. For many years, I had been indirectly involved with the FAI when the Irish team were playing away matches. As part of the travel company carrying the officials and media crews I got to know many of the TV presenters, radio commentators, press guys/girls and photographers and that is where I knew Michael from. I remembered him as a really great guy.

Meeting him at this time helped to settle my nerves a little as we reminisced over the next 90 seconds or so of places such as Estonia, Amsterdam and a World Cup play-off in Brussels in 1997. For a brief moment I forgot where I was, but with professionalism Michael went from mid-sentence talking about a trip we shared to Iran for a World Cup play-off in 2007 to discussing the trials of Cork GAA with the listeners once directed by Cooper.

Then our moment of introduction arrived. Matt looked up and his eyes focused on mine. I felt like a rabbit caught in the headlights. After introducing us and the nature of what we were attempting eight months hence to his listeners, his first question was very much to the point.

"I'm tempted to ask, are ye mad?"

I was keen to speak first to settle my nerves and Ken was fine with that. Thankfully I managed to mouth a reply and we settled in fine afterwards. He seemed fascinated by our ambitious plan but I think he thought we were a little crazy. As we exited less than 10 minutes later, he invited us to come back once the challenge was completed.

Launch number one was now out of the way and already over 200,000 people knew of our ambitious plans. The second launch was more local and came just two days later. This time the attendance was in our own hands consisting of friends, family and local media. It was a success.

Over 200 people had been invited and they all turned up. By the end of the night 38 people had registered to run. That might seem small. Not so. Just because Ken and I were into running we could not expect that others would want to run 13 or 26 miles with us. We were also asking people to raise a considerable sum for the charities. On the night we had several offers of help as people volunteered their services or advice as well as offering sponsorship. The jigsaw was starting to come together.

For the remaining four weeks of 2009, every lead was chased down and every newspaper and radio station that we could get access to was contacted. By the end of December, 175 people had signed up.

CHAPTER 23
CLEAR FOR TAKE-OFF

"SO what do you want with an old fart like me?" The voice was unmistakeable. It was Michael O'Leary on the other end of the phone.

You don't need me to tell you how much of a business one-off genius O'Leary is. He is a giant of the PR world and the CEO of probably the most successful airline on the planet, Ryanair. His airline thrives on publicity and no one knows how to go about getting it better than the bould Mick.

Like ourselves, the O'Learys grew up in Mullingar. I knew his dad Ted from the golf club. Indeed his mum Ger is a very close friend of my own mum's. A lovely lady.

Michael is someone I didn't know so well. When we were growing up in the 70s and 80s two of Michael's siblings, Eddie and Valerie were regular visitors to our house. However they were more friends of my older brother and sister, Tom and Mary.

When we first started to hatch the plan that would involve marketing this challenge, we hoped to get Michael on board. I was sure that he got a million requests for such things and I didn't want to risk a refusal. Due to the family friendship, I didn't want to overstep that boundary. As luck would have it, an opportunity arose well before most people knew anything about our plans.

I was at a charity cycle in Mullingar in September '09 and bumped into Eddie, Michael's younger brother and Eddie's wife Wendy, both renowned horse breeders. My sister Dorothy had already informed Wendy of my plans. All three of us are members of the same triathlon club and so we see each other regularly.

"Go on, tell Eddie what you're planning," Wendy urged, laughing as I sat down beside them.

"What are you talking about?" I asked innocently.

"About the marathons," she replied, laughing.

"Oh, you heard," I said.

"Yeah, go on, tell him."

"What the hell are you planning now?" intervened Eddie, trying to make out what we were saying. He knew of my previous exploits.

"Oh the marathons, next year. I am organising an event called the 32 Marathon Challenge," I explained.

"And tell him how many of them you are running, Gerry," Wendy asked.

"All of them," I informed him.

"Over how long?" asked Eddie

"32 Days," I said.

He looked at me in total disbelief.

"You're mad, you know that," he said.

"I know, but what the hell. We are doing it for a great cause and we want to get lots of people to raise money for charity."

"Would you run with us?" I asked trying to fill my first place in the event long before we had even gone public. "Wendy is running," I declared boldly as I looked at her hoping she would back me up.

"Not a chance," he retorted, "I'm not a runner, but I'll get Mick to do it if you like."

Bingo!

Six weeks after meeting Eddie and Wendy, my phone rang. It was late one Thursday evening. By the end of the phone call, Mick had come on board by agreeing to endorse our event publicly. He had also agreed to do a photoshoot and to run two half-marathons with us, one in Dublin and on the final day in Westmeath.

What a coup this was I thought to myself as the line went dead.

I knew that having Michael on board would give the event great credibility. He had a wide range of appeal not just to the person in the street, but he was also an attractive personality to any potential sponsors.

He had suggested holding off on a press conference and the photo shoot until mid-January. It was by now late November. The media only had room for two news items, Christmas and the upcoming

Government Budget. Michael felt the press would be hungrier for a good news story then.

I made contact with his office the first week into the New Year and we agreed on Thursday January 9th. He was holding a Ryanair press conference in a city centre hotel at 11am but expected to finish within 30 minutes. We were asked to be ready from 11:30 onwards.

Given that the Ryanair news story would presumably be published on the Friday we invited media from two Sunday publications, the *Sunday Tribune* and the *Sunday Independent*. In addition, RTE's Darragh Maloney agreed to do an interview with Michael, where he would publicly confirm his involvement in our event.

Darragh is better known for presenting RTE's flagship football programme, *The Premiership*. He also presents a nightly sports show on RTE Radio 1. He had helped us earlier by hosting our launch in Mullingar and was delighted to be given the opportunity to interview Michael.

I arrived at the hotel an hour ahead of schedule. The Ryanair press conference was in the room immediately beside reception. I went to reception on arrival and asked which room had been reserved for us.

"Oh, you're on the seventh floor, sir," said the receptionist.

"What?" I replied. I was horrified. The last thing I wanted was to risk annoying the Ryanair entourage by asking them to take a lift seven floors up. I had only 20 minutes of his time and I did not want to waste 50 per cent of it getting him from the ground floor to the top of the building.

I decided to check out the room regardless for suitability and accessibility. I began sweating profusely after five minutes of searching the seventh floor when I still hadn't located the meeting room. Finally I found it, but on inspection I was certain it wouldn't work. Apart from being hard to find, it was tiny and had no natural light. We had got a company to make up a seven-foot cardboard map of Ireland to be used as a prop and I couldn't even get it in the door. I raced back to reception and asked to be moved to another location.

"I'm sorry, that is the only room available. All our other meeting rooms are booked up," I was informed firmly.

I explained why I was in the hotel and the fact that we would only need the room for 15 to 20 minutes, but he said there was nothing he could do for me. I paced up and down the lobby, stressing out more and more with every step. Here I was, having landed a major coup by getting one of the greatest PR men on the planet here. I had only minutes to solve this problem and no solution was on the horizon. To make matters worse his press conference would soon be winding up and our media were starting to arrive. I could see them enquiring at reception for directions to the meeting room.

Just then a friendly concierge approached.

"Excuse me sir, I couldn't help but overhear your difficulty. What about using the restaurant? Breakfast has finished and we can easily move the furniture around to allow you to do what you wish with the room."

I could have hugged him.

"Where is the restaurant?" I asked.

"There," he said pointing to a room not five feet from where I was standing. Within seconds of inspecting it, I knew it was perfect.

Ten minutes later we were ready to rock.

By now Darragh, the journalists and two photographers had arrived. All we needed now was the main attraction. It was 11.45 and we had expected him 15 minutes earlier.

I started to worry. What if he actually was not here? I certainly hadn't seen him come in earlier. Just then I got a brainwave. Michael travels by taxi when he is in Dublin and I knew what it looked like from seeing it in Mullingar.

I nipped to the front door of the hotel and right outside in the drop-off area was his taxi. Sure enough, moments later he made his entrance. I had brought along additional props. I knew he would have to agree to it but I didn't think a pair of shorts, a 32 Marathon Challenge t-shirt and a pair of running shoes would upset him too much.

"Hi guys. How is everyone?" he asked. "Blooming hell Gerry, you have more media here than we could muster for our own press conference," he said loudly, trying to make me feel at ease.

Darragh spent 10 minutes recording a piece for his radio show. "Well how mad are Gerry and Ken?" was Darragh's first question to him.

"Clearly they are crazy but then Gerry's family are all a little mad. I know them from Mullingar and they are into crazy things like Ironman Triathlons and the like. Clearly there is a screw loose."

I looked at him and he seemed to be enjoying himself. I knew his time was limited though, so as soon as he was finished, I introduced him to the two journalists who were there.

Alison O'Riordan from the *Sunday Independent*, Ireland's biggest-selling newspaper was first up. Her first question went something along the lines of... "So Michael, I hear you are running with the lads. Can you confirm that you are and if so, what your training consists of?"

"Oh yes, I am definitely running. In fact I am in regular training. Five pints a day, copious amounts of cigarettes and regular sex."

I wondered if she would print that word for word. She did.

Next up were the photographers. I handed him the running shorts, which he willingly took. I was just about to direct him to the gents but his trousers were already around his ankles, changing in full view of all in the room. He had never been shy, had our Michael.

"Ok, Gerry, what other props have you got?" he enquired.

I pointed in the direction of the giant map of Ireland.

"Brilliant, what else?"

"Eh, a stopwatch," I offered.

"A stopwatch?"

"Is that all? We want to get this front page, don't we?"

Michael then shouted in the direction of one of his staff members to get some additional props which he felt would make a good picture.

A few minutes later the two photographers were salivating at the pose which involved Michael, two cigarettes hanging out of either side of his mouth, a bottle of vodka in either hand, with Ken and I holding him aloft. It was vintage O'Leary and vintage PR.

Twenty minutes after making his entrance, he was gone.

CHAPTER 24
GOING THE ALL-IRELAND ROUTE

AWARENESS of the event was now reaching a bigger audience. A photo of Michael with Ken and I got great coverage in the *Sunday Independent* and the *Sunday Tribune*. This really kick-started the registrations and by the end of January we had almost 300 signed up to run.

Ken and I chased every possible lead to get more. Brothers, sisters, parents, cousins and friends both at home and abroad were encouraged to sign up. We were unrelenting in our efforts.

On the presumption that hundreds more would join us we had to begin to piece together a huge logistical plan. A big undertaking, it would take us six months to put it together. We were determined that anyone who registered would have an unforgettable race-day experience. This was not a regular city marathon with thousands and thousands pounding the roads. It would be the same physical challenge however, for all participants. We were also asking these people to fundraise to participate. We had a responsibility to ensure we provided them with a great day out - in a safe environment.

After work, training and family life we were by now putting in three to four hours every day on logistics. We were making new contacts every day, mostly on the phone, some face-to-face. We knew that getting awareness out to running clubs was a possible rich source of new people joining as well as learning about running routes. The charity also sent posters and information leaflets out to hundreds of running clubs, gyms and other sports clubs to stimulate interest.

Two of the more daunting challenges were finding 32 different routes and trying to get sponsorship from a hotel in each county. The first was a massive undertaking. For this, we enlisted the help of close friends Brian Boyle, John O'Reilly and Brian Ivory. They were all good organisers and were not afraid to put their names forward to help. Our first task was to find 26 route co-ordinators. We had managed to delegate the job of finding routes in Northern Ireland to another contact Colin Telford, who had local expertise.

We quickly identified contacts in Longford, Carlow, Kerry, Limerick, Kildare, Offaly, Clare, Galway, Roscommon, Monaghan and Donegal. As a follow up to the poster campaign we had called some running clubs in the remaining counties to ask them if they knew anyone who might help and if they could suggest any routes to us. After a further six weeks, we came up with nine more names covering as many counties.

Some route co-ordinators actually came forward and volunteered. Richard Donovan in Galway, Willie Burns in Offaly, Richard Chapman in Limerick, Pádraig Sherry in Monaghan, Vinnie Glennon in Roscommon, Ken Dunne who organises the Dingle Marathon in Kerry and Alan Logue, a man involved in the Burren Marathon in county Clare. Their enthusiasm, assistance and knowledge was a great help and a great boost to us.

The routes that we needed to find or create were not typical marathon routes. This would be a very 'intimate' marathon series. It would average at only 25 to 30 runners each day. We would have no road closures like you would in regular marathon events. We would however had to cover all the same safety aspects. We could not simply turn up and run from A to B on a busy main road without any preparation.

One of the first things we decided on was multiple loops in order to halve or quarter the number of marshals needed on any given day. We had to get this message across to our contacts locally. This was part of our master plan that with very little exception could not be tampered with.

That meant we needed to source courses measuring 6.55 miles. Where four loops was not an option, a routing of 13.1 miles for a two loop or 4.366 miles for a six loop circuit would need to be identified and mapped. Some of it was easy such as Carlow where locals Ken and Ann Hickey found a scenic River Barrow trail. They simply measured 3.275 miles in one direction and doubled it for one loop.

One of the more complicated counties was Wicklow. For starters we had no running contacts there. Brian Boyle identified a possible person who might help. His name was Eamon Breen. Together with his work colleague Tony Salmon they volunteered to co-ordinate the 'Garden County' marathon.

I met them one afternoon. We had sent a checklist of things to consider in advance so I was delighted when they told me that they had a possible routing already identified. We jumped into the car and drove around the seaside town of Bray. The route was quite complicated though, meandering all over and around this lovely coastal location. On the day I was there the town was exceptionally busy. I knew however, that the Wicklow marathon was scheduled for a Sunday morning, so the town would be much quieter when we returned.

Over a few hours we identified potential pitfalls, such as dangerous junctions or road crossings, appropriate water station locations, public toilet facilities etc. One set of toilets on a four loop route is actually four toilets. Similarly, two water stations on one loop is actually eight stations over 26 miles. Areas requiring marshals and a suitable race headquarters were also identified as we drove around. Both Eamon and Tony displayed a 'nothing will phase us' attitude. Their professionalism was very reassuring. Come Sunday 4th July, we would not be disappointed.

By having multiple loops, the task of measuring each course was less time consuming. We asked all route co-ordinators like Eamon and Tony to GPS the route (map and measure) and to forward it onto Ken's brother Barry, who was looking after the website. We were anxious to present as many routes as possible on the site so that local runners could get the flavour of the proposed routing. On each race day, Ken and I would also carry GPS watches purely as a precaution.

As I bade farewell to the two lads, I asked them if they had any good hotel contacts locally who might sponsor our one-night stopover. They suggested and even offered to speak on our behalf to the Martello Hotel on the promenade in Bray. I explained our requirements and they told me to leave it with them.

Hotel sponsorship was something we devoted significant time to. We would have a rotating crew of 14 or 15 people travelling with us. By basing our headquarters at a hotel it meant we would have a location for registration as well as post-race massage for all the athletes. The Irish Society of Chartered Physiotherapists had very kindly offered to provide complimentary post-race physio massage to all runners. The hotels could provide us with a room. Hotels could also provide us with shower facilities as well.

We also needed these venues to be close to a population centre for our bucket collectors. Having emailed all our coordinators a checklist in advance, we asked each team in early May to visually inspect each route.

My next port of call was Cork. Fota Island was my destination, I was there by invitation. The general manager John O'Flynn had actually made contact with us in early March. He had spotted a photograph promoting the event in the Sunday newspapers. "What can we at Fota Island do to help?" was his question to us over an email. The contents of the email stunned me. The management at Fota Island had obviously recognised the magnitude of the charity challenge we were undertaking. I arrived into the hotel foyer to be met by an old acquaintance of mine who had lived in Mullingar for a number of years. Adre Vosloo, a South African lady had moved to Cork two years previously. Adre was the only person I knew living in that county. When we rang her asking for help, she volunteered without hesitation. We had also arranged to meet John to discuss our Cork stopover and to try to find a suitable marathon route.

By the end of the meeting, FOTA were not only giving us a bed on the eve of the marathon for the entire crew, they also offered to map a four-loop marathon route around the estate. John added that he would run a half-marathon with us himself and promised to encourage the staff of the Spa and Leisure Centre to run with us as part of a relay.

On the drive home, I got a great feeling that the event was really starting to take shape. It gave me a surge of confidence to know that Fota was willing to go to such lengths to support us. This generosity gave us great ammunition when we made contact with other hotels looking for sponsorship.

One of the first things we had done was to ensure the website projected an image of a big professional event. This, we hoped, would encourage people to participate and help persuade sponsors such as hotels to come on board. In February, March and April and whenever we had a spare moment, we picked up the Golden Pages and simply rang hotels in the towns we had chosen as marathon sites. I soon developed a successful sale pitch which worked 99 per cent of the time.

In my first 'cold' call, I asked to speak to the general manager or the hotel owner. This ensured that I would be put through to the person who ultimately made the decisions. My next tactic was to undersell the event a little but to sow a seed of the magnitude of the challenge and the fact that it was for charity. Next I told them about the well-known faces we had backing us. It was great to be able to say that the likes of Keith Duffy of Boyzone, the 2009 Rose of Tralee Charmaine Kenny, Michael O'Leary and Eamonn Coghlan were already on board. Not just that, they were running too. I gave them the website address and simply asked them to take a look.

Thankfully by now, we were also able to put on the site sound bites from programmes on RTE Radio, Today FM and Newstalk shows on which the event had been discussed. These soundbites were strategically placed on the homepage. I explained to each hotelier that we were looking for them to become an associate sponsor by way of accommodation. I am proud to say that the support we received from hotels all over the country was overwhelming.

Within a few days of leaving Wicklow, Eamon emailed to say the Martello Hotel in Bray had committed to supporting us. Another task completed from one of several thousand boxes we had to tick.

CHAPTER 25
WORKING OUT THE WAY AHEAD

TRAINING for this challenge was by the nature of the event always going to be 'extreme' but that was one part that we both eagerly looked forward to. As documented earlier, Ken and I had served various apprenticeships leading into this challenge. In addition, we both knew a massive volume of training lay ahead. Running two marathons in a row sounded hard. We had committed to running 32.

The year 2009 was great for Ken and I in terms of achieving our sporting goals. By the end of that summer, our bodies needed rest and recuperation but without winding down entirely. From November to January we ran between 50 and 55 miles each week to keep ourselves ticking over, before commencing a strenuous 23-week training programme starting on February 1st.

For that programme and for ultra-running advice we needed to speak to an expert. We found that man in the west of Ireland. Richard Donovan, a 43-year-old Galway man was a world record holder. A year previously he had beaten the record of one of the world's great adventurers, Sir Ranulph Fiennes. Richard now held the record for running seven marathons in just six days. What was unique about the record was that he ran them on the *seven continents of the world*.

Richard immediately agreed to piece together a training programme for us that would have us in peak physical condition on the day we arrived at the start of our first marathon, then giving us the best chance of getting through the 32-marathon challenge.

The first day of spring - the first day of our official training. It was a Monday, which was ideal. It allowed us to mentally prepare ourselves over the preceding weekend for what lay ahead for the following 23 weeks. The programme Richard sent us was a spreadsheet with many colours offering different distances and tempos of runs on different days. I opened it as excitedly as young Charlie opening his Willie Wonka chocolate bar. The programme looked very tough, with each day filled for the next 161. Ninety-five per cent of it involved running with a small amount of cross training of swimming and cycling.

There was also the odd rest day thrown in for good measure thankfully. I immediately spotted some interesting runs he had scheduled for April.

"Now that looks interesting," I thought to myself.

As part of training, Richard had pencilled in three different runs of '31 miles' distance. That was a defining moment in realising the magnitude of what lay ahead. Ken and I studied the programme with heavy concentration. It made complete sense but would involve a massive commitment. Each three-week training block would see our runs rise by between five and 10 miles per week. Week one had 50 miles of running, week two 60 miles and week three had 70 miles. Week four then dropped back down to 40 miles to allow for a little recovery. The next three week block started at 70 miles and so on. That was just the start. Soon it would hit three digits.

There is nothing like having a goal written down in front of you. When that goal has a map attached to guide you there (our training programme), the journey is easier to mentally visualise and prepare for. I went to bed on that Sunday night excited that we were starting our dedicated training programme.

The next day we hit the roads in earnest. Ken would do the bulk of his training in Dublin and me in Mullingar. The mileage climbed quickly. From the Double Ironman a year earlier, I already had a large volume of training in the legs. A lot of that had come from hours and hours on the bike. Over the spring, we built up our mileage each week. In February, an average week involved 60 miles of running. In March, it hovered towards 80 and by early April it was in excess of 90. That would still be well short of our peak mileage.

Excerpt from my diary of Thursday 18th February

'Early morning workouts are nothing new to me. I relish rising at 6am eager to train and to experience nature at a time when it is unseen by many. Since the start of the month we have been raising the bar. A tasty 70 miles is on the menu this week. This morning I had 12 miles run before tucking into a breakfast of porridge with sesame and pumpkin seeds sweetened nicely by a few spoonfuls of honey. All done before 8am. What

a great way to start any day. Perhaps my enthusiasm was helped by a rest day yesterday. My legs were burning a little on Tuesday night so I felt it prudent to take it easy yesterday. Three consecutive days from Sunday where we clocked a total of 35 miles on the feet had to be respected.

Runs of 10/12 miles and higher are now almost a daily routine. It is amazing how the body can adapt to such challenges once you combine experience, exercise and a focused mind. The menu for the remainder of this week has plenty to whet the appetite culminating with a tasty 18-miler on Sunday next (Feb 21st).'

February and March went great. For one thing there was the weather. Some people dislike frosty mornings. I love them and the spring of 2010 had them in abundance. It was simply a matter of finding suitable terrain to avoid slipping. For that eight week period I did most of my running along the banks of the Royal Canal which flows through Mullingar, meandering and weaving its way past a variety of landscapes that rarely leaves you bored. On many mornings I was privy to a beautiful sight of a frozen canal at six am. Every morning that I ran, I silently gave thanks for being blessed with great health. On those mornings I tried to think of people less fortunate than me who were possibly lying on a hospital bed or for whatever reason might have been unable to do something as simple and enjoyable as running.

Towards the end of March we headed towards 80 miles per week. Normally when training for a marathon, a runner's training is centred around one long run per week complemented by three or four shorter runs. For our challenge we had to do two long runs every week. Sometimes this was Wednesday and Saturday, other times it was consecutive days over a weekend to simulate fatigue.

Early morning runs of 10 miles or more were done without as much as a thought. Then the weekend might see us run a full marathon on Saturday followed by another half-marathon the next day. Some weeks saw us do back-to-back marathons on consecutive days. It was tough but the truth is we were both totally focused and relished every metre. Never once did we skip a session.

For the entire training period, I was fortunate to remain injury-free. Ken was not quite as lucky as an old injury flared up in March, meaning sometimes he couldn't run for a period. As an indication of his commitment to achieving our goal, he refused to stay stationary during this four week injury period. Instead, he laced up his runners and walked the entire distance each time. To appreciate just what that entailed, one of those weekends meant walking back-to-back marathons of 26.2 miles on Saturday and Sunday. Both walks took him over seven hours each. I always knew he was tough. Later in July, our entire crew would realise just how tough he really was. He would soon display a mental and physical fortitude that would truly astound us all.

By early April we were about to start our peak period of training. Every Sunday evening I would plan my diary for the week ahead. The run mileage per week was already set in stone. What needed weekly structuring was work, college, organising the logistics of the event, family and rest time in between. I have never known a period where my life was so busy. Looking back it was a crazy time but I saw the 32 Marathons Challenge as the ultimate reward for our efforts and we were determined to ensure that we had every angle covered.

On Sunday 4th April, I checked my timetable for the coming week. I was in the middle of a very busy period. Not only did we have all of the logistics of the event to continually drive, but I had to work, train and I was back in college studying hard for exams which were now just a matter of days away. The exams were for a course I had enrolled in to qualify as a fitness instructor.

For a few years now, people had begun asking my advice on a range of sporting training topics. I felt it was correct to get the proper qualifications. In addition I really enjoyed it. The timing for an academic challenge though could have been better. It was proving very time-consuming, requiring two weekly commutes to Dublin as well as every second Saturday. On April 10th, I sat my last big exam but it meant I was away all day. I had two late-night music gigs to do also, which meant working beyond 2am.

"Why the music gigs?" I hear you ask. Well, by early 2009 my property business was suffering hugely. I had no 'second idea' as a back-up when the property market crashed. I needed to find another revenue source - quickly. In May, I started a new business from scratch. I chose something that had been a hobby around 20 years previously. I went back to being a DJ.

One thing in my favour was there had been a resurgence in the popularity of 70s and 80s music and I knew it like the back of my hand. What I had to relearn was the DJ equipment and modern computer music technology. I learned fast. With a small financial investment behind me, I went in search of my first gig. It wasn't long coming: a Friday night in a Mullingar hotel which was launching a 70s and 80s late night bar. It helped that I knew the hotel owner.

As fate would have it, I was about to meet someone very special in those late night surrounds. The venue was full on the opening night with perhaps 250 people strutting their stuff to Boy George, Creedence Clearwater Revival and a bit of Tina Turner. I was very nervous on the night but I was able to hide behind the music. The crowd seemed to be loving it.

One group sitting right in front of the DJ area caught my attention. There were four in the group, three girls and a guy. One of the ladies came up for a request shortly after 1am. Jacinta O'Neill was celebrating her qualification as a primary school teacher that very day. Jacinta and her fellow classmates were out letting their hair down. As you've learned, I'm not someone blessed with the ability to talk comfortably to people in social situations and in particular to someone I'm attracted to. However, somehow I found this situation different. Jacinta's easy-going and friendly personality shone through immediately when she requested a song... U2, I think it was.

I was unable to talk for long as I was under too much pressure applying my turntable skills and deciding whether Sister Sledge could follow Bruce Springsteen (not recommended) and wondering if slow sets were still acceptable (sometimes, but only close to 2am for some reason). Jacinta and I chatted for a short while after the gig and a hot date was arranged. Hot for me anyway. I wasn't sure if she would see it that way.

I was never much of a ladies' man and had a very short list of what I would classify as serious relationships in my life. Only two before this one. A little shy in personality and just short of her 30th birthday, Jacinta had long black hair and striking good looks. We started dating immediately. Her main hobby was long country walks so we shared a love of the outdoors. I liked the fact that she saw the good in everyone and every situation around her. It was a lovely quality to possess. We have been together ever since.

But being a DJ did not suit my lifestyle with the late nights putting paid to early-morning weekend workouts, something I loved. My 5am and 6am weekend run and bike starts would have to be rearranged. I needed sufficient income to meet my commitments in challenging times. A friend of mine, Karl Pentony, had a great expression for where I found myself.

"Must is a great master," he says. When you absolutely must do something you will usually find a way. Well I had to find another source of income and luckily for me I did.

On examining the timetable on Sunday April 4th, 2010 I saw the next weekend had a 15-miler on the Saturday, followed the next day by a full marathon. To make matters more challenging I was working late on Friday and Saturday night and I had college in Dublin on the Saturday too. On top of that, I had been asked to do a public speaking commentary at a triathlon event in Mullingar on Sunday morning which would mean being on my feet for five hours solid. How could I expect to run a marathon after that?

I decided to change the schedule and switch days. I was determined to complete the full run mileage for the week which was in excess of 80 miles, so I pencilled in a full marathon for the Wednesday as this was the only day it would suit. I ran 11 miles on the bank holiday Monday; this was relatively short but it had been preceded by a 20-mile run the day before to finish the previous week's running total.

Tuesday I woke at 5.45am to the sound of rain hitting off the window. It was bucketing outside so I decided to head to the gym instead. I managed just eight miles on a treadmill but that would be fine. Tuesday night I had to head to Dublin to attend my last college lecture. Getting home after midnight, I decided to forego a 6am start as I needed an extra lie-in until 7.30.

Over the previous four days I had run 63 miles so I was feeling a little jaded and there was the matter of 26 miles the next day. I was sore that Wednesday morning but the forecast promised a beautiful day, which lifted my spirits.

I decided to take the next three days off from work to cram some last minute study. I hit the books shortly after 8am and did about four hours of study. By lunchtime I was feeling mentally drained. I had no option however but to head off for a four hour run that would see me cover the 26 miles. I had to lift myself mentally for this as I was not overly enthusiastic heading out the door.

As I was leaving. Dorothy called and enquired as to how long the run would be.

"Twenty six miles," I told her.

"Grand," she replied. "See you later."

No "Wow" or "Blooming hell, that far?" or "Isn't that a marathon?"

That evening I reminded her of her reaction. She said that my commitment to training was such that she didn't see it as anything out of the ordinary.

I completed the full 26 miles but only after calling Dorothy and asking her to meet me on my route home with some energy drink. After 10 miles I left the bottle I was carrying beneath some undergrowth to give my arms a rest for an hour or so. Could I find it when I returned? Not a chance.

The marathon itself was ok. It was a day for just digging deep and getting the job done. The sun felt lovely on the skin so I could scarcely complain. About five miles in, I had an unwelcome visitor. My route took in some of the Royal Canal. A mother of a new born calf who was grazing on the canal bank mistakenly thought I was coming to take her newborn baby from her. She came after me with anger in her eyes. I legged it down the embankment and as I did so, luckily for me, the cow slipped. I seized the opportunity to clamber back up the bank and sprint away as fast as possible. Now that I had passed her on this narrow part of the canal bank I could continue on my merry way and I relaxed my pace, turning around to see where she was. As I did so, I got the fright of my life. She was running towards me once more and was barely 10 metres away, snorting loudly. I had to sprint for about a minute to be certain of making good my escape a second time. Luckily, cows don't do long-speed sessions so she was no match.

Having the exams behind me freed up some much-needed hours for other labours. I had many duties to keep me extremely busy. There was still a small amount of property-related activity from which I was eking out a very small income. I was also working one and sometimes two nights a week at DJing, not getting home until close to 3am. I was also carrying out some work on behalf of the Westmeath Sports partnership, where a colleague Craig Sterrit and I would coach primary school pupils in a road safety cycling course. And of course Ken and I were continually piecing together the logistics of the challenge which was now only a few months away. That is aside from our training, which was up to 80, 90 and by late April, in excess of 100 miles of weekly running.

The 3x31-mile training runs that Richard had pencilled in now loomed large on the horizon. The first of these training runs was scheduled for Sunday 14th April, the day of the Great Ireland Run in Dublin's Phoenix Park. In the days leading into this weekend, I ran 10 miles on Thursday and 14 miles on Friday. Saturday's training spin was only five miles before Sunday's big run. But that five miles was only half the story.

I had worked until 2am on that Friday night but had an appointment in Dublin first thing on Saturday morning. I was pretty tired by the time I arrived home a little after 6pm that evening, I had only managed five hours sleep the night before and I knew I had to go out and work again within four hours. That would be fine under normal circumstances but not on this occasion. I started to plan the next 20 hours of my life. My schedule required a 5-mile run on that evening so I had no option but to hit the road. After the 45 minute workout, I decided to go to bed for a few hours but I couldn't sleep.

My mind was in overtime stressing about how the hell I was going to manage to run 31 miles the next day on only four hours sleep. This was the first real bad time I had had since training had commenced three months previously. I pride myself on being a very upbeat individual, always trying to seek positives out of every challenge. As Saturday wore on, I struggled and became very moody that evening. I was exhausted yet I had to go out to work until 3am. All I wanted to do was put my jaded feet up and sleep but I couldn't. Here is how the next day unfolded.

2.40AM Got to bed.

3.20AM Finally fell asleep.

7.10AM Alarm goes off and I rose feeling good mentally but my legs were still a little tired from the previous days' exertions. Jacinta drove me up to Dublin to allow me to sleep on the journey.

8.25AM We arrived into the Phoenix Park in Dublin and I met Ken at the Papal Cross.

We had arranged to meet two friends, Pat O'Hara and Malcolm Craig, whom you will remember from the Ironman France 2008. The lads had promised to run at least an hour with me. Ken was in the middle of some niggling injury woes so he decided to adopt a mixture of run/jog/walk as part of his day, leaving the rest of us to do our own workout. It was sad seeing Ken go off on his own as I knew he wanted desperately to join us but it was a measure of his determination that he remained so disciplined.

We started off doing a quick inner lap of about eight miles of this c.1,700 acre park. It was a gorgeous morning and the sun spent the first two hours trying to burst through the clouds with partial success. Eight miles later, a toilet stop was required, coincidentally by all three runners. Great timing. There was no need to run behind the trees as there were approximately 50 portaloos to choose from. The Great Ireland Run was on in the park at lunchtime which was part of our reason for being there in the first place.

I had arranged to rendezvous with Jacinta in the city centre where she would join us in a run back to the Park. Having her share my journey over the previous 12 months had been fantastic. Apart from being super company, she loved the fresh air and being out there in natural surroundings. Early in the spring of 2010 Jacinta would join me on many long runs by cycling alongside me as I ran. Both of us were benefitting from the workout and it meant we got to share lots of time together. Organising the event was very time consuming but this meant I could train and spend time with her.

Jacinta had by then settled into her first full-time job as a primary school teacher. She had secured a placement in Gainstown School, just outside Mullingar. She has a gift in being able to communicate with children. My own nieces and nephews always gravitated to her on family occasions. It was her wonderful ability to relate to them at their level which marks her apart.

Malcolm and I left the surroundings of the park to meet up with Jacinta. As we left the park, Pat bade us farewell.

I turned to Malcolm.

"How are you feeling?" I asked

"Better than you look," came the cheeky reply. "Reckon I am good for another hour," he replied. Malcolm intended to run an hour or so. But 13 miles in, he scarcely looked out of breath and was running with apparent ease. I was very grateful to both Pat and Malcolm for coming out to run, chat, joke and take my mind off the job in hand. Malcolm has great endurance ambitions too. I spent the next few miles telling him why he should consider putting a Double Ironman on his list.

"Go away, ya lunatic," was his reply on at least two occasions as we ran by the Four Courts and headed towards Grafton Street. We met

Jacinta as arranged and she was already limbering up by the Molly Malone Statue as we arrived.

A relative newbie to running, she certainly looks like a runner with a 'slight' frame built to run a marathon or two without much bother. Jacinta's goal that day had her registered to start in the Great Ireland 10km run a few hours later. She had driven me up that morning which meant she had quite a few hours to fill. She had got the bus into the city centre to do some window shopping and decided at the last minute to run back with us as part of a long warm-up. Her longest run before this had been 10km a few months back so this would be a big step-up in distance for her.

It was quite surreal running around Grafton Street on what was a busy Sunday morning. Grafton St was virgin running territory for us all and we did get a few strange looks as we meandered through the crowds. By now we had 15.5 miles done and both Malcolm and I felt great. Half an hour later the three of us were back in the Phoenix Park. By then, Malcolm and I had completed approximately 19 miles. We ran back to the car to pick up some more refreshments before continuing on to complete another six miles.

The first part of our day would see us run a total of 25 miles. Phase two would see us tackle the 10km or 6.25 miles of the Great Ireland Run. Because Ken had started an hour or more before us, by 12.30pm all three of us had completed 25 miles. Ken remarked that he was actually feeling great, a welcome update. At 12.30pm, Malcolm took his leave. He had come to run an hour with us but stayed for four.

The Great Ireland Run was an event that had in excess of 11,000 participants. The organisers had very kindly given both Ken and I free entry. Not only that but they had requested us to record a piece for a TV programme which was being broadcast all over the country. At the start line, an official motioned towards Ken and I and started asking us 20 questions about what we were undertaking. All the time, he was feverishly taking notes. I wondered why. Then it all made sense. As he put his pen away he took from his pocket a microphone and started talking into it. The motivational music that had the 11,000 crowd enthused and pumped up was lowered and he started talking into the microphone, his voiced amplified a thousand times so that he could be heard for a mile in every direction.

He was the official race announcer and was now telling the thousands of people all around us of the challenge that we were preparing for, the fact that we had run 25 miles just to get to todays start line and encouraging people to join us in the summer. He then completely caught me unawares and asked me a question I wasn't expecting and thrust the microphone to my mouth for a response.

I muttered something probably inaudible but we both received a huge round of applause nonetheless after he summarised once again the challenge we were facing.

The gun went off and we started the final leg of that day's journey. We had not run for about 30 minutes and I was a little concerned that my larger muscles would have seized. No such worries however as we both immediately felt comfortable.

After a kilometre, Ken and I were amazed at how strong we still felt. If anything we felt even better than an hour before. We ran at just under an eight-minute mile pace which was a little over a minute faster than we had done the first 25 miles in. Slightly too fast perhaps, but we really did feel that good. Forty-eight minutes after starting we crossed the finish line and again the race MC was there to encourage the huge crowds to give us a big cheer. It was a brilliant finish to a truly memorable day. I live for days like this, and I never ever forget how fortunate I am to have the health to do it.

The rest of April and early May would see us climb towards our highest mileage of 111 miles. I looked into my training log, in which I kept short narratives to describe how each week was going. The following extract from my diary was filed under the heading "Tough Week."

Excerpt from my diary of Friday 14th May, 2010
'This week is just three miles short of our peak week in terms of mileage

to be reached. 108 miles of running. The schedule says we have seven days. To make matters even more challenging, I have only six days available. A prior arrangement to attend a function means I couldn't run on one of the days so since Monday last I have been tweaking the schedule each day to ensure I reach the required total.

A run of 16 miles on Monday followed by 10 miles on Tuesday. Another 16 miler on Wed with a full marathon of 26 miles of running Thursday. Ouch!

Friday was tougher again. Not in terms of distance but mentally it was a really challenging day. I had scheduled 20 miles but when I woke up that morning having played a late night music gig until 1.00am, my calves ached badly after three hours of standing in the same position. I had a busy morning in town catching up on a few bits and pieces and only got home after 4pm. I had to be back at work for 10pm that night so without delay I headed off to complete another 20-mile run thankfully set amidst a beautiful sunny Friday afternoon with a lovely 15 degrees Celsius of heat to warm up my aching lower limbs.

When I left the house I knew it would be a tough session. My heart wasn't in it, my head wasn't in it and my calves were not too agreeable either. They were very sore.

After four miles I wanted to come home but I knew I couldn't. In addition I had arranged to meet a running pal, Jarlath Mahon. Together we ran 12 or so miles before I bade him farewell. Several times over that distance I had to ask him to either slow down or worse again to walk for a hundred or so metres, such was my pain. It was a really hard day.

When he left, I realised I was only four miles from home. I limped the rest of the way, my calves aching with every crushing impact from the hard road surface. The run took me 3hrs and 14 minutes. I was quite proud of this run as it was definitely the hardest of that 32x32 training schedule.

Despite my discomfort the post-race routine worked well. This consisted of a five minute 'cold' bath followed by a self-induced massage of the calf muscles. A protein shake consumed and within an hour, I was feeling strong again. Good job as I had to go back out to work and I still

had another 20 miles of running to be done the following day.
Blooming hell, what a week.

By May 30th, we had reached our peak of training. We still had four-and-a-half weeks to go but in that time we dropped down from our highest mileage plateau to where a three-week taper would begin.

CHAPTER 26
PLUGGING AWAY WITH THE RADIO STARS

BY now the logistics of the event were in full swing and registrations were climbing, albeit slowly. By this stage we had nearly 600 names and people were still registering every day. Our goal was 1,024 but we were still optimistic we would achieve it. Runners are usually late in registering even if they have already pencilled in their participation. Thankfully, our event would be no different as we would soon find out.

To keep it in the public eye the charity had arranged a photo-call with Keith Duffy, Eamonn Coghlan and Ray D'Arcy to announce the fact that we had hit the 600 figure. We had already met Eamonn and Keith and Ray wasn't a complete stranger. Presenter of one of Ireland's most popular morning shows, commanding more than 200,000 daily listeners, he had already mentioned our run on the show. Several times my phone received texts from friends saying Ray had given us yet another plug on his show encouraging people to register. When we met, he could not have been more friendly and more complimentary. He is known as someone who is into running, having done a few marathons himself. It appeared to Ken and I that he had adopted us out of a fellow runner's respect for the challenge we were about to put ourselves through.

He promised during our brief photo-call to have us on his radio show at some point. We were delighted as it would offer great publicity to the event, thus raising awareness and funds for the charities. By now radio interviews were a regular occurrence and I was slowly getting accustomed to them. One night my phone rang a little after 10 o'clock. It was Ken. He told me that he had just received a call from Newstalk who wanted to interview us on the Breakfast Show.

"When?" I asked.

"Tomorrow morning at 7am," came the reply.

"Blooming hell," I thought to myself. But it was better the following morning rather than a week away where I would have had time to sweat up over it.

By 5.30am the next morning, I was wide awake having had a

great night's sleep. "Hmm, maybe this is not as bad as I feared," I commented to Ken as we journeyed into the Newstalk studio.

On arrival, we were greeted by the show's producer Chris Donoghue whose opening line was the by-now "are ye flaming mad?"

"Perhaps," I replied.

He said he couldn't resist having us on once he had seen one of our posters in his local bike shop. Next into the room came the two presenters, Claire Byrne whose smile lit up the room and Conor Brophy who showed a great interest in what we were doing. I held a bottle of water tight in my grasp as we were motioned into the studio 20 minutes later. I tried to block out the thought of all those people listening to me speak.

Conor opened the interview by asking me how the idea had come about. As I explained, I noticed a look of inquisitiveness appear on Claire's face.

"Wait a minute," she said. "Is it 32 back-to-back marathons??"

"Yes," Ken replied.

"Wow!" she offered. "Is that possible? I saw the Eddie Izzard documentary last week and he did 41 of these things over 50 or 55 days and his body was just broken at the end and he was in a dreadful state. Have you thought about that?"

I read about Izzard's efforts while he was in the middle of his challenge. What he managed to do was truly astounding. Here was a guy who, in his own words, had no sporting background and not much preparation. He simply wanted to do something that would get people to sit up and take notice and in the process raise funds for a charity in the UK. I first learned of it in September 2009 when he was on the Northern Ireland leg and watched with great interest the remainder of his ordeal. He went through the horrors physically and a follow-up documentary illustrated the pain he endured. His final totals were very impressive - 43 marathons in 51 days and over £1.3m raised for Sports Relief.

During the interview, Ken explained about the apprenticeships we had served and the fact that we were bringing a very professional six months training programme to the table. As I sat in the chair listening attentively to my friend, my mind started to wander. It dawned on me where this challenge was bringing us and what it was doing for us. This was a show I listened to most mornings and here I was being interviewed on it myself. Just then I noticed something in my own body. My heart was beating at a regular pace, I had no shake in my hands and my voice was calm as if I was talking over breakfast in my own kitchen. 'How far I had travelled,' I thought to myself.

Just then Claire threw a question in my direction but the only word I heard was 'nutrition.'

I had to think fast. "Yes. Proper carbohydrates, fats and adequate protein to rebuild the muscles as well as proper post race physio will be very important," I replied. She seemed happy with the answer so I guess it was relevant to her question. Phew, I had dodged a bullet!

With that the interview finished, Claire and Conor thanked us profusely off air for coming in. Claire said that she would love to have us on again. As we were leaving we got word that the station editor wanted to see us. "Oh," Ken said. "Do you know why?"

"Don't know," came the reply but he said you were to call to his office before you left.

A few minutes later we were introduced to the station manager, a Donegal man named Garret Harte. By coincidence he was running a half-marathon the very next day in Manchester.

"Geez, lads, that is some challenge ye are undertaking."

He seemed taken with our event and told us that the station would follow us for the 32 days and give regular updates to their listeners. As a follow on, Garret contacted us shortly after to say that *The Breakfast Show* would actually follow the challenge for the duration by doing a weekly live interview with us.

CHAPTER 27
MAPPING AND MANAGING THE BIG EVENT

EARLY in June Ken and I started our taper period where our run mileage would be significantly reduced. This was done so that we would arrive at our start line on 2 July in peak condition, having rested considerably following the demands of the previous months.

I have always found tapering hard to do. I rely heavily on adrenalin and I find in taper that all my energy leaves my body. During this period I develop lethargic feelings and phantom pains. Paranoia, call it what you like. However, we had little time for rest.

By late April, Irish Autism Action had taken over a lot of the logistics. They had assembled a superb team of 10 or so people, all of whom brought expertise in a variety of ways. None were more hands-on than Kevin Whelan, the CEO, who had assumed the captaincy of the ship we were about to set sail in. He made the big calls and crucially secured sponsors for the side.

One of them was 'The Expert Group' of electrical stores. They had at that time 63 locations nationwide and saw the obvious benefits of sponsoring an event that would reach into the heart of each of these locations. Marks and Spencers had assisted Irish Autism Action before and came forward again offering food, water, sports drinks and t-shirts for the runners. In addition The Lagan Group, Ireland's leading privately-owned constructions material supplier also helped by way of financial sponsorship. One of the directors, Jude Lagan, as well as his wife Kathy would also lace up their runners and run with us.

Just a few weeks before we started, Kevin managed to source another sponsor 'Just Mobile', a new mobile phone company who were about to launch in Ireland. They brought with them a financial commitment and enthusiasm in the form of two of its directors, Stuart Kelly and Donal Lawless. Stuart and Donal made regular appearances as we travelled the length and breadth of the country.

Through our own efforts Ken and I managed to get 'product' sponsorship from Nike, courtesy of their account executive Ronan Gourley and we were also fortunate to secure additional product sponsorship from Oakley sunglasses. John Russell, the MD for Ireland, was very generous in supplying 34 pairs of Oakley sunglasses with the marathon logo engraved into the glass. There was a pair for Ken and I, and one to be raffled every day of the 32 for the runners who joined us.

Our backroom team pulling all the logistics together consisted of Niall Murphy, Sarah McInerney-Buckley, Colette Charles, Aisling Garry, Freddie Grehan, Ann Reilly, Colin Telford, Carly Ferguson, Johnny Davis and Dara O'Reilly Daly. Yes, it needed that many. The workload was enormous. Everyone gelled brilliantly and each person recognised their own tasks and responsibilities.

We had to design, source and order finisher t-shirts, certificates, medals, water and food for the runners. In addition we had to organise transport, livery, a gantry, medical cover, hospital contact, hotel confirmations, rooming lists, physio coordination, insurance, high visibility clothing and porta-loos.

As this would be a national event we had to present a detailed safety statement to An Garda Síochána Headquarters in Dublin. We also had to write to each council for a permit to do a bucket collection. Our jobs list covered such a wide range of topics, literally an A-to-Z. One of the more sizeable tasks was the necessity to communicate important information to over 700 runners who had registered by this time. This communication would outline meeting points and times for each of the 32 days. It was a crazy time but everyone worked tirelessly to ensure that this was done.

By now we had mapped and managed to put all but two county routes up on the website. Ken's brother Barry had done sizeable work in this regard and our professional website was the result of his labour as well as the original design of Tanya O'Neill, a friend from home. Barry was unbelievable to us and quietly performed hundreds of vitally important tasks related to the website and the registrations over a six month lead in period. Never once did he question a request.

Three weeks before the first marathon we held the first of three final logistics meetings where our team put the finishing touches together. That meeting lasted eight hours.

Another week passed and soon the time to pack was upon us. The final few days were hectic. We were due to run our first marathon on Friday 2nd July. Tuesday and Wednesday were busy spent packing and ensuring that the final jobs were all done. Thursday finally arrived, the day before the off. That day was unbelievably stressful.

CHAPTER 28
FIGHTING OFF THE NEGATIVES

2PM, THURSDAY 1ST JULY, 2010

I was troubled.

We had less than 24 hours to kick-off. I pride myself on having a very strong mind but at 2pm I was all alone in the car and I really felt the strain.

It was a combination of many things. Unexpectedly we had to go to Dublin at 5am on the eve of the start for a radio interview. This was not ideal as it meant only five hours' sleep. It also meant I was way behind and on the Friday there were 50 small things needing to be done. I still had 25 left to do at 2pm. The clock was ticking, we were leaving Mullingar at 5pm. It was getting to me, plain and simple.

I pulled over to the side of the road and I closed my eyes. I thought back over the past year and what 'we' had achieved. Ken and I, Jacinta, my family, Ken's family, the charity, close friends and the crew. Everyone had done so much. Now there was a huge amount resting on the shoulders of Ken and I.

I thought back to the original idea, conceived in August 2008. Into my mind came memories of the launch, the media work, the creation of the website, the registrations, scouring the length and breadth of the country for advice, route, runners and accommodation. Thousands of man-hours worked and thousands of miles travelled.

It was not just running 32 consecutive marathons. There were 16 road crew waiting to offer us sweat and toil, 32 different routes awaiting our feet, over 100 indirect local crew eager to help, almost 750 runners to run with and over 1,050 marshals and volunteers eager to play their part.

It was then I noticed my heart rate was beating much faster than a resting heart rate should. I could feel it pounding out 130 beats per minute from my chest. This was not excitement. This was not adrenalin. This was fear.

The above is not to seek sympathy. After all, I had gotten myself into all of this. I had nobody to blame but myself. I was doing it voluntarily, nobody was forcing me. I sat in the car and bit my lip to prevent tears. I genuinely felt scared. Perhaps this would do no harm. I simply had to channel it into positive energy. After all, there was nothing to fear but fear itself.

I needed a moment alone but only briefly. I also needed to share this fear with someone so I turned and faced the car towards Jacinta's house. Twenty minutes later she was there offering her unconditional support. She had done so since the first day we had met 15 months before, and she would do so 24 hours a day for the next 32. Early mornings and late nights lay ahead of us all. Town parks, dirt tracks, canal banks and cornfields, we would navigate them all. Medical clinics and physio waiting rooms, we would soon sit in them all. Poignant moments and stunning backdrops, we would see them all. Missed signposts and wrong turns, we would take them all. Human fortitude, we would see it all. Oh, and fun too. We would have great fun!

It was all ahead of us, we just had no idea. Sure, we thought we did, but in reality we hadn't a clue. The best laid plans are just that, plans. The reality is in the experience and the experience is in the journey.

Welcome to the 32 Marathon Challenge.

CHAPTER 29

NIGHT OF THE LONGEST DAY

7PM, SUNDAY 1ST AUGUST, 2010
THIRTY-TWO DAYS LATER

I lay on the bed nauseated and devoid of any emotional attachment for what the next 24 hours would bring. Running one more marathon was the furthest thing from my mind. I was on the eve of the greatest sporting achievement of my life, but it was a million light years from my thoughts.

I could hear and see the repeating drip slowly inserting its contents into my right arm. Its benefits I would soon enjoy, but for now all I could think of was throwing up. An hour earlier I had leapt from the car, afraid my stomach's contents would destroy its interior. We were 200 metres shy of the medical clinic on the outskirts of Mullingar when I asked Jacinta to pull over with great haste.

Just hours earlier, Ken and I had finished our 31st marathon in Leitrim. My stomach was all I cared for at 7pm on that Sunday. It felt like it had Mike Tyson's fist clenching in it and his grip was vice like. It was a pain I had never experienced before and I really felt it.

The doctor had diagnosed food poisoning or gastroenteritis, nothing more, nothing less. I knew I would get over it, that it was but a minor blip but at the same time I felt awful. I lay on the bed for three hours drifting in and out of sleep, allowing sufficient time for the full contents of the drip to enter my body. Jacinta and I checked out of the medical clinic a little after 11pm.

Thirty-two days earlier, a little after 6pm we had checked into the Longford Arms Hotel on the eve of our first marathon.

THE DEVIL IS IN THE DETAIL: COUNTY BY COUNTY, DAY BY DAY

Friday 2nd July 2010	Longford	Tuesday 13th July 2010	Tipperary	Saturday 24th July 2010	Antrim
Saturday 3rd July 2010	Dublin	Wednesday 14th July 2010	Laois	Sunday 25th July 2010	Down
Sunday 4th July 2010	Wicklow	Thursday 15th July 2010	Kildare	Monday 26th July 2010	Armagh
Monday 5th July 2010	Carlow	Friday 16th July 2010	Offaly	Tuesday 27th July 2010	Fermanagh
Tuesday 6th July 2010	Wexford	Saturday 17th July 2010	Galway	Wednesday 28th July 2010	Monaghan
Wednesday 7th July 2010	Kilkenny	Sunday 18th July 2010	Mayo	Thursday 29th July 2010	Louth
Thursday 8th July 2010	Waterford	Monday 19th July 2010	Roscommon	Friday 30th July 2010	Meath
Friday 9th July 2010	Cork	Tuesday 20th July 2010	Sligo	Saturday 31st July 2010	Cavan
Saturday 10th July 2010	Kerry	Wednesday 21st July 2010	Donegal	Sunday 1st August 2010	Leitrim
Sunday 11th July 2010	Limerick	Thursday 22nd July 2010	Derry	Monday 2nd August 2010	Westmeath
Monday 12th July 2010	Clare	Friday 23rd July 2010	Tyrone		

DAY 1

LONGFORD

FRIDAY 2 JULY, 2010
838.4 miles (1,349.27km) to go

Longford Town
Gerry   4 hours 38 minutes
Ken   4 hours 38 minutes

Every journey begins with the first step.

Old Chinese Proverb

"I'M going to teach them some mind-tricks to help them get through the tough days."

Magician and mentalist Keith Barry was chatting to the RTE News crew at the front door of the Longford Arms hotel. He was a friend of the charity's and had come down to see us off and to add his profile to the first day. We never got the opportunity to ask him for those mind-tricks but within a few days I would have to employ some old ones of my own.

Four hours earlier the alarm had gone off. By then I was already in the shower having slept soundly in room 105, a good-sized bedroom on the first floor of our hotel accommodation. Given that this morning would see the start of the greatest sporting challenge of my life, I was surprised at the ease with which I had gone to sleep.

It was a little after 6am on Friday July 2nd, 2010. Marathon number one was now just four hours away. I picked out a pair of runners. They had a number '1' written in my handwriting at the side.

Three other pairs were in my gearbag numbered 2 to 4. Nike had been very good in providing us with abundant shoe and clothing apparel. It would all be needed. I had spent the previous four weeks breaking in the four pairs I would constantly rotate for the next 32 days.

We arrived into the breakfast room a little before seven as excited as children on Christmas morning. It was quiet though, with only a few staff in attendance. Our request for porridge was greeted warmly and soon we were sitting down to a delicious breakfast. Midway through the meal however, the room became the centre of organised chaos. By 7.15am the restaurant area was full. Family, close friends and crew arrived along with the first of many runners who would join us on day one of our challenge. Perhaps we could all be forgiven for being over enthusiastic on day one. Three or four cameras clicked over our shoulders. I felt embarrassed. After all we had yet to run a mile.

In the melee I forgot to finish breakfast. Only at mile 15 would I realise it. I had consumed little more than a three-quarters bowl of organic porridge, nothing more. An amateurish mistake but thankfully one which had no major ill effects.

By 8am, the lobby area was a hive of activity. Registration had been set up and was been ably manned by Colette Charles and Aisling Garry from Irish Autism Action. Spreadsheets with names and other data as well as race numbers (blue for full marathon and orange for a half) were numerically stacked. Sunscreen, blister pads and route maps were all available just in case. Every morning for the 32 days we would see the same events unfold. By 8.30am the lobby was full, abuzz with activity and atmosphere. As 10am drew ever closer we called everyone into the main bar area to give the first of our athletes' briefings. The first day would see 25 people join us at the start line.

Into the room came runners, crew, family, friends and well-wishers, perhaps 100 people in total. I had pictured this scene many times before on long training runs and now it was finally here. There was no planned order of speakers. It was simply organised about 30 seconds before Kevin Whelan spoke to the gathering. He thanked everyone for their attendance and expressed gratitude to our sponsors. His words were brief and with that, he introduced me.

I stood on a stool and surveyed my audience. Over the following seven or eight minutes, I summarised the efforts of a multitude of people over the preceding six months when the bulk of the logistics were pieced together.

I expressed hope for what the upcoming 32 days would bring and I spoke passionately of the gratitude that Ken, the charities and I felt towards the runners who had registered, trained, fundraised and turned up on this day to run with us. Without them, I explained, we wouldn't have had an event. Finally I pointed out how we might be able to overcome any difficult moments that might lie ahead.

"Every time I go running," I said, "I remind myself how fortunate I am to be able to do so because I have been blessed with good health. It is something I will never take for granted."

I finished by suggesting that our challenge should be put into context. It would be nothing when placed beside the challenges faced by children with autism, families of children affected by autism, or anyone who has been affected either directly or indirectly by cancer.

With that, Ken got up and spoke from the heart about his gratitude that we had arrived here ready to tackle an amazing challenge. Moments after he spoke, the crowd exited to the start line which was literally outside the front door. As Ken breathed in the fresh air from outside he felt someone tugging at his shirt. It was Adam, his four year old nephew.

"Uncle Ken, I want to go to the toilet," the young man requested.

"Interesting timing," Ken thought to himself. Nothing to do though, but escort the young man and assist him with his request.

Five minutes later and with gathering family, friends, runners, local and national media including RTE television, all waiting at the start line, there still was no sign of my running partner. I guess we should not have been surprised. After all, Adam's needs were far more important at that moment.

That night over dinner we laughed as Ken explained how he encouraged Adam to be as quick as he could as he sat on the loo. The more Ken encouraged haste, the more Adam chatted, oblivious to Ken's urgency. Ken said that despite his stress to be somewhere else, it brought a realism of sorts, reminding him that life is sometimes not meant to be hurried and it gave him a chance to settle his nerves.

A little after 10am, we were off. We ran the main street of Longford town for the first 500 metres of our first marathon. In our plan we were to run on the footpath but unknown to us, our route co-ordinator Brendan Doyle had persuaded the local Gardaí to shut down the main street for a five-minute period.

By 10.20am we were on the banks of the Royal Canal away from any traffic hazards and noise with a lovely landscape to keep us entertained for the following four hours or more.

Amongst those keeping us company on the first day were three of my siblings, Tom, Mary and Dorothy. Tom the oldest and Dorothy the youngest in the family, had both been running for many years. Mary, older than me by two years, had been a revelation in training. As I mentioned earlier she had committed eight months previously to getting into shape for her half-marathon. A lady with no running experience, this would be a step well outside her comfort zone. Undeterred by a back injury and a six-week ban on running as ordered by her doctor, she was here and was determined to walk 13.1 miles. It was a display of resilience which we would see re-enacted by many people every day for the next 32.

Another sister Katherine, would also do her bit later in the month for our challenge by completing two half-marathons herself. Our route coordinator's wife, Madeline Doyle also made her half-marathon debut in Longford, having trained very hard for over four months.

Also running that day was Mary's close friend Catherine Mooney, whose only son John had been diagnosed with autism. Catherine had brought an amazing work ethic not just to her training but also to her efforts on the day. She was one of the first people I had told about the challenge almost a year before. Without hesitation she committed her support. Mary kept me updated regularly over the spring months on how Catherine had brought rigorous training into her life to ensure success at her first marathon. We would be very fortunate over the following four-and-a-half weeks to have hundreds and hundreds of people like Catherine Mooney join us, all motivated to run for a variety of reasons.

In Longford Catherine, with her nephew Daniel running beside her smiled all day long and a little after 3pm she crossed the finish line, having completed her first ever marathon. Quite rightly, she was a very proud person indeed.

For Ken and I, Day 1 was all about being patient. We were chomping at the bit in anticipation of the first day, we were in the best shape of our lives and now finally we would get the opportunity to realise our dream. After 13 miles we both commented that we felt tired. Coincidence? We soon realised it was simply our bodies dusting off a few cobwebs as we hadn't done a long run for the previous two weeks. By mile 18, we both felt strong once more. After 4 hours and 38 minutes we had completed the first marathon, 26.2 miles down, only 812.2 miles to go. The time for our opening run was something we had planned in advance. For both of us, it was a very comfortable pace. We knew it would be a long month ahead and that we had to be patient. The opportunity to run faster marathons would come.

After all, we had 31 more still to do.

DAY 2

DUBLIN

SATURDAY 3 JULY

812.2 miles (1,307.1km) to go

Phoenix Park

Gerry   4 hours 24 minutes

Ken   4 hours 24 minutes

IT'S unlikely the Ashling Hotel just opposite Heuston Station in Dublin had ever seen anything like what happened at 9.0am on Day-2 of our challenge. Enter one Michael O'Leary. You will recall my previous encounters when the Ryanair supremo had promised us some fun.

Boy did he deliver!

At many of the modern marathon events you often see fun runners dressed up as pumpkins, pints of Guinness or lollipops. Well on this particular morning, dressed principally in white, Michael arrived with a large bandage over his head, a white t-shirt with the words 'old fart' emblazoned across his chest, all held together with two red braces and an oversized pair of football shorts.

Having Michael endorse our event opened many doors. Now true to his word he was there again, with his runners laced up, ready to join us for the first 13.1 miles of the run. At 9.30am he was outside the front door of the hotel, arms wrapped around Eamonn Coghlan, posing for a scrum of photographers.

Conscious of not delaying our fellow runners who were waiting patiently in the lobby, we headed back in to start the second of our race briefings. We had a group of 100 or more before us. Three or four minutes into our talk, the doors of the bar burst open. It was O'Leary.

"I noticed you started the athletes briefing without the main athlete," he boldly interrupted. The entire room erupted with laughter. It was a very funny moment and certainly lightened the already friendly atmosphere.

My brother Tom was there too, back for a second half-marathon in as many days. Just three days earlier he had become a proud dad for the first time, his American wife Orla having given birth to a beautiful girl whom they had called Juliana. I took the opportunity to congratulate him publicly whilst explaining to the crowd that fatherhood had come to him later than most. He was 47 years old.

"Yeah, it just goes to prove that the Duffy brothers have spent far too much time running and not enough time making love," O'Leary bellowed. Again the crowd laughed heartily. Tom and Michael are good friends and our audience could see immediately it was all in jest.

Michael would later finish the half-marathon in just under two hours, a very impressive time. Eamonn Coghlan ran with us as well, covering five miles despite carrying an injury. We were very grateful to him.

Our run that day was in the Phoenix Park, the setting for our 31 mile training run the previous April. It was a lovely Saturday morning with a temperature in the very late teens. Six loops of a 4.37 mile circuit were negotiated by Ken, myself and the 65 runners who joined us which included four of my cousins Emer, Moya, Susan and Fionnuala as well as my Auntie Mary and her friend Frances O'Shea.

The physical effort of Marathon Number 2 was quite manageable for Ken and I. On the final two laps we were joined by Brendan Doyle, our route co-ordinator from Longford and now a part of our road crew. He wanted to get a run in before getting back to post-race duties.

"You're not going to believe who called," he said.

"Who?" We enquired.

"Dublin Zoo."

"What?" I replied "Why?"

"Apparently the music at the finish line is upsetting the giraffes."

We crossed the line in 4:24, perhaps a little fast, but in reality we both felt very comfortable at the finish. Lap five for me was the toughest of the six, for Ken, the last one felt more challenging. Back to the hotel for a much needed ice bath and some physio, after which we packed the bags and headed to Wicklow for our third marathon.

The giraffes were glad to see the back of us.

DAY 3
WICKLOW

SUNDAY 4 JULY
786 miles (1,264.94km) to go

Bray
Gerry   4 hours 30 minutes
Ken   4 hours 30 minutes

NEITHER Ken nor I had ever run three marathons in three days so we had no idea what lay ahead of us in Bray, Co Wicklow. We woke up to a really overcast and blustery morning. Just as we appeared at the start line however, the clouds cleared and the sun came out.

There was a super turnout yet again including six members of one family. Alan Earls, a Wicklow native and also a great friend of the charity had recruited many of the runners. They included five of his own brothers and sisters. A friend from Mullingar, Shane Pearson also made his debut at the full marathon distance.

The Wicklow stage was a four lap circuit around the town and was very challenging. Eamon Breen and Tony Salmon, two new friends, managed the logistics with military precision. The day itself was hot, even hotter than the previous day and the urban environment made it feel even more so.

Each lap ended with a run along Bray Promenade where Alan Earls had arranged Irish Dancers, a DJ and a singer to keep the runners motivated. Not only that but Bray Fire Brigade came and helped with the bucket collections. A real team effort.

We navigated miles 53 to 78 on our 838 mile voyage in Bray. It was a tough course and very hilly. The last lap of four really got to us with the downhill section from Bray Head a killer on the quadriceps muscles. Finally 4 hrs 30 mins after we started, we crossed the line. Within seconds we were in the Irish Sea cooling off. It was a treat we had promised ourselves on the three previous occasions that the sea had come into view. The water was freezing but it would help by doubling up as an ice bath.

NUTRITION

Our ability to run a marathon everyday was a combination of many things. For starters we had completed many tough challenges leading into this event. We had also trained hard for the preceding six months, leaving no stone unturned in our programme. We had ourselves mentally prepared in the months before and we had long since adopted a mindset that it was achievable. Finally there were a host of other ingredients that needed to be added into the mix each day of the 32. One of these was nutrition.

Since we finished, I have constantly been asked about our nutrition during the event and what it consisted of. People wondered how many calories we needed to consume and what we ate. Nutrition would play a huge part. Early in 2010 we had been fortunate to be introduced to a nutritionist, Barry Murray, a native of Dublin, in his early thirties. Barry had graduated from UCD with a BSc in 1999 and later completed a MSc in Sports and Exercise Nutrition. He is now based in Loughborough University in the UK. His speciality is in nutrition for endurance sports and he is also an accomplished athlete competing in running, cycling and triathlon events.

Over a number of meetings he gave us a fascinating insight into what he believed would help us in our quest. The daily schedule outlined below is what we planned based on his advice and recommendations, mixed with personal preferences and tastes.

For the purposes of explaining this as simply as possible, Barry has written the 'science' behind our choices for ease of understanding why we ate and drank what we did.

BREAKFAST

Typically two hours before we started each day we sat down to breakfast. A good breakfast was a key component to give us a solid foundation for the day ahead. Principally this consisted of a foundation of fruits such as grapefruit or mandarin oranges etc. Next up was two bowls of organic porridge, raisins, a variety of milled seeds such as flaxseeds, pumpkin seeds, sunflower seeds and goji berries, all blended with honey. A delicious combination. This was a regular breakfast before the challenge so it was nothing new to either of us. Breakfast was usually topped off with some toasted brown bread and every second or third day we would throw some scrambled, poached or fried eggs to add variety and some extra protein into our diets. We usually had a cup or two of tea or coffee as well.

BARRY: *'Breakfast is arguably the most important meal of the day although because of the uniqueness of this event, for Ken and Gerry the most important meal would be the one post marathon. Breakfast is key as liver glycogen stores need to be replenished after the overnight fast. In terms of nutrition, low GI (glycaemic index) prior to exercise is key to control blood sugar levels and provide a sustained release of energy. Oats have a low GI score and are therefore a good option. Foods such as seeds are rich in essential fats and help the absorption rate of glucose into the bloodstream, helping the sustained energy release. Protein is also a key requirement as amino acids consumed before exercise can help aid recovery, prevent muscle breakdown and improve fitness and endurance adaptations. Therefore Ken and Gerry made conscious efforts to include complete protein sources with every breakfast. Finally caffeine, in the form of tea or coffee, has been shown in numerous studies to improve performance when taken prior to exercise. It has been shown to increase fat metabolism, reduce rate of perceived exertion and increase carbohydrate delivery rate to the muscle.'*

TEN MINUTES BEFORE START - A BANANA

BARRY: *'Most of the fuelling before a race such as a marathon is done the day before. Breakfast is normally only a top up on fuel stores. Carbohydrates, particularly fast release sugar type foods should not ideally be ingested in the hours leading up to a race start. This is because it causes a high blood glucose level which results in the body releasing insulin to remove it. This happens quickly and can result in hypoglycaemia (low blood sugar levels) before you race. Therefore it is better not to take in any sugars during the 60-90min window in the lead up to the start. However if an extra carbohydrate is required, then it is ok to eat something fast-release such as a banana, within minutes of the start.'*

START LINE - A HOMEMADE GEL

This consisted of two tablespoons of honey and a small portion of sea salt mixed with 500 ml of water. This would be consumed over the first three to four miles each day. Ken actually had two of these every morning. The first was in the last 10 minutes before starting and then the second was over the first five miles or so of each run.

BARRY: *'Gels are an easy and quick method of ingesting sugars and electrolytes. They typically deliver 20g of carbohydrate and small amounts of sodium. The aim with Ken and Gerry was to ensure that their foods and sports supplements came from natural wholefood sources. I showed them how to create their own natural gel. Honey contains glucose and fructose while crystal sea salt contains sodium and trace minerals. Therefore the correct amount of honey with sea salt mixed in water provided them with the optimum natural race gel.'*

DURING RUN - ENERGY BARS, FIG ROLLS AND BANANAS

At about eight miles I would begin eating a regular energy bar which had c. 450 calories for energy/45g of carbohydrates. Such was its size it would take me four or five miles to consume it. On alternate days I chose to eat fig rolls. In the second-half of the run I would eat at least one and maybe two bananas and between one and two 'Nakd' bars – which is a wholesome totally natural bar packed with raw fruit, nuts and oats. I always carried a 500ml bottle of still water which I sipped at regular intervals. This was to ensure I never became dehydrated.

BARRY: *The main nutrient requirement in terms of energy production during an event such as a marathon is carbohydrate. This gets oxidised and converted to glucose which gets converted to ATP (i.e. energy). The body oxidises carbohydrate at a faster rate than we can match with carbohydrate consumption. This is due to the rate of limiting steps such as gastric emptying and the rates at which glucose can be transported to the muscle. Studies have calculated this rate to be 60g/hr of carbohydrate that we can actually consume and use. An average banana would typically contain 30g of carbohydrate while a flapjack or Nakd Bar contains 40g. Thus, the aim was to ensure that Ken and Gerry were consuming a combination of these foods (in addition to their gels) that provided roughly 60g of carbohydrates every hour. It should be noted that this is not an essential requirement. However, given that Ken and Gerry were completing 32 consecutive marathons, it was important that they kept properly fuelled.'*

In a later chapter I will go into detail about what we did 'post race'. After each run we consumed a smoothie, a juice and two dinners. Notice I used the plural here. We were after all doing a lot of exercise each day, so it was crucial that we ate a lot.

DAY 4

CARLOW

MONDAY 5 JULY
759.8 miles (1,222.77 km) to go

Bagenalstown
Gerry   4 hours 38 minutes
Ken   4 hours 38 minutes

"SURE what else would be doing on a Monday morning," I commented to David Devine.

I was trying to distract David from the obvious discomfort the poor guy was in. He had told me earlier that he never ran more than nine miles in his life and he was only planning on running a half-marathon. By the time I made this comment to him, we were on mile 19. He had just kept going.

An architectural technician by profession, he and I shared the same bank along the river Barrow just outside the small Carlow town of Bagenalstown on this leg of our run. This was the home of Ann and Ken Hickey, two great people who were actively involved with many charitable causes. They were co-ordinating activities and loved it so much, they volunteered to crew for many more of the next 28. At the finish line a little before 3pm, they had arranged to present Ken and I with a crystal memento from the local town council. It was a heartfelt gesture that we both hugely appreciated.

Ken and I had met up in the car park of the Lord Bagenal Hotel in Leighlinbridge at 6:45am. It was a lovely morning with vitamin D sun rays pouring down onto our faces and the water glistening from the adjacent river. We paced its bank whilst talking live on air to Claire Byrne and Ivan Yates on the Newstalk Breakfast Show.

Yates, a former government minister turned radio anchorman was very sceptical of our ability to complete the 32 marathons. He declared it both impossible and foolhardy when we had been in the studio in Dublin for an eve of race interview five days earlier. Many others doubted our ability to finish it too. Ken and I were strong in our determination to prove them wrong.

"Well, I wish ye good luck but I will be checking the obituary pages for the next 32 days to see if ye are in them," was his parting comment.

David Devine was one of many people whom the Hickeys had encouraged to sign up to run a half-marathon with us. David and 19 other runners joined Ken and I for the Carlow leg. People every day said the event had inspired them. Well it was also true in reverse. Ken and I were overwhelmed by meeting complete strangers who had signed up for the gruelling challenge for many different reasons.

David had capped his training for a half-marathon at nine miles, perhaps a fraction short of ideal. To make matters even harder, by the time I tried to distract him from the discomfort he was in, we were finishing the 3rd loop.

Four loops along the river bank was our routing. The surface was lovely and grassy underfoot, not to firm or too soft. It was exactly what the calves needed after the hard surfaces of Dublin and Wicklow and with no traffic to navigate or to worry about. David's lower leg muscles might not have been so agreeable. It was obvious he was feeling it. An hour or so earlier he had said he was going to try to continue beyond a half-marathon. Now we were coming to the end of that loop and he was contemplating going for one more. Madness for sure but he was a grown man. Who were we to argue?

A little before 3pm he crossed the line having completed a full marathon of 26.2 miles. Quite rightfully, he received a hero's welcome from the local community who had turned out in great numbers.

Ken and I crossed the line just a few minutes before David in 4hrs 38mins

MEDICAL COVER

Each day we had medical facilities at our side. A fully equipped ambulance was a critical back-up to have. Given that we had runners every day pushing themselves to do such a challenging distance we were paranoid about safety for them and for our crew. Neil, Keith and Paddy, our medical crew, rotated their time and expertise. We were glad to have them watching over us.

Four down, 28 to go.

DAY 5
WEXFORD

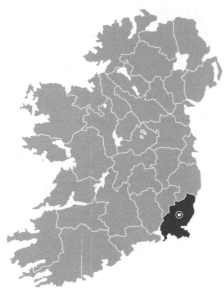

TUESDAY 6 JULY
733.6 miles (1180.61 km) to go

Enniscorthy
Gerry   4 hours 32 minutes
Ken   4 hours 32 minutes

AS a setting for a radio interview, this was indeed a strange surrounding. Ken and I were standing in the middle of a cornfield.

Earlier we had been told to expect a phone call from a well-known radio personality. The exposure it would give us and the awareness for the charity meant that we had to have as little background noise as possible. The N11 road from Enniscorthy out to Oilgate was our course and it was a very busy environment. Five marathons in and we had yet to find two comparable routes.

Jane and Graham Porter, organisers of a local Wexford half-marathon were our Wexford marshals'. When we contacted them three months earlier they promised us that everything would be safe in their hands and just to turn up. Two people whose enthusiasm and love of running was infectious, they were true to their word. I told them afterwards we would never forget them for their help and I meant every word.

The N11 was noisy and to cap it all the day was quite windy too. To confound the challenge, no one had turned up to run with us. We were grateful then that one of our crew, Niall Murphy, did. Niall had not only volunteered to come with us for the entire 32 days, he was happy to lace up his runners at five minutes' notice for the full 26.2 miles challenge. We knew he was fit and had trained hard but he was scarcely out of breath during the marathon.

We were on the return leg of the first loop when my mobile phone rang. We jumped over the fence into a nearby cornfield to shelter from the noise and the strong wind that was on our backs. It was Ray D'Arcy from Today FM, the host of one of the biggest morning radio shows in Ireland. Like Jane and Graham, Ray had been true to his word. Here he was calling us live on his show, 11 miles into our fifth marathon.

"You may have heard about this challenge. Two lads doing 32 marathons in 32 days. Gerry Duffy, Ken Whitelaw. Good morning lads, where are ye today?"

"Good morning Ray," Ken immediately replied. "We're doing good, 11 miles done already only 15 more to do and we are just outside Enniscorthy, Co Wexford."

Ray was a fan of running and regularly extolled its virtue to his listeners. Over the following five minutes he asked us a multitude of questions about the background to the challenge and about our experiences in the first few days. Over 200,000 people listened every morning to his show, among them many of my own family and friends. Later we heard from them that his comment to his listeners when we finished the call was: "I've met those lads and they appear to be... perfectly normal."

As an indicator of the huge listenership he enjoyed, the noise that greeted us from hundreds of tooting car and lorry horns for the remaining 15 miles was continuous. We even ran by a van selling strawberries where the young salesman offered us a complimentary punnet each. He had heard us a few minutes earlier on the radio.

For the second half of the run, a friend from home laced up his runners and kept us company. Not just that, but Darragh Thornton also brought a camper van which he left with us to the end as well joining us for a further five days as part of our support crew.

I found the going tough, the hardest so far. I had to work hard and dig deep both mentally and physically. From mile 18 to the finish, I experienced significant lower body pain. I knew I would be able to finish but I really felt it both in the legs and in the head. My mind drifted constantly and I had very little enthusiasm for the run. Perhaps I was feeling sorry for myself. Maybe the physical pain I was feeling was impacting on my mind. It was my first bad day.

I adopted the technique that the hypnotist had taught me many years before to ensure I finished. It was a tool I would draw on quite a few times later in the month. Each day we started at 10am or a few minutes after, which meant we would be finishing around 2.30pm. This then, became my main focus. Whenever I was in a difficult place mentally, I used the 2:30pm technique. I knew that time would eventually arrive so I simply focused on that.

At the finish were some unannounced friends from home, the Bates family. Eric And Catriona Bates as well as their two young children Eric Junior and Cáit had come over from Tramore, where they were holidaying after they had heard our interview on Today FM. Realising they were only 30 miles from where we were running, they jumped in the car and drove to Enniscorthy to cheer us home.

We crossed the line at 14:32pm, just 4hrs and 32mins after we started.

DAY 6
KILKENNY

WEDNESDAY 7 JULY
707.4 miles (1138.44 km) to go

Inistioge
Gerry 4 hours 51 minutes
Ken 4 hours 51 minutes

OUR location in Inistioge, Co Kilkenny was also the location for the movie adaptation of Maeve Binchy's *Circle of Friends*. On this leg we made 15 new ones. If you have never been to this village, you are missing out. It is a really beautiful place.

Our second marathon course that involved six loops, this woodland trail ensured yet another unique environment for our sixth day on the road. It was a tough course as it climbed and fell constantly over rough terrain. Little did we know what trouble it would start. Given the tricky underfoot conditions, we decided to drop the pace conscious of the many days that lay ahead.

A special mention to four ladies who all enjoyed different running experiences today; firstly to Kate Giblin who completed her 8th marathon and to Teresa Daly who completed her 32nd (what a coincidence). Thirdly to my other half Jacinta who ran her first ever half-marathon. The previous evening she expressed a desire to try her luck. Her first ever official 'run' race was the previous Christmas in the Phoenix Park. She had run a 10k race then but she would more than double that distance in Inistioge. Jacinta had trained for a half marathon so at the 13.1 mile mark she joined Ken and I and a small but happy group of runners who had 13.1 miles still to do. As I spotted her limbering up whilst waiting to join us, her enthusiasm was obvious. To be truthful, I feared for her achieving her goal. It was not that I doubted her. She is a very determined lady. Rather, I knew something about this route that she did not. She had picked the toughest route of the six up to then, to try her luck.

For the first of her three laps, Jacinta chatted happily to us and to the other eight or nine runners. It was great having her there running alongside me. I could tell by her smile that she was enjoying the experience. In the lead in to the challenge, Jacinta had fundraised just like everyone else. Now she was out doing her bit for herself and for the charities.

She had brought much to the challenge in many ways. She was a vital member of our crew and assumed so many roles every day. She was my mentor, my counsellor, our nutritionist, a baggage handler, a chef, a timekeeper, a diary contributor, a chauffeur and a motivator. In addition, she cycled a large part of each route to keep Ken and I company and to ensure we had the necessary nutrition during each run. Above all she was my girlfriend and a true friend. She was and is simply a joy to be around. Always enthusiastic, always bubbly, always encouraging and always there.

In the second lap of the three, I noticed she grew quieter than she had been. This was a sign that she was really starting to work to achieve her goal. With a little over four miles to go she began her third and final lap. By now she was well outside any physical comfort zone that she might have experienced before. She was suffering as most do when going a maiden distance. It is in the last third of any race that the real work begins. In the half-marathon, that is from 10 miles upwards. Now she was there. There were no words from her for the final 45 minutes or more. Others talked, she just listened. As we ascended and descended the rocky trails over those final three miles, her breathing like mine, and like the rest of the group became more laboured. Now it was my turn to act as a motivator.

As we eyed the finish line there was another very special moment as my mum joined us for the final 200 metres. My mum had been a constant source of support from the very first day I had told her about the challenge. I was nervous telling both my parents but their enthusiasm never waned. Indeed my mum also fundraised herself and got many of her friends to contribute to the cause. This was her fourth day to watch us and she would make efforts to get to many more before we would see Mullingar again on the last day. Crossing the line with her and with Jacinta beside me was very memorable.

With her arms held aloft and a smile beaming with pride, Jacinta O'Neill crossed the line a little after three pm, her half-marathon completed. Her goal had been well and truly accomplished. We were all proud of her. Although it was only 100 metres or so, her journey back to race hq was slow. It is not uncommon for muscles to seize up once the body shudders to a halt after such demands. She was starting to cramp up just like I did. Now it was her turn to struggle onto the physio table. It was a running joke with the crew about how I was unable for any tolerance for pain on the plinth. Now it would be her turn.

Before that however our physio for today insisted we walk 500 metres to cool our limbs in the adjacent River Nore. It was a very hot day. The cooling waters were lovely. There to chat while we chilled were Sean, Deirdre, Jamie and Tom Fallon, all friends from Mullingar. They had driven down especially to lend their support.

Ken and I had finished the run in 4hrs 51mins, our slowest to date. The routing required extra energy and the climbing and dropping on hard, rocky terrain had exacted a toll on our legs. We slowed our pace down a little but the last hour was a long and hard struggle. Ken couldn't pinpoint a particular area of soreness but we were both very glad to finish.

Afterwards we were fortunate to be hosted by Avril Lenehan of Lenehan's Bar, a quaint old-worlde hostelry in the middle of the village. Eddie Kehir, the legendary Kilkenny hurler, was there to greet us on our return after the marathon, having earlier blown the whistle to start us off.

Also assisting was a man who would come and run with us on two more occasions. Brian Keane, a Dubliner who has made his home in

'OTHER THINGS MAY CHANGE, BUT WE START AND END WITH FAMILY' ANTHONY BRANDT

DRIVING MRS DUFFY: *Mum and Dad, just after they got married in August 1961*

TRIO OF TROUBLE: *My three sisters, Mary, Katherine and Dorothy*

FORE! *'Perfecting' my swing in 1981*

THESE BOOTS WERE MADE FOR WALKING: *Dad in Mount Tahat, Southern Algeria, Central Sahara*

WHAT A SWEATER: *Photographs such as this made me recognise I had a weight problem*

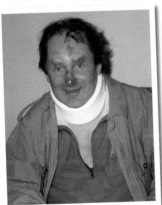

TOP OF THE POPS: *Dad after his dreadful fall in Scotland in 1994*

DOTING PARENTS: *My brother Tom with his wife Orla and their new baby daughter Juliana, who was born two days before we started the marathons*

A FAMILY AFFAIR: *My three sisters Katherine, Dorothy and Mary with my mum in June 2008*

LIFE BEGINS AT 70: *Dad has been involved in sport throughout his life. Here I am with him and Dorothy competing in a triathlon in Lilliput, Mullingar. He was 71 in this photograph*

GENERATION NEXT: *Andrew, Gerry, Rebecca and Mark, my nephews and niece*

THE FIRST STEPS: *I look a little nervous as I make my way to the start line for the 2007 Dublin marathon, my first ever*

LIFE THROUGH A LENS: *Enda Munnelly was not only a friend and a bike mechanic but a film director too*

BEFORE THE FALL: *My property business, 2005*

'THE WORDS 'CAN'T' AND 'QUIT' VANISH FROM T[
AND THEIR DEFINITION OF A GOAL IS NOT A DESI[

MAKING A SPLASH: *A swimming frenzy at the start of Ironman France 2008. Dorothy and I are in*

HOSE YER MAN: *Nice was hot, hot, hot*

NICE TO KNOW YOU: *Some of the gang from Ironman France*

THLETES' VOCABULARY, JT DESTINY' IRONMAN.COM

there... somewhere!

SWISS ROLE: *Dorothy prays for divine help in Ironman Switzerland in 2010*

TWICE AS NICE... DOUBLE IRONMAN UK, LITCHFIELD, 2009

STARTER: *304 lengths of the 25m pool*

MAIN COURSE: *My spirits plummeted 168 miles into the 224-mile cycle*

DESSERT: *By mile 47 of the run, pain had well and truly arrived*

RAISING AWARENESS WOULD NOT BE EASY, SO WE ROPED IN A FEW WELL-KNOWN FACES TO HELP

MARKING OUR CARDS: *Announcing that 600 runners had registered to run with us for the 32 Marathon Challenge, with Eamonn Coghlan, Keith Duffy and Ray D'Arcy*

A BIG HELP: *'You're some animal' were Paul O'Connell's words to Ken; Johnny Donnelly, ex-Sawdoctors band member, ran with us in Cavan*

THERE'S SOMETHING ABOUT MARY: *With ex-Olympic gold medallist Mary Peters; and myself and Ken with 2009 Rose of Tralee Charmaine Kenny*

BUTT MICHAEL: *Michael O'Leary knows a thing or two about PR and here he gives myself and Ken a hand with raising awareness of the 32 Marathon Challenge at the launch. Cheers, Michael!*

KEN AND I SHARED MANY AMBITIONS

COOL CUSTOMER : *My running friend and challenge compatriot Ken Whitelaw*

FIRST IMPRESSIONS : *Ken's debut marathon in 2006, an impressive 2 hours 54 mins in Edinburgh*

KEN'S BACKING TEAM: *Ken's parents Paddy and Celine in Wexford; and his brother Barry*

DAY ONE AND BEYOND: A JOURNEY OF 838 MILES BEGINS WITH A SINGLE STEP...

My nephews Mark and Gerry show us the way in Longford

It's beetroot, honest!

Family and friends help us set sail on our journey

Who wants ice-cream? A hot sundae in Wicklow (Day 3)

Tony Kinlan proudly got this pic on the first take!

POIGNANT MOMENTS, STUNNING BACKDROPS MISSED SIGNPOSTS AND HUMAN FORTITUDE...

WATER'S EDGE: *Ken cools down in Kilkenny. Some incredibly difficult days for him lay just around the corner*

WHISTLE BLOWER: *Charmaine Kenny starts the Kildare marathon*

HAND IT TO HIM: *Willie Burns had Offaly rocking on Day 15*

ICE, ICE BABY: *A 10-minute immersion in ice and a juice were important ingredients to ensure a quick recovery*

ALL THE YOUNG GUYS: *The Rhode minor football team lent their support in Co Offaly*

ABSOLUTE BEGINNERS: *Catherine Mooney (3), Tomas McCormack (4) and Simon Hutchinson (6). Between them, they ran 12 marathons. None of them had ever run one before*

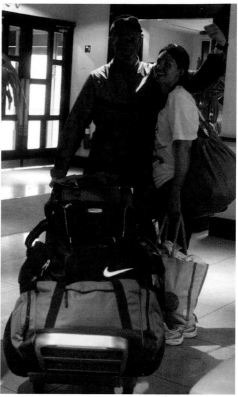

MY GIRL: *Jacinta helps me out in Waterford*

SIGN OF THINGS TO COME: *No wonder we got lost on the way from Clare to Tipperary*

TOUGH DAYS SHOULD BE CELEBRATED. IT'S ON SUCH OCCASIONS WE DEFINE OUR CHARACTER

EYEING THE PRIZE: *No pain, no gain, our physio Noeleen promised in Mayo*

ROSCOMMON TOUCH: *Terry Greene (720) dusted off her shoes 14 years after her last marathon closely followed by Clare's Michelle O'Halloran*

DONEGAL DELUGE: *We were thrilled to be together once more on the wettest day of the 32*

DERRY AIR: *Myself and Ken with Fiona McCann and her children Niamh and Sean*

LUCY AND THE SKY: *I grabbed a quick hug from my niece Lucy prior to departure in Derry*

LITTLE WONDERS: *With Aoife O'Brien, Peter Murphy, Shauna O'Brien, Caoimhe O'Brien and Eleanor Murphy in Tyrone*

IT'S THIS WAY: *Niall encourages Jacinta at the end of her first full marathon in Fermanagh*

NORTHERN LIGHTS: *Gerry Kelly and a happy band of Sunday morning full and half-marathon runners in Downpatrick*

UP DOWN: *With Joe Quinn, our co-ordinator in Co Down. An ultra marathon runner and a man who has inspired many people to take up running*

IT MAY BE HARD TO COMPREHEND BUT WE REALLY WERE ENJOYING EVERY MARATHON...

WOOF DAY AT THE OFFICE: *Our physio Noeleen Bourke never let Ken out of her sight. Chris and Keith Roddy and the Siberian huskey Tyson were also in tow in Drogheda*

RADIO WAVES: *Ray D'Arcy put on his runners to do a half-marathon in Cavan*

TIME OF MY LIFE: *My fastest single marathon was on Day 29 in Meath*

RUNNING UP THAT HILL: *Ken on the climb on the penultimate day in Leitrim. Sean Fallon and Colin Clarke took the easier option!*

COUNTDOWN: *As the challenge neared the end, the number of runners swelled. We had 95 in Leitrim*

GO TEAM: *We had a massive crowd of 205 runners for the final marathon in Westmeath*

WE DID IT: *At the finish line with Ken and his niece Caoimhe*

OUR CREW KEPT THE SHOW ON THE ROAD

HAIR-RAISING: *Stuart, Jacinta and Brendan brought much humour and fun to the challenge*

ONE DIRECTION: *Niall Murphy and Colin Telford helped navigate us around the country*

THE THREE AMIGOS: *Alvaro Ramirez, Freddie Grehan and Kevin Whelan, the CEO of IAA*

HANDY MEN: *Well I'm no dentist but I'll take a look if you like! Freddie with Ken's dad, Paddy*

LIGHTS, CAMERA, ACTION: *Ken's mother Celine offered great support throughout the 32 days*

SO SOLID CREW: *Some of the crew. If they look tired, that's because this was Day 31 on the road*

this idyllic village, was a huge source of local knowledge and help. In addition, he placed regular messages of encouragement on our Facebook page. Another local man, Denis Cormac, also helped. Denis was typical of so many people whom we met on our year long journey. I got his number from a mutual friend and thankfully for us, he took the call. He and I stumbled across Inistioge when we were out looking for a suitable route back in May. This man had never met me before, yet he embraced our challenge without question. It is impossible for me to mention all the people like Denis who helped along the way. There were hundreds. Without people like Denis, Brian and Avril, we could not have done it. Community spirit is alive and well in Ireland.

PHYSIO

Early in March we received a phone call from a lady called Sinead Fennell in the Irish Society of Chartered Physiotherapists (ISCP). She had learned about the event through a mutual friend, Noeleen Bourke, a chartered physiotherapist based in Mullingar. This was the same Noeleen who had helped me on the road to recovery in early 2009.

The ISCP wanted to do their bit for charity and took it upon themselves to organise voluntary physio not just for Ken and I in the build up and during the event but also for every runner that would join us. It was an incredible gesture as well as a huge undertaking by them and it was a key element in our success. To know that every day our tired limbs would get a professional rub-down from a chartered physio was a great comfort to us all.

Ken was in some discomfort getting onto the physios plinth after the Kilkenny marathon. This would be the start of some challenging times for him. At first he barely noticed the discomfort but on the final loop he had felt some muscle tightness. Little did we know just what an impact this would have over the following days. He was in excellent hands post-race today though, as the Kilkenny senior hurling team physio was waiting for him. Teresa McGinn worked on him for over an hour before we loaded up the car and headed further South.

Kilkenny was our sixth marathon, we were almost a week on the road. An Olympic silver medallist in the marathon from the 1984 Olympics was waiting to start us at our next port of call. Our destination as we left Kilkenny was the location for our seventh marathon, Waterford.

DAY 7
WATERFORD

THURSDAY 8 JULY
681.2 miles (1096.28 km) to go

Waterford City
Gerry   4 hours 42 minutes
Ken   5 hours 35 minutes

I HAD fallen asleep. It was a Sunday I think, in 1984. It was about midnight when I drifted off, unable to keep my eyelids open. The next morning I jumped off the couch and ran to the radio. How could I have fallen asleep on this night of all nights?

I was a 16-year-old sports addict. I had waited up to watch the final event of the 1984 Olympic Games, the marathon. The next morning I turned on the radio for news and heard Jimmy Magee's now legendary commentary being replayed over and over again on RTE Radio: "Caldwell, Gilroy, Byrne, McCourt, Russell, O'Callaghan twice, Tisdall, Delaney, McNally, Tiedt and Wilkinson. Now for the 13th time an Olympic medal goes to an Irishman, John Treacy, the crowd stands for the Irishman from Viliarstown, in Waterford. The little man with the great heart, the winner, and what a winner, John Treacy."

"This was a great idea, well done," were John Treacy's opening words to us when he arrived outside the headquarters in Waterford. Slight of stature just like I imagined him to be, John is now head of the Irish Sports Council. No stranger to fundraising for charity himself, John recognised the uniqueness of the event and we discussed it in some detail as we made our way to the start line.

I felt honoured walking beside an Olympic silver medallist. The memories came flooding back. Perhaps Ken was too young to remember but not me. I could even remember Limerick five years earlier in 1979 when Treacy completed back to back World Cross Country Championship victories.

Along with Ken and I were eight other runners. One of them was Amanda Mansfield whose son had been diagnosed with autism at two years and nine months. Now five years on, he was in mainstream school and was doing excellently. Despite their success, Amanda was back many years later, still doing her bit by raising funds for autism charities.

Our route saw us navigate two loops of 13.1 miles. It turned at the beach in Tramore and brought us back to our base at the Kingfisher Leisure Centre, on the edge of Waterford city. It was at the 13.1 mile turnaround point that Ken's marathon challenge started to unravel. Treacy was always someone who displayed huge courage and great heart throughout his career. From mile 13 onwards my running colleague would have to display similar qualities. As we turned to head in the direction of Tramore for a second time, Ken let out a cry of pain. Within metres he was forced into a walk, his distress obvious. Our worst nightmare from a running point of view had just arrived.

On the plinth in Kilkenny, Teresa our physio had expressed concern about some soreness Ken was starting to feel in his left quad muscle. In addition, Ken had mentioned over breakfast that the pain hadn't gone away.

KEN: *I tried to jog after a minute or two but the muscle just couldn't support my running weight. Although the legs were reasonably okay for the first half of the marathon, at mile 13.1, I let out a sudden shout of pain. A knot was developing in my left quad muscle, above my knee, and it seemed to become very painful very suddenly.*

Siobhan, our Waterford physio came out onto the course and applied some heavy strapping in an attempt to ease it. "You go on," Ken said to me, his face etched with discomfort. "There is no point in both of us walking. I'll be ok, I'll walk for a mile or so and then I'll pick it up again."

I felt guilty leaving him there but his point was a valid one. I was feeling fine and he had the company of our crew member Darragh and John O'Reilly, our route co-coordinator for Waterford.

"Ok , I'll see you later," I replied.

I turned and headed for Tramore. My heart went out to him. I knew it could just as easily have been me left there. It was simply the luck of the draw.

It was vital that we both gave ourselves the best chance of finishing this challenge. So much of our journey still lay ahead and we had so much riding on our ability to finish it. The less time spent on our feet, the more time for recovery. Also, one of the full marathon runners was waiting patiently for me to resume. Joe Kelly, a pharmacist from this part of Ireland was one of the first to register to run with us over six months ago. He and I ran the second half together.

As I got off the plinth almost three hours later, a 4hrs 42mins marathon completed, Ken still had five miles to go. By now his father Paddy was keeping him company. On hearing of Ken's travails, Paddy immediately put on his walking shoes and got a lift out onto the course to join Ken, providing comfort to his son when he needed it most. So many miles lay ahead of us and Ken would have to be mentally strong. Running a marathon every day was hard enough. Having to walk some or all of it was immensely harder. Longer on the feet and longer on the mind. Ken was a runner at heart and I knew deep down walking would not appeal to him at all. This was the first really big test of the challenge. Tough times were always going to come, now they were here.

Having Paddy to keep him company was great for him as they jogged the last few miles. Paddy later confessed that this was his first time to run or jog in over 40 years. He must have been fit though. In 2009, he and Ken's mum Celine completed the famous Camino De Compostelo Pilgrimage walk in Northern Spain and France. Over seven weeks they had covered a distance of some 600 kilometres. They walked an average of 25km every day. Five hours and 35 minutes after starting our seventh marathon, Ken crossed the line with his dad in tow.

I had climbed off the plinth 90 minutes earlier. I felt my muscles had tightened considerably, much more than on previous days. Perhaps it was the fact that we had run seven marathons in seven days or maybe it was the constant pounding of the hard road surface for 26 consecutive miles. The fact that I hadn't had an ice bath was another possible reason. Ten minutes later I was in the sea just up the road in Tramore, cooling the aching lower limbs. I started to feel its benefits immediately.

Afterwards Paddy had cheekily insisted on getting on the physio table himself. The physio, presuming he had ran a full marathon, asked him had he done his stretches and stretched his quads.

"Now where would they be?" came the reply.

Jacinta and I loaded up the car at 4.30 pm. It had been a long day for everyone. As she studied the map to navigate our way out of Waterford, my mind drifted. We were starting to have some unexpected tests thrown at us. The euphoria of the first few days was distant now. We were a travelling party with only 20 per cent of our job done. The seven days since the previous Friday in Longford had felt like a month. Every day was a long one. We rose around seven and never got to bed before 11pm. So much had happened since and so much labour from everyone on the crew. Yes, it was a great adventure but it was a challenge. I guess it was meant to be hard.

Paddy later told us he had noticed the severe discomfort Ken was in. The reality of the situation was becoming apparent. His injury was starting to be a cause of worry. That night we were concerned, very concerned.

DAY 8

CORK

FRIDAY 9 JULY
655 miles (1054.12 km) to go

Fota Island
Gerry   4 hours 37 minutes
Ken   7 hours 35 minutes

I WAS in shock. It was Jacinta who first noticed the plain white envelope on the desk, next to the TV.

"What's that?" she had said moments earlier.

"Probably just a special offer from the hotel or something," I replied.

"Open it," she suggested.

It was a personal letter addressed to Ken and I. When I saw who it was from, I was stunned.

It started... *"When I was informed by the general manager of Fota Island of your fundraising activities in support of autism, I had to write to applaud your efforts."*

It was from a sportsman. A very famous sportsman. *"I can't even imagine what it would be like to run 32 consecutive marathons."*

The letter was from a famous golfer whose own life had a few years before, been directly touched by autism.

"I think I could probably stretch to one... but I would need a golf cart for the other 31 probably. Seriously though, I am in awe of your determination to raise funds for a cause that you'll know is close to my heart. My son Ben is quite severely affected by autism so I know the effect

it has on families. And one of the things that shocked me was how common this condition is and how little is known about its causes. Knowing there are people all over the world trying to do the same thing is very heartening."

It was from Ernie Els, the South African golf professional and one of the greatest players the world has ever seen.

It finished: *"I send my best wishes to you both and I hope you achieve your goals."*

Wow! I was thrilled. I am a big fan of his and had watched him perform many times. When his son Ben was diagnosed, Els and his family moved to America to set up their own charity the "Els for Autism Foundation" to raise awareness of the condition. The letter gave us a great lift after a very challenging day in Waterford.

Just five minutes earlier and before checking into our rooms, we bumped into another well-known person in the lobby, the man we had last spoken too from a cornfield in Wexford two days before. It was Ray D'Arcy. He was broadcasting from Cork the next morning and for 10 minutes he questioned us eagerly on our experiences to date.

The next day we were met by a very wet morning in the south of Ireland. A large gathering was there nonetheless. Among them was the general manager of the FOTA Island resort, John O'Flynn. John had promised many months earlier to run with us and he was true to his word. Our running pace was similar so I spent the first two hours or more in his company. Here is a man who really knows how to run a business. The FOTA resort is in a beautiful environment where the staffs' courtesy to their guests is exceptional. John and I enjoyed an interesting conversation and by the end of it we had solved all of the country's economic problems.

For the second half I was joined by a friend from home, Dara Caffrey. He had arrived down the night before with his young son Rian. On reminiscing onto the dictaphone that evening, I recorded below my own comments as we drove from Cork city to Killarney on a very wet Friday evening.

"I could possibly have run 4hrs 20mins if I had pushed myself but not much more. All my research shows that I should be getting faster but I am not feeling it yet. Sure I am feeling good, but a sub-four, I can't see it just yet."

My time in Cork was 4:37. I had an enjoyable run as the staff had presented us with a gorgeous route that criss-crossed the entire estate through a mixture of wooded trail as well as the championship golf course.

If Ken was to draw any inspiration from Ernie's letter, the timing was opportune. The poor guy needed a lift as he endured a torrid day. Our concerns on the drive to Cork the previous evening were well-founded. We had started at 10am and he finished just after 6pm. Given the nature of the challenge we had set ourselves, he was unable to rest his body between marathons. As a consequence the injury he had picked up on Wednesday had resurfaced on Thursday. All day Friday it worsened.

Just one mile into the run he knew he would have to walk most of the distance. The first steps showered him in pain. He jogged slowly more in hope than anything but it soon became apparent that this injury was quite serious. At the two mile mark his jog turned into a moderate walk and a moderate walk soon turned into something resembling a shuffle. He was in too much pain for anything more. As a result of having to walk he would have to use different muscles. Consequently, he began to feel pains in his shins. His time too would plummet.

Gone was the comfortable 4hrs 30mins for him. He would spend over seven-and-a-half hours on the course excluding one unscheduled physio stop of 30 minutes. For many of those miles, Ken had his sister Alaine to keep him company. Although five months pregnant she had driven down from Mullingar the night before to give Ken a welcome boost. Ken only found out later how tough it was for Alaine to see her younger brother suffer. She was in tears before getting back into her car to begin the three and a half hour journey back home that night.

We had great support in terms of runners in Cork. Among them was Trish Cronin who came to run a half-marathon. On seeing Ken's plight she insisted on walking an additional 13.1 miles with him just to keep him company.

KEN: *It was frustrating because I was physically fit enough to run 32 consecutive marathons. I was perfectly psyched up to run 838 miles in a month. I wanted to be running. I didn't want to walk any of it, let alone full marathons. But the challenge now was to keep the spirits high, stay positive and keep moving forward. One step at a time.*

Each step brings me closer to home. I had to block out the fact that the crew were delayed by my slow pace. I was holding everyone up. There was little I could do but keep plodding along. Gerry and I both knew that injuries were the only unknown factor in all of our plans. Our training got us to the start line in peak condition. No amount of fitness however would prevent a niggle developing into a problem on our 7th consecutive marathon.

An unfortunate by-product of all the walking was that by the last few miles of the day my shins were starting to get very tight and sore. As if the knot in the quad wasn't challenging enough, the pain in the shins was quickly becoming more of a worry."

Ken's injuries were now the subject of much discussion among our crew. A physio from Cork, Oswald Schmitt, a man who once swam the channel, came to our aid to try to offer some relief to Ken. Ken's mum and dad, Celine and Paddy, accompanied him to the clinic. Both in their early sixties, they had been with us since the very first day. By now they were a vital part of the crew, carrying out a multitude of daily tasks. Their son's pain was mirrored all over their own expressions. It was draining them mentally as much as it drained Ken physically. They were both putting in 14 hour days. It was the last thing they needed or indeed their youngest son at that stage.

We checked into our hotel in Killarney very late that night. By now, Kens difficulty was filtering into everyone else's psyche as well. We all felt for him. Watching my running partner suffer was difficult. He was enduring so much but was still as determined as ever to continue. Jacinta and I ate a meal in our room. We were exhausted and felt quite deflated. I did a video diary before retiring and outlined how morale was sinking just a little. I hoped the next day would be better.

For Ken, it would actually be even worse.

DAY 9
KERRY

SATURDAY 10 JULY
628.8 miles (1011.95 km) to go

Killarney
Gerry   4 hours 21 minutes
Ken   9 hours 6 minutes

DON'T tell anyone but I'm a softie. Around 10pm on our journey up to Limerick I became quite emotional. Despite the beautiful surroundings of the Killarney National Park, this day was just horrendous, the worst by far. Moments before, I had sent Ken a text in the car behind. My reasons were twofold. One was because it was from the heart, the second was to try to give him a boost.

"Ken," I wrote, "today you reached legendary status in my eyes. I am in awe of what you did."

Even as I wrote this, tears were welling up in my eyes. I guess if you were not there you could not have understood. To confound the challenge that Kerry would give my running partner, it was also perhaps the wettest day of 2010 or at least it felt like it was.

Eleven hours earlier we had been joined by a group of about 20 runners including a friend from home Darragh Moore, who was making his marathon debut.

Perhaps it is better if you hear Ken's thoughts about what unfolded.

KEN: *I kept an open mind over breakfast, not letting the tough day in Cork get to me. Over the previous months of training, pounding the roads,* *paths and canal banks, we had not only been getting physically fitter with every passing week but we had also, almost subconsciously, been preparing our minds to take on this massive challenge.*

We found that when each marathon was done, it was 'parked' and left for another day to think about and relive. It was a question of focusing on the one ahead of us the next day which was the marathon around the 'National Park'. My plan starting off was to walk the first mile, just to get the legs and body warmed up before trying to jog the remainder. Within the first few steps however, I knew that I was in for a tough day. My shins were sore from the start. The knot in the quad had improved somewhat overnight but was still not strong enough for me to run on. So I had a long slow, 26.2-mile walk ahead of me. And in the rain, again!

Shin splints are a worrying injury to get at any time and the usual recommendation is to stop exercising, ice and rest. But I didn't want to rest. So I walked, and walked, and walked as tenderly as I could. It was a slow walk too. I wanted to walk as fast as I could to get to the finish line quicker but the shin pain just wouldn't allow me to go at a strong pace.

My cousin Simon joined me for his second marathon of the challenge. He walked the first 13.1 miles with me. At the half way point I took a break as he started a jog. We had arranged our physio to come out onto the course to treat me so while she was massaging my shins and quad on her plinth, I took the opportunity to get some grub into me. As I was eating, I could hear the cheer and applause for Gerry as he crossed the line of his 9th marathon – in a time of 4:21. I was happy that he had another successful run in the bag but I just wanted to jump off the plinth and start running myself.

After a change of clothes I set off again, this time with my brother Barry. He proved to be great company and tried to distract me but it was almost impossible to take my mind off the pain my lower legs were feeling. By mile 14, I tried new ways of relieving the shin muscle by hunkering down every 500 metres or so with my knees on the ground and my toes stretched out behind them, using my hands on the ground to keep my balance. It was very sore but it did give momentary relief.

At mile 16 Barry and I were moving slowly along when I asked him to return to the van for a bit of food. A minute or so after he left I got an awful dart of pain up my lower leg. It was so severe that it took me by surprise and immediately worried me. Without taking one step further I sat down on a large stone beside a stream. I realised then for the first time that it was now a real possibility that I wouldn't be able to continue. If that pain was to remain, there was just no way that I could walk another step.

I sat silently and I said a little prayer. I didn't want to stop. I had the energy, fitness and determination to continue. I had put a year's work into this. But I felt that the outcome of this little break was beyond my control. Then after five minutes I straightened up again and tentatively took my next step. To my relief the pain was bearable. So I kept on walking, slowly.

My mum joined us for the last eight miles. She is such a positive person that it is hard to feel sorry for oneself in her company and her chat was just what I needed. Kevin Whelan and his son Peter joined us for the last few miles and I was quite happy to let the conversation flow around me as I concentrated on taking each step. The last miles just got harder and slower. It was taking me between 25 and 30 minutes to walk each mile.

Grainne, our physio, came back out to the course at mile 21 out of concern for me and gave me a quick treatment. She kindly offered to stay until I finished but I felt that she had given enough of her time, so I thanked her and declined. A cousin of Gerry's, Tony O'Callaghan cycled alongside me for a few of these miles offering encouragement at every turn.

It was a tough day but I got there. Gerry and Jacinta came back out onto the course to see me home and even though it was still raining, Gerry walked the last few hundred metres with me. I had started that morning at 10am. It was 8:50 that night when I took my last step. I had spent 9hrs 6mins walking the distance. The remainder of the time was taken up with physio and clothes-changing stops."

All of our crew will never forget the Kerry marathon. It was gut-wrenching to watch. What is even more amazing is that never once when Ken was in company did he let his spirits drop. It was so unusual that I felt he did it purely to keep everyone's spirit up. His fortitude in the face of such distress was heart-rending. Not only did he have to walk, he had to walk slowly with every step a mountain. Given that he had effectively walked the last 65 miles (since the half way point on Thursday) he was now developing a whole new set of injuries. He had to change his running stride to compensate for the initial pain in his quad. As a result his shins endured a lot of pain and discomfort.

As we drove the two hours from Kerry to Limerick, morale was at its lowest point since we had started eight days before. Something had to be done, otherwise Ken would not be able to continue. Time to make a phone call.

Thankfully, the person at the other end answered.

DAY 10
LIMERICK

SUNDAY 11 JULY
602.6 miles (969.79 km) to go

Limerick City
Gerry   4 hours 45 minutes
Ken   7 hours 43 minutes

"The real glory is being knocked to your knees and then coming back. That's real glory"

Muhammad Ali

WE were all up early. Ken was on the physio plinth before 7.30am. Our hotel which was located on the edge of the university campus was only a short five minute drive to the start line.

Noeleen Bourke, our Mullingar-based physio, was the person who had taken our phone call the night before. Faced with the prospect of Ken not being able to continue, we had to think of something. The collective wisdom was to ask Noeleen to come down and do some late night physio on him. At two hours notice, she drove down to meet us. She arrived in at 11pm, Ken soon after from Killarney. It was close to midnight before she began working on him and almost one o'clock in the morning before he was faced with the final task of the day, the 'ice bath'. It had been an unbelievably long day, one he would later describe as "the toughest ever on my feet." Despite being immersed in ice in the bath, he was so shattered, he fell asleep.

Sunday 11th July was a lovely sunny morning with the previous day's miserable weather a distant memory. Despite the sunshine however, morale was at its lowest ebb. Three laps into the four required, our crew member Darragh Thornton spotted an unmistakable 6' 5" figure walking out of the 50 metre pool and gym complex on the grounds of Limerick University, the Race HQ for our 10th consecutive marathon. Darragh raced over as he was keen to get Ken a morale boost. Ken was actually in the back of the support ambulance undergoing a quick bout of physio and taping when he spotted the pair of them approaching.

"Just come over and say hello," Darragh suggested to the rugby Lions skipper Paul O'Connell, when he informed him that there were two guys close by who were running their 10th marathon in as many days.

"Sure," said the Munster and Ireland legend.

"In 32 days?" he asked disbelievingly when Ken explained the challenge we were undertaking. He was genuinely interested and when he heard about the extent of what we were undertaking, he got up and said simply: "You're some animal." If only he knew.

After the harrowing day that Ken had endured on Saturday, we waited with baited breath to see if Noeleen could somehow bring him back to life. Noeleen was a vital part of our crew long before the actual event started. Not only had she offered me a weekly physio session for the six months leading into this challenge, here she was yet again giving up her free time to come to our rescue. Without her help, it is doubtful if Ken could have continued. Ken also received some acupuncture to his ear, to help ease the muscles in his legs, from Alvaro Ramirez, a doctor who was lending his support. They were slightly painful to receive, but the new piercings weren't too noticeable.

Now to see how he reacted when he stood up again. The first few steps would give us some insight into whether he would have the opportunity to run or at least jog again. The early signs were cautiously encouraging as he managed a very light jog for the first 6.55 miles. Still well short of being injury free, crumbs of comfort were on offer and his happy face swallowed them up hungrily. What a joy it was to see him happy again.

After two days of heavy rain, the day offered a pleasant morning on the banks of the River Shannon. At the start line to wish us well were my dad, my three sisters, my cousin Amanda with her daughters Heather and Grace and lots of nieces and nephews. Andrew, my nine-year-old nephew was by now a team mascot, having attended seven of the first 10 marathons. For this particular one, he even ran six miles with us. A group of a dozen runners joined us for our 10th marathon as well as some welcome faces from home. My other nephews Mark and Gerry as well as my 10-year-old niece, Rebecca, ran about six miles as well and I loved having them there. It was very special.

Mark and Andrew have had a great athletics role model in their family. In 1996 at the Atlanta Olympics, midway through the heats of the semi-final of the 5,000 metres, an Irishman led the field around the Olympic Stadium. On his shoulder was none other than Venuste Niyongabo from Burundi. Niyongabo would just a few days later claim Olympic Gold in the 5000 metres. The Irishman was Cormac Finnerty, an uncle to Mark and Andrew. Cormac's brother Enda, is married to my sister Mary. More of Enda in a few marathons.

On this day too some friends from home arrived in the form of Sean Fallon and Colin Clarke. Their job they felt was to keep me distracted for the second half of the marathon. It worked. I only knew the lads a short time. Sean had a sporting background, representing Ireland twice in Aussie Rules and was heavily involved in an Aussie Rules club called the Midland Tigers. Only new to running, he had taken to long runs for marathon training with ease.

Colin and I had shared a coffee a year before. It was the first time we had met. He admitted that he was new to running and he had come to me for advice. He wanted to shed a few pounds and perhaps have a gentle introduction to triathlon. On learning more about his ambitions, I told him he might consider attempting a marathon. He thought I was mad. Well I wasn't and he did. This was his third run with us. He and Sean had run a full marathon with us in Dublin on day two, a half-marathon in Kilkenny and they would do another full marathon before we finished our quest. An impressive tally by both men.

Also joining Ken and taking on his first marathon was his close friend, Peter Droog. Recognising that he really needed some company and some distraction from his pain, Peter stayed with Ken for the entire 26.2 miles. It took seven hours and 35 minutes. Peter had trained like all the other runners to run a much faster marathon. Never once did he leave Ken's side however, which was a huge gesture.

As the day progressed, Ken had to mix in some walking and a few stops for additional physio but he was relieved just to have any kind of forward momentum. I was more fortunate and thankfully remained injury free crossing the line in 4:45. It was a hard last six miles but nothing compared to what my younger stable mate had to endure since the previous Friday.

ICE BATHS

I mentioned earlier that a part of our strategy involved a 10 minute ice bath each day. This was something we actually grew quite used to. I never lasted longer than seven or eight minutes but I am certain that I did enjoy the benefits. We felt it was a vital part of our strategy towards ensuring quick muscle recovery. In Waterford on day seven, the cold water of the Irish sea had an immediate effect of easing the stiffness in my lower limbs. Of that I was sure.

Ken actually grew to love the ice-baths. I think by week three, he was actually concealing a toy boat and rubber duck in his gear bag to keep him company. In Limerick, our ice bath was actually the same facility used by the Munster rugby team. If it was good enough for those boys it was good enough for us as well.

That night en route to Clare, I logged onto our Facebook page to see what people were saying about the challenge. By now we were getting a large volume of feedback from thousands of people who each night were logging on to find out how our days were unfolding. We tried to keep this as up-to-date as possible, which was an additional challenge given all the other stuff we had to do. A friend from home, Brian Boyle, perhaps summed it up best. That night he wrote...

"Ken, you're starting to make this s*** interesting."

DAY 11

CLARE

MONDAY 12 JULY
576.4 miles (924.4 km) to go

Ballyvaughan
Gerry   4 hours 30 minutes
Ken   6 hours 13 minutes

LOGUE'S Lodge in Ballyvaughan, Co. Clare, was the starting point for our 11th run and by the time we were ready on this Monday morning there was quite a buzz from the 23 runners and their families, all gathered at the start line.

The evening before we had watched Spain defeat Holland in the soccer World Cup Final. Our host Alan Logue, was the owner of the hotel. Alan was a man who contacted us early in 2010 to offer us any assistance he could. He gave it to us in abundance, feeding us, providing us with lodgings and then running a full marathon with us.

A typical day would see our legs reach out for the bedroom floor a little after 7.30am. By now we were well settled into our early morning routine and the alarm had been moved forward by an hour or so. Since Day-4 in Carlow, for the first minute or so I had to walk around the room like an elderly man. My calves each morning felt like they were still asleep despite the rest of my body being awake. It took only a minute of two though to get them back to normal.

Our sizeable crew normally started to appear at breakfast shortly before eight o'clock. Given the distance we were from home and the amount of time spent on the road, we had all built up a strong bond.

THE CREW

First up was my other half Jacinta. As I alluded to earlier, Jacinta played a key role in this challenge. Ken and I owed her a huge debt. Already she had one half-marathon under her belt and another running milestone for her was just around the corner.

Ken's parents, Celine and Paddy, brought much-needed humour as well as a great work ethic to our challenge. Paddy, a former secondary school English teacher, was a quiet man whose main sporting passion was fishing. He was calmness personified and never let things get to him as he performed a multitude of tasks every day. He disappeared for an hour midway through each marathon. It took me a few days to realise where he was headed. Was he gone to the bookies or to the pub? Not at all. He was simply gone off to have a quiet read of The Irish Times newspaper and a brief snooze in the back of the camper van. Hardy a criminal offence.

Celine, like Jacinta, was a multi-tasker and such a positive person. She did so much for everyone. One of Celine's main hobbies was photography. In the early days she had the camera shyly protruding from her jacket pocket, only taking it out when Tony and Stuart, the two event photographers, were distracted. One day though, I spotted her studiously taking notes as she observed the two professionals at work. As the number of photographers rose during the event and as her confidence grew towards the latter days, her shyness with a camera disappeared. By then she was out in front of all the professional snappers shouting the orders as to how Ken and I and whoever was in that day's photographs, should stand. How quickly she learned. In the end I think I even spotted Stuart and Tony taking a few notes.

Two Offalymen, Freddie Grehan and Niall Murphy, brought experience and a 'can do' attitude to every task. Freddie, a huge GAA fan and a good golfer, was in charge of all the event logistics and Niall was his right hand man and director of operations. Freddie had 30 years experience in the overseas travel business and the logistics of bringing large groups to foreign destinations. At the end of this challenge I am not sure which he would say is harder, global travel or doing 32 counties in 32 days.

Niall was first out on the course each morning and last off it in the evening. One of the last things he did every day was to inspect the next day's course and ensure it was as safe as safe could be. On a number of occasions he expressed concerns and made last minute changes to the proposed routing. Clare was actually one of those days. We were immensely grateful to have both men on our team.

Close friends of ours, Brendan Doyle and Darragh Thornton, were also on board. Both men had a significant running background. Brendan was a co-organiser of the Longford Marathon, one of Ireland's premier marathon events. Both Brendan and Darragh ran with us on more than one occasion. In fact Brendan ran two full and half a dozen half-marathons.

Ken's older brother Barry, appeared on a number of days too. Barry, a very keen wind surfer had been a crew member since the launch way back in November. Apart from being a vital shoulder for Ken to lean on during the lead in, he was also a big help with the website among other things. We had to change it a hundred times over six months with constant updates. A quiet man who did massive work and never looked for thanks.

Our crew did not finish there. As I mentioned, the faces changed constantly. Two men who never left our side were Pat Whaley and Joe Whelan. Both Westmeath men quietly laboured every day doing the lifting, the dragging, the pulling and the driving, never seeking attention or thanks.

David Cahilan, a pal of Ken's and a father and son in the forms of Mervyn Rundle senior and junior, who were friends of the charity's, also shared many days with us, offering us the vital muscle we needed.

The charity crew also constantly changed. Over the duration, four ladies would share the duties. Aishling Garry, Colette Charles, Kerry Boyd and Sarah McInerney-Buckley. A man who appeared a dozen or more times was a Nicaraguan doctor who lives in Clare called Alvaro Ramirez. Alvaro does a lot of work in conjunction with Irish Autism Action. He had administered acupuncture on Ken a number of times in the hope of relieving some of the pain he was in.

Back at base Freddie's partner Ann O'Reilly, was answering the phones to deal with so many late enquiries about the event. All of the team were great. No egos and no complaints. We were all sharing a very unique journey and nobody wanted to leave.

By now we had almost 900 participants registered and thus a sizeable logistical and physical effort was a daily requirement. Everyone on the crew worked tirelessly, with each day lasting 14 hours or more. Registration usually started around 8.30 each morning under the care of Kevin Whelan, Sarah and/or Colette. Kevin was present every single day. If he wasn't registering, he was co-ordinating photographs for our sponsors. Once that was completed, he and Sarah would head out onto the streets with David to supervise the bucket collections.

Two photographers accompanied us for the event and they became great friends. At this stage we had a sizeable following on Facebook and the hundreds of photographs that Stuart McChesney and Tony Kinlan took, received much favourable comment on the web. Stuart was an ultra marathon runner himself. Nothing unusual about that until I tell you that nine years previously he had suffered a very serious mountaineering accident. As a result of the fall he developed a neurological disorder called 'Transverse myelitis' caused by inflammation across both sides of one level, or segment of the spinal cord. For nine months Stuart lay on a hospital bed staring at the ceiling and at one stage was told he would never walk again. He refused to accept his fate however and over the following two years through rehabilitation, he slowly made a full recovery.

Perhaps they should make a film about Stuart. He ended up marrying the nurse who helped him in his rehab and two soon after became three as they have since had a little boy called Alex. Stuart brought much laughter to us on many occasions and also sent Ken and I the odd text when he wasn't there. This was hugely inspirational to both of us.

Tony was a 21-year-old Dublin born photographer. He wasn't there on day one but joined us soon afterwards. It took him a day or two to find his feet. I think at first he thought we were all mad but within a week or so, he was as absorbed in the event as much as any of us.

Tony and Stuart had a field day in Clare where the route in the Burren was hard to beat for scenic beauty – a combination of cliffs, limestone landscape and a sea vista had us looking in every direction for at least the first 13 miles. From there on though the conversations started to dry up, the heads lowered a little and the mind became more focused on the task at hand, putting one foot in front of the other.

The beauty of having a four-lap course, as it was in Clare, is that you get great support more often than you would on a one- or a two-lap course – not only from our crew but also fellow runners and those who travelled to cheer them as well as Ken and I.

For the first 11 days more than 400 people had already run with us. We met wonderful people who provided enormous energy and motivation for Ken and I to feed off. Our cup overflowed on this run. First up was a close friend of mine, Jim Hickey, who came to run a half-marathon. At 13 miles, he made two confessions. Firstly that it was his 43rd birthday that day and secondly, that he was going to run the full 26.2 miles. A little over four-and-a-half hours after starting he completed his second ever marathon.

A man making his debut in his 'first ever running event' was a close friend from Clare, Declan McInerney. Declan was one of the people whom I had called six months before, after drawing up a list of potential runners. When he answered the call, he told me I was mad, as he had no background in running. Within a week though, he rang back to say he had changed his mind, had registered and was about to start his training. He was a former golfing friend and a plus-two handicap golfer. No mean feat. That golf handicap was attained in Lahinch, a very tough links course on the west coast of Ireland.

Declan's wife, Rachel, had been diagnosed with cancer a few years before but was by now thankfully enjoying recovery. That was Declan's reason for running a marathon. Rachel's warm smile and personality lit up our day in Clare. What an inspiration both of them were in Clare and for the next few weeks. Rachel would continue to post messages of encouragement online, for the remainder of our journey.

Before finishing I must mention Pauline O'Halloran. Her family had a direct link with autism and so, with no prior experience she was here ready to tackle a half-marathon. Not only Pauline, but she had her four sisters and a few friends in tow. They had a ball. Not content with just doing the 13.1 miles for the first time ever, Pauline and her friend Fionnuala O'Buachalla joined Ken for his final loop. Their support carried him through those final tough 6.55 miles.

Ken's time was 6:13. Over dinner in Clare he confessed that given what he had endured over the previous four days, this marathon time meant as much to him as his personal best time for the marathon of 2:54:31. I had a small wobble; nothing major but from mile 14 to 21, I struggled somewhat. I even had to walk for about 300 metres or so. Funny thing though after the 21st mile my energy returned and I was able to take the pace right up again, finishing strongly. I crossed the line in 4:34. We all agreed later that night that we had a very memorable stay in Clare.

Only three weeks to go.

DAY 12

TIPPERARY

TUESDAY 13 JULY
550.2 miles (885.46 km) to go

Clonmel
Gerry   4 hours 23 minutes
Ken   5 hours 39 minutes

THE Comeragh Mountains overlooking the picturesque town of Clonmel, formed a stunning backdrop for the next run, a distance that would take me 4hrs 23mins to complete. My times were consistently improving now and thankfully so were Ken's. He was in good form once more and we felt confident he was edging back to full fitness. His time of 5hrs 39mins was a huge improvement given the turmoil he had experienced.

The route was tricky, set amidst some minor roads and some hard shoulders. Our starter, former top jockey and trainer Charlie Swan, looked on in shock when he was told the extent of our 32-day challenge. He was a friend of a friend and was delighted to add some profile to our brief stopover in Tipperary.

Kevin Kenny, a renowned chef from these parts, met us in his adopted county of Clare. He ran a marathon with us in Clare and another in Tipperary, 52.4 miles over two days. His second run was slower but that was to be expected. He had our full admiration as he was the first person to undertake such a challenge with us.

Mark Carroll, a friend from home who was in the area on business, spotted us on the road and pulled over to cheer on all of the day's runners. Ken had the company of a work colleague Maureen Hally who had taken a day off work duties to do a half-marathon.

I was feeling myself getting a little stronger each day. We had over 20 runners in Tipperary but for the second loop I found myself alone. Their pace was simply to strong for me. Barry, Ken's brother accompanied me for four or five miles on his mountain bike. The rest of the time I spent alone with lots of time to think. It was strange as we were so used to having company.

Ken spotted a cornfield on the second of two loops and nothing would do for him but to jump over the wall to reenact a photo opportunity scene from the movie *Gladiator*. Our photographer Stuart duly obliged.

DAY 13

LAOIS

WEDNESDAY 14 JULY
524 miles (843.29 km) to go

Emo
Gerry   4 hours 20 minutes
Ken   4 hours 58 minutes

IN my diary the first paragraph read...

I've started to look over my shoulder now. I feel like the swimmer in the Jaws movie waiting to be pounced on. Ken is on the prowl and I have to ensure I stay ahead of him.

I am joking of course, but how fantastic is the underlying meaning to what I am saying, and so richly deserved. Ken, like me, had put his heart into this event. For 12 months we had toiled every day. Early mornings and late nights we had spent piecing the logistics together. At its core was the challenge of completing 32 consecutive marathons and Ken was a runner at heart. He deserved to be running and now he was again. Truly fantastic. As he crossed the line in 4hrs 58mins he smiled from ear to ear. That was how much 'just to be running again' meant to him.

Over the course of the 32 marathons we were privileged to run in some historic settings. Emo House is situated in a small village just outside Portlaoise. Bequeathed to the state in 1994, it is a neo-classical mansion, formal and symmetrical in its design and was built as the home of the first Earl of Portarlington. The gardens at Emo are magnificent and are as well presented now as they were when first designed in 1790. It formed the backdrop for race HQ in County Laois.

Teresa McGinn, our physio from Kilkenny, returned to visit us in Laois and ran the final three miles with Ken. Ken was delighted as he could see by the expression on her face just what a personal achievement this was for her.

The routing was one of our most challenging to date. I would place it third in terms of difficulty, just behind Kilkenny and Wicklow. A course that meandered the perimeter of this lovely estate had a hard surface to add aches to already overworked legs and two climbs that were extremely testing. One of them was locally nicknamed the 'Dog Pound'. I have no idea why, but suffice to say if any dogs chased us, we were done for. It was that steep, we would have had no escape.

A strange thing was starting to happen. I felt stronger not weaker in Laois. It is worthy of note because it was day 13 and because of the severity of the testing course. It was hard, very hard. The road surface offered no recovery. Despite the challenging route, I ran my fastest of the 13 marathons, crossing the line to applause from two of my sisters Mary and Katherine as well as my dad. A most satisfying feeling engulfed me when I examined the watch. The gradient should have meant a marathon of perhaps 4:30 or more. My watch read 4 hrs and 20 mins. I really was starting to feel as if I was elevating to a new level of fitness. Hard to believe, but true.

I felt our bodies had now exited the physical 'comfort zone' of marathons one, two and three. We had trained to be able to do a lot more, we just hadn't actually done it yet. I thought back to my first ever run of over 21 miles not that many years before. That day I had felt a pain that had never returned. By the end of week one we were becoming accustomed to running 26.2 miles every day. For sure, Ken was having some challenges but these were not 'ability' related. Ken was a superior athlete to me. He was just unfortunate in that he picked up an injury that worsened.

In week one, my average time for each marathon was 4:36, by week two it had actually begun to quicken. Marathons 8-14 were ran in an average time of 4:23, 13 minutes per marathon 'faster' than the first seven. My body was definitely becoming used to the grind of running a marathon every day. I was getting stronger. I could feel it.

On our journey from Laois to Kildare we made a short detour to Mullingar. It only involved a minor diversion from our planned route. I didn't go back to my house as I felt I risked losing the adrenalin we were experiencing if I did so. It was a risk I did not wish to take, after all we had 19 more marathons still to run.

I wanted to say 'hi' to some of my family who I knew were in town. We agreed to rendezvous at my sister Dorothy's new multi-sports and triathlon store. Her new shop 'Tri and Run' had just opened a week before and I had yet to see it. There to meet me were Dorothy and Enda as well as Tom and Mary. A brief family reunion of sorts.

DAY 14
KILDARE

THURSDAY 15 JULY
497.8 miles (801.13 km) to go

Maynooth
Gerry   4 hours 15 minutes
Ken   5 hours 12 minutes

A FRIEND from home, Katherine Kenny, sent me a text the evening before.

"Reading your blog today left me speechless and full of admiration, you guys are amazing and inspiring."

It was one of hundreds of messages we were getting daily from family, friends and complete strangers. Every night our Facebook page was inundated with messages of support and we treasured them all. Words of encouragement mean so much. It is when you are on the receiving end you realise it. By now, close to 2,000 people were following our journey on Facebook and approximately 8,000 more on the website, where we posted a daily diary.

In 1980, a man from Mullingar called Louis Kenny ran an Irish marathon record of 2:12:21. Katherine, who had sent me the text, had married Louis's brother, John. Louis's marathon record stood for many years. Louis and Katherine's niece Charmaine Kenny was the 2009 Rose of Tralee and Charmaine had agreed to run with us in her home county of Kildare.

We contacted Charmaine through Katherine months earlier. Over the next few months in her capacity as the 2009 Rose,

Charmaine did some public relations work for us that helped build awareness of the event. On the morning of our 14th marathon we met her and the other 21 runners in a lecture hall in the historic grounds of the National University of Ireland in Maynooth. A local friend Sean Kelleher had managed to get us access to use this impressive facility as our race headquarters.

Brian Keegan sped through Dublin airport twice in a 24-hour period. A Kildare man living in London, he was one of the first to sign up and roped his brother John in as well. Brian got a late flight the evening before and now was standing next to Charmaine at the start line. Later that night he would be back in his bed in London, his contribution made and a 32 Marathons' medal to set off the sensors at the airport security area.

One of the greatest satisfactions Ken and I got over the 32 days was to see so many people running a half or a full marathon for the first time. Brian was a case in point. By the time we had finished the 32 marathons, more than 750 had ran their 'debut' full or half-marathons. Every day people thanked Ken and I for helping them achieve this. We offered in return a metaphor. Perhaps we had set the dinner table by organising the run. It was the runners themselves however, who went into the kitchen and cooked the dinner through months and months of training. Also, it was those same runners who ate the dinner by running 13.1 or 26.2 miles with us. All we did was set the table.

I managed to shave another five minutes off the previous day's 4:20, finishing in 4:15, my fastest to date. Ken had a few more niggles and was later, he confessed, becoming slightly concerned again. He found the final loop of 6.55 miles very hard and had to stop twice for physio en route. He was still pleased, however, to have another marathon completed, this time in 5:12.

On the five minute walk to post race physio my mind drifted. I knew it was July 15 and I quickly calculated that this monumental emotional and physical experience had yet to reach the half way point. That in itself was a hard concept to grasp. The two weeks we had been on the road felt like months. It was just that every day was so abundantly filled. Running the 26.2 miles was just one part of the experience. There were the early morning rituals of reigniting our muscles gradually. There was the meeting of so many new people every morning. The routine of saying our pre run 'thank yous' before setting off on that days run. The camaraderie for four hours and beyond full of chat and lots of humour. The post-race nutritional routine, rub down, packing up, navigating our way to the next destination, eat two dinners, unpack, unwind and close our eyes all over again.

Sure, I was enjoying it, I relished every minute. Even the hard moments. It was hard though to comprehend that we had another 18 more marathons still to run. That was difficult to digest. This challenge was nothing if not long and hard. I took stock, however, realising with gratitude that we were living our dream. Despite the challenge, both Ken and I recognised the fact that we were on the trip of a lifetime. Notwithstanding his injuries he remained every bit as enthusiastic as I. This is something that I expect we will look back on in future years with great memories and a sense of pride that we were a part of it all.

Another group of friends Louise McCartan, Robert Fagan, Frank Dillon, Grainne O'Neill, Marc Butler, Peter Mooney and Mairtin Savage joined us on this leg. John Conroy thought running his first ever marathon on his 35th birthday would be a good idea so he made it happen. As we were setting up in the grounds of the college, a friend from home Anne Coleman noticed the commotion outside. She had no idea we were running that day in Maynooth. Nothing would do her but to jump on her bike and cycle a few miles with us.

As we took in the grounds of Carton House, which the Mallaghan family had kindly given us permission to include in our routing, I thought back on my previous years of golfing pursuits. 'The Monty' golf course, named after its designer Colin Montgomerie, was a particular favourite of mine to play and now we were meandering through it. A few golfers looked on in bemusement as we ran up the main avenue on four occasions. We looked back in amusement at a few of their golf swings.

The next day Charmaine, fresh from a 2:03 'half marathon', sent a text.

"Hi Gerry. Hope you both got on well today. Incredible feat that requires incredible strength of mind. Am in awe of the pair of you. Keep it up. Looking forward to Westmeath already!"

DAY 15

OFFALY

FRIDAY 16 JULY

471.6 miles (758.96 km) to go

Birr

Gerry	4 hours 18 minutes
Ken	7 hours 59 minutes

AS I left the foyer of Dooleys Hoel in Birr at 7:30pm on this Friday evening with a 4:18 marathon under my belt, Van Morrison was warming the air reminding us that 'There'll be days like this'. How apt the lyrics were because for Ken unfortunately it was a case of deja vu. Once again our friend had to fight the injury demons and as usual he did it with a courage that was difficult to fathom.

His day had begun so brightly, but after 10 miles his sporting world had crumbled yet again. An agonising second loop of 13 miles on quiet country roads were taken at a snail's pace, his lower limbs screaming for rest. He would spend one minute less than eight hours on the course, his only reward being another very long bout of physio.

KEN: *After seven miles in Birr I was forced to walk. Another knot in my quad had developed. This time however, it was in my right leg rather than my left but in almost the identical spot. I got it bandaged on the course which gave me some relief but the leg was not strong enough to take my running weight. I was faced with another 19 mile walk. Once again, not long after starting, my shins started to make themselves known. By mile 10, I was in a similar amount of discomfort as in*

Killarney National Park; every step was sore. But I had good company; my brother Barry, Willie Burns, my mum, my father, Kevin Whelan and the Bates family whom we had last seen in Waterford, all came out to join me once they heard that I was in need of company.

Once again my sister Alaine had driven down to visit. This time Adam, my four year old nephew, joined her. Alaine had driven out to the course and pulled into a car park up ahead and waited for me. As I approached Adam ran to me and taking my hand, asked me to run along with him, but I couldn't. I could see that he was a little confused; here I was in runners and shorts, looking the part, but I wasn't able to run. So he grabbed my brother's hand and went for a run with him instead. His energy and innocence cheered us all up no end. I was told later that Alaine almost didn't come out to the course, upset as she was, knowing that I was in pain. But I was glad she did.

Earlier that morning, the entire square in the centre of this beautiful midlands town was filled with people. It was obvious they had taken this event to their hearts. A huge crowd greeted us, motivated to be there for sporting reasons, autism reasons and because Willie Burns, a close friend had told them to be there. Willie pledged his support eight months earlier; his only request was that we would have it in his home town.

"I'll have the place rocking," he had promised us, and boy did he do just that.

We had looked forward especially to this day as two of our crew, Niall and Freddie, were from this neck of the woods and the glint in both of their eyes over breakfast boasted proud Offaly roots. A turnout of almost 80 runners, joggers and walkers truly amazed both Ken and I. We had to call in additional assistance at registration to ensure we started on time.

One of the many highlights of this leg included a massive relay run involving the young footballers from Rhode GAA. Under the supervision of Niall Murphy they had fundraised a huge sum for our cause and we were immensely grateful. Also there was Martin Kelly one of only eight people to have completed all 30 Dublin City

Marathons and Dave Kavanagh, the former Offaly and Kildare GAA star, who ran the second half of the race with yours truly. Both Ken and I were stunned to see an army sergeant called Mick Devanney running too. Nothing unusual in that until I tell you he ran a full marathon in 5:04 carrying a full 'army chess rig' weighing 20lbs around his shoulders.

At the start we had Michael Duignan and Brian Whelahan, two former Offaly hurling giants, we had Charlie Swan back yet again to cheer us on and we had Pauline Curley who had represented Ireland in the marathon in the 2008 Beijing Olympics.

Long after myself and the other runners had finished, Ken was still out on the course. It would be close to 7pm before he would finish taking into account time he had to have physio administered. We had started a little after 10:30am.

KEN: *The last mile of the day was the toughest mile of the whole month. I had been on my feet for almost eight hours. I was tired, hungry and sore. My shins ached with each and every step. The pain was relentless and constant.*

I remember thinking with a mere 500 metres to go, that I wasn't going to make it. I just wanted to stop. I tried to hide the pain from my parents who were walking slowly beside me but they caught the grimace on my face. Coming into the town square we walked past the pub where many of the runners from earlier in the day had gathered for a barbeque and pints – it sounded great craic and it smelt good. But I walked on, finishing to a quiet but welcome round of applause. I was delighted to have that day over.

By 8pm we were ringing Noeleen yet again. This time we asked her to drive not 'south', but 'west'.

DAY 16
GALWAY

SATURDAY 17 JULY
445.4 miles (716.6 km) to go

Galway City
Gerry   4 hours 37 minutes
Ken   5 hours 40 minutes

WITH about six miles to go in Galway, it was like someone ran a knife just fractionally beneath the skin on my left shin bone. I leapt from the road onto the footpath when I felt the presence of the razor-like pain which continued for the final seven miles. Given Ken's travails, I was paranoid about injury and so I sweated with worry until Noeleen could take a look. She diagnosed muscle soreness, nothing more and so I ate my dinner with my mind at ease.

After the day Ken had just endured and the late night physio Noeleen had administered, he had gone to bed on the eve of the Galway marathon absolutely shattered. Although he always woke up ready to tackle another day, this morning for the first time he was worried as soon as his right foot hit the ground. He still had pain from our day in Offaly and even walking to the restaurant for breakfast caused him discomfort. Noeleen had him on the plinth by 8am and although her work helped loosen the shin and ankle a little, he still wasn't happy as we drove to the start line in Galway City.

His spirits were lifted slightly by the good number of people who had come to run/jog/walk with us. Several more friends had driven from Mullingar to join us. Unfortunately he had to miss another race briefing as he was getting his ankle strapped - this was one morning he didn't mind missing it - he needed to focus on just getting to the start line.

He started off tentatively, at the back of the group. Each step of the first quarter mile or so was sore and worrisome. He would later tell me that during the first few minutes it was the first and only time during the whole challenge when he would question what he was trying to do, running a marathon when it was sore just to walk. Thankfully though and somewhat miraculously, the pain in his ankle seemed to dissolve from about the half mile point. From there on the run became almost... enjoyable.

I had gone on ahead and was flanked by a great group of friends and fellow-runners. Declan Mulderry was taking on the 13.1 mile distance for the first time whilst Deirdre Fallon was also successfully making her debut at the same distance. Further back Ken had the company of Double Ironman crew member, Enda Munnelly. We all knew Enda didn't enjoy running but he committed himself to run a full marathon with Ken. Many of the later miles went by with few words spoken between the two. Getting to the latter part of a marathon the mind becomes very focused on one thing - getting home using the least amount of energy.

Ken was thrilled to say that 5hrs and 40mins after Enda and he set off, they crossed the line together, both with big smiles and Ken holding the hands of his niece Caoimhe and nephew Adam, by now another team mascot.

I had finished a little over an hour ahead in a time of 4:37, fortunately with no injury to dwell on. Just behind me was another crew member from my Double Ironman in 2009, Jarlath Mahon, who finished his first ever marathon.

At the finish line, my sister Katherine asked me to introduce myself to an elderly man who had waited patiently for two hours to meet us. "Hi," I said, "My name is Gerry Duffy. You wanted to see me?"

The man before me was quite elderly.

"Hello, young fella," he said. "I have a few bob for you. It's not much but I did my best. I heard about ye on the radio and I rang the charity for a sponsorship card. Here it is, I wish it was more."

With that, he turned and left.

I examined the card and its contents. Every line was full and each displayed a different handwriting. Every name had a euro or more beside it, a total of just over €20 at the bottom.

Suddenly I realised the magnitude of what I was reading. On reflection, it would prove to be one of the most uplifting moments of our journey. This man was perhaps 80 years old. What's more, he didn't even know us. How much effort must it have taken for him to gather his contribution?

Over 20 people had been approached for donations. That was at least 20 times he had to explain what it was he was collecting for. I watched him disappear from view, in humbled and stunned silence.

By now we had 16 marathons done. Sixteen still to go. You will recall my comments after marathon number 13 in Laois.

"A strange thing was starting to happen. I got stronger not weaker on this run."

It may be hard to comprehend, but I really was enjoying every marathon. I found my body had long since adapted to the challenge of running 26.2 miles every day. Yes, there were a few days when my mind was elsewhere and finishing was a challenge in itself. Wexford was a case in point. I guess you would not be human if this did not happen at some stage.

Nonetheless, by July 17th and the half-way mark in Galway, I really felt I was getting stronger. Unlike my companion, I was fortunate to have had only a few minor niggles to deal with. Noeleen and the other chartered physios were quickly able to remedy these.

In the weeks leading into the start we had spoken at length that the only thing we could not control were injuries. Ken did have some major injuries but these were just that, injuries. They did not take from his ability to complete the challenge. He was every bit as fit physically and mentally as I, only his challenges were even greater.

DAY 17
MAYO

SUNDAY 18 JULY
419.2 miles (674.63 km) to go

Ballina
Gerry   4 hours 23 minutes
Ken   4 hours 50 minutes

A FACEBOOK message that night read: "Every step now is a step towards home." It was a very positive message that we would recall many times over the following days. We were now at the half-way point.

Every day when we got into the car, Jacinta and I would reflect on the day's events. We thought this unique experience could not continue being as good as it was proving to be. We were wrong because it did, and Mayo was no exception. The River Moy just outside Ballina provided a perfect backdrop for marathon number 17.

It was a two-loop circuit of 13.1 miles on a flat but very attractive course. Ken's injuries continued to heal, thanks to some more brilliant work from Noeleen. The twinge in my shin resurfaced again after an hour, or about six miles into the run and it stayed for the remainder. I was concerned. After I finished, Noeleen had me in some discomfort on the plinth but no pain without gain. She predicted an easier passage for me the following day.

I managed to cross the line in 4:23, all of which was spent in the company of Johnny Donnelly, former drummer with the famous Irish group, the Sawdoctors. Johnny had his own marathon challenge on the go where he was endeavouring to run 60 marathons in as many months, a very long and arduous challenge for which he deserves huge acknowledgement. To compound the difficulty he faced, he was running his marathons all over the world. Raising funds and awareness for micro credit projects in the world's poorest regions is the cause he was championing and his fundraising had already exceeded his original target; a true testament to his efforts.

Two veterinary surgeons who never met each other before ran side by side in Mayo. One of them was my brother-in-law, Enda Finnerty, who was running his first ever marathon. As I mentioned in the narration of the Limerick marathon, his younger brother Cormac had represented Ireland in the 5,000m in the Olympic Games in Atlanta back in 1996. The other vet was Tom Horkan, a local man who was running his 32nd marathon and his sixth marathon in just six months. What made it all the more inspiring is that Tom was 70 years of age.

Another debutant led the field home. A former footballer of some prowess, Aidan Gorry had only taken up running relatively recently. In Mayo he crossed the line in 3:42 with his wife Eileen and his three daughters Nicole, Sarah and Lauren proudly watching. This was the first of two marathons he would run 'that week'. At any other time to say you would run two marathons in a week would be hard to comprehend. In the context of this event though, it was becoming 'quite normal'.

The Race HQ for the day was Ballina Rugby Club and a huge number of locals turned up to help. If Ken had finished a few minutes earlier he could have enjoyed a delicious array of refreshments for all the runners and their supporters; it was a day where community spirit and friendship came out in bucketfuls.

A far bigger sporting occasion than ours was held in Mayo on this day. Roscommon were crowned Connacht football champions an hour after Ken and I crossed the line. A friend, Colm Connaughton, was at the game having earlier fulfilled a promise made to us by running a half-marathon in our company.

A final word about our hosts, Mary Horkan as well as Liz and Alan Murphy. They are the organisers of the River Moy half-marathon which is held each May. They plotted the route, they brought marshals, water tables and they also made everyone welcome in their pub and restaurant 'Crocketts on the Quay' just outside Ballina. The pub's beautiful interior was surpassed only by its culinary delights that fed our crew royally.

DAY 18

ROSCOMMON

Boyle

Gerry	4 hours 11 minutes
Ken	4 hours 44 minutes

FOR some strange reason I can remember a lot of it in minute detail.

We had left our house at about 5am. It was a Saturday, I think, in 1979. My brother Tom who was 17 had left with some friends two hours before, eager to get the best view. Into the yellow car, an old Fiat Mirafiori, we climbed. There was my mum and my dad, my sister Mary and me an 11-year-old kid, still a year off boarding school. Katherine, my six-year-old sister and Dorothy who was just four, were left behind with our neighbours, the Johnsons. They were too young to come with us. It was going to be a long day.

We had to park in Lucan or Leixlip I think, on the outskirts of Dublin, and from there we were herded like sheep onto a fleet of waiting buses. As we arrived, a giant roar bellowed from the skies. We looked skyward and directly over our heads, we saw a massive jet plane with the familiar Aer Lingus shamrock logo emblazoned on it. It was beginning its descent into Dublin airport. We still have footage on my dad's old video camera of the jet as it came into view. Our interest was just minutes away from touching down on Irish soil and Ireland was very excited.

As we climbed the hill, the panorama that was about to unfold was still hidden from view but our excitement was overwhelming. As the vast expanse became visible, the hairs on my young arms stood aloft. It was a mesmerising sight. There, in front of me were hundreds of thousands of people. This is not some 11-year-old's imaginary folly. This was fact. There were over a million people in there. I know by now you have guessed where we were? It was September 29th, 1979. The occasion? A Mass. Pope John Paul II was celebrating it. We were in the Phoenix Park, Dublin.

If our distance from the stage was anything to go by, we had left it late. Such was the expanse, binoculars were required. I recall we had a sticker handed to us as we went in, with a corral number on it. I was envious of my brother later that night. His sticker read 42 which meant he was up much closer than we were. I recall that this meant he was just 42 rows from the front. We might have been 1,042, I'm not sure. All I know is, it took hours for the main man to drive within metres of us. He was travelling in a bullet-proof vehicle specially built for the occasion.

Ken Whitelaw would be born just two months later.

1979 was also the last time my family had holidayed in Lough Key Forest Park in Co Roscommon. Thirty-one years later, Monday 19th July 2010, my family were back in Lough Key again. We had picnicked and holidayed there as children and it was for this reason that I chose it as the location for our Roscommon marathon, our 18th day on the road. This occasion rekindled wonderful childhood memories for me.

KEN: *It was an earlier start for us this morning as we had to travel about half an hour to the course. Before leaving the hotel, Gerry and I took a call from the Newstalk 'Breakfast Show' to give Ivan and Claire an update. The only problem was that we had almost no reception on our mobiles where we were staying. I was thinking of walking around the hotel to pick up a signal but about five minutes before we were due to go on air, the heavens opened and it started to pour down so I phoned* the station from reception. I hadn't seen Gerry all morning, and I couldn't get in touch with him, so I thought I'd have to do the interview on my own.

When we went live, Ivan said hello to both of us. I was just about to correct him when I heard Gerry's voice on the other line. Gerry told us that he was standing under a tree outside in the spills of rain as it was the only place he could pick up any signal on his phone. It took all my strength not to laugh when I looked out the window and saw the poor fellow getting soaked!

Our route was around the grounds of Lough Key Forest Park. Gerry and I both love running on woodland trails and they don't come much better than the trails around the lake and parkland here. Not only were we distracted by the superb scenery around the lake and the great company of fellow runners, but on top of all that the route was flat, a welcome respite for my legs.

We were delighted to be joined by so many familiar faces from home: Brigie McCabe, Breda Daly, Michelle O'Halloran, Nuala Daly, Wendy O'Leary, Eimear Foley, Martina Kennedy, Liam McGlynn, Mick Duggan and Enda Mimnagh, all members of Midland Triathlon Club. Their support really gave us a boost. A special mention also to Terry Greene who ran a full marathon with us - her first one in 14 years and to a friend of Gerry's, James Martin, who came to run one lap of four and ended up running, much to his own surprise, a half-marathon.

James later posted on Facebook: "I just got caught up in the occasion. This event does that to you. It's infectious. In fact I will be back for one more before ye finish."

A big thanks to three people; Louise Scullion, the manager of Lough Key Forest Park, Vinnie Glennon who had quietly co-ordinated activities in advance of race day and Finbarr Feeley who was up at 5am marking out the route for us. Not only that but he joined me for the last 13 miles.

Gerry ran a 4:11, his fastest time to date. He puts this down to a combination of the terrain, his body getting stronger and the fact that he has been fortunate enough to remain injury-free.

I ran a 4:44, six minutes faster than the previous day, so I am heading in the right direction. Like Gerry, I can finally feel that my legs *are beginning to become accustomed to the daily task of running 26.2 miles. My ankles could be stronger but compared to the last 10 days or so, I'm feeling great. I have noticed that I'm beginning to run on my toes more, rather than my normal heel strike, but this is to take a bit of weight off my ankles.*

We finished off the day with a dip in the lake to cool down followed by a nutritious feast put together by a nutrition friend of ours, Andy Smith. All in all, a great day.

DAY 19
SLIGO

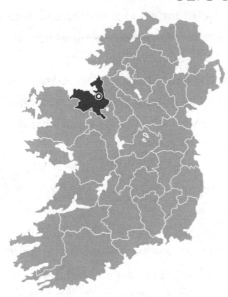

TUESDAY 20 JULY
366.8 miles (590.3 km) to go

Ballygawley
Gerry   4 hours 9 minutes
Ken   4 hours 26 minutes

THIS event was certainly getting noticed. I woke up this morning to see our event splashed all over the *Irish Independent*. Word was spreading and the fact that we were now in Ireland's largest selling daily newspaper meant that more and more people were becoming aware of our challenge. There is a well-known song in this part of Ireland called 'The Hills of Donegal'. Well the hills arrived a day early in Sligo. Ballygawley, south-east Sligo to be precise. Starting at the main entrance to the Castle Dargan Estate this course would prove to be very challenging to the 30 or more runners who participated.

It had us constantly running a number of very strenuous climbs with very little relief on the reverse side as our quad and calf muscles balanced our frames. A route change at the last minute was necessary as the course we had previously planned would, on inspection, have required us to have oxygen on standby because it was so challenging.

We noticed a pattern developing in recent days. More and more people were signing up late or in some cases just arriving on the morning of the marathon. We were grateful to have their companionship and their funds to give to the charities. It was a win-win all round.

At the start line were some very enthusiastic friends, some old, some new, such as Conor Flanagan who was running his third marathon with us in just eight days and Andy Hamilton who sat on my shoulder for the duration. Also present were Garret Murphy from Mullingar as well as Malcolm Craig and Pat O'Hara (from the 31 miler back in April).

Pat had gone on ahead of us in the early miles but waited at the final mile marker for us to join him on the run in. I think he was slowing down myself and taking a breather but he says it was in the interest of a good finishing photo opportunity. Hmmm!

Once again in my diary I commented about just how strong I was starting to feel. Over the previous few days my times were edging ever closer towards the four hour mark.

As I chatted to people at the finish line, Freddie Grehan turned to get my attention. "Look," he said pointing behind me. He was laughing. I turned and there panned out on the grass gasping for breath were my three running companions from the marathon. The final 200 metres to the finish had a sizeable hill to be negotiated. It knocked the stuffing out of them. I went over and ribbed the boys about their lack of fitness, all in good humour of course.

Immensely grateful to have remained pretty much injury free for the last 19 days, my strength was noticeably increasing, as we made our way through each day's exam paper. This was definitely the hardest course to date and the hills were genuinely very tough. Still, both Ken and I recorded our best times by some margin, his in the last two weeks and mine of the entire 19 marathons. For the record, Ken finished in 4:26. I was only just ahead of him and was still doing some post race stretches when he finished. My time was 4:09, two minutes quicker than my previous best effort.

A special mention to the amazing Marie Barrett, a mammoth fundraiser, joint route co-ordinator for our Dublin marathon and this marvel of a lady ran a full marathon step by step with Ken, despite signing up and training for only a half. Also a mention to the entire Murphy family of eight, who stood on the side of the road in the rain cheering Ken and I and proudly holding aloft the posters they had made for us earlier that morning.

As we neared the finish line with about a mile to go, I was joined by a son of the aforementioned Murphy's. His name was James and he was 12 years old. Over that last nine minutes or so, James and I chatted continuously about sport. When we crossed the line, Freddie had the foresight to present him with a souvenir, a 32 Marathon Medal. James was thrilled. An hour or so later, after I was finished with physio and having served my penance in the ice bath, I was walking out the front door of the hotel when I met James.

"Sorry Gerry, can I ask you something?

"Sure," I replied.

He took out something from his pocket. It was wrapped in plastic and was still unopened.

"I got this medal, but I would like you to present it to me."

Wow! That was a moment I would remember long after the challenge was completed.

Another milestone tomorrow as we head for number 20.

NUTRITION (ANOTHER SERVING OF...)

Earlier in this section of the book, I spoke about the nutrition we consumed prior to and during each marathon. The following is what happened after each marathon was completed.

FINISH LINE - A SMOOTHIE

An absolutely crucial time where we had a 20-minute window to consume a nutritious c.1000ml portion involving a 'super smoothie'. Barry stressed the importance of a replenishing protein shake which we would need to consume literally at the finish line. This he said would allow our bodies to immediately start rebuilding the muscles ahead of the next day's marathon.

Typically the ingredients consisted of a table spoonful of a natural whey protein mixed with honey, sea salt and various fresh fruits which we chopped and changed regularly. Usually the fruits were drawn from the following list - bananas, pineapples, blackberries, blueberries, apples, and kiwis. In addition another vital ingredient was a knuckle size portion of ginger to add some bite to the concoction and to aid muscle recovery. Early in the challenge I mixed in some natural yogurt, but I didn't find it that agreeable so after four or five days I removed it from the list.

BARRY: *Arguably the most important part of exercise is what you do afterwards. The recovery process is where all the training adaptations take place which improve fitness and ultimately performance. It is also the stage where the body is 'switched on' to intake food in order to refuel and repair. Sports Scientists and Nutritionists talk about this '15-20 min window.' In general, the sooner the better. Two things are required.*

1. Simple Carbohydrates to refuel muscle glycogen stores.
2. Easily Digestible Protein to repair muscle tissue and aid physiological adaptations.

In this instance, it is important that the carbohydrate source is a fast releasing sugar. Fruits contain easily digestible sugars as well as helpful vitamins, minerals and antioxidants. Fruits are also alkaline in nature and therefore help neutralise the acidic environment caused by exercise. The protein used was Whey protein which is a by-product of cheese production.

It contains all the essential amino acids and has a high biological value (which means the amino acids are absorbed well). Ken and Gerry were provided with reference sheets that outlined the required quantities of these foods that would supply the necessary carbohydrates and protein. This ensured that they optimised their recovery after each marathon.

For this meal Jacinta and Celine would prepare a variety of ingredients to make this smoothie as nutritious and as consumable as possible for Ken and I. Both of us looked forward to it each day as much as we would an ice-cream. It was delicious.

JUICE

Each day we ate two dinners. Just before the first of these however, we drank a juice consisting of some or all of the following: Beetroot, carrots, spinach, broccoli, apples, flavoured with lemon juice.

> **BARRY:** *Fruits and vegetables are alkalising and help control the pH of the blood. Most other foods that are commonly consumed such as grains, meat, fish are acidic. In addition, strenuous exercise caused production of acid so therefore the control of the pH balance of an athlete is vital. A low blood pH (high acid) is known to cause calcium loss and muscle degradation. Increasing the alkalinity of the blood helps to prevent this. Hence, Ken and Gerry ensured that in addition to their regular fruit/vegetable consumption with their main meals, they had a further supply of alkalising foods in the form of a homemade juice.*

POST-RACE DINNERS

Barry had prepared a pre-event strategy that would involve us consuming not one but two dinners each day. In principle this involved one meal predominately apportioned with protein followed later each evening by a meal mostly consisting of carbohydrates.

A typical meal would involve fish (usually salmon or sea bass) with potatoes (regular and/or sweet) as well as a multitude of vegetables, with a preference for greens where possible. We also had chicken regularly because it was packed full of protein ensuring the muscles were rebuilding immediately after each marathon and ahead of the next day.

We had a 90-minute window after the finish line smoothie in which to eat a larger meal but given that we were in a different location every day, this was not as simple as might first appear. Our first meal was normally eaten around 4pm or thereabouts. Once we had that finished we usually loaded up the cars and camper and headed to our next port of call. By 8pm or 9pm most nights we were busy looking for somewhere else to eat when we would repeat the process all over again.

BARRY: *The smoothie Ken and Gerry consumed after each marathon was step one of their daily recovery process. The next was their meal. As mentioned earlier, the post exercise stage is when the body is best able to uptake and absorb nutrients. Although this is at its highest level in the immediate window after the finish, it still functions well in the couple of hours post exercise and tapers as the day progresses. I advised Ken and Gerry to eat their biggest solid feed of the day in this period.*

Simple carbohydrates are the preferred choice as they are quickly converted to glucose. The glucose is then transported to the muscle and converted to glycogen where it is stored and ready, waiting to be used the next day. Lean proteins were also included in the meal to provide amino acids and vegetables, in particular green vegetables, were recommended due to their alkalising affect. These two feeds for Ken and Gerry, the liquid smoothie and solid meal, consumed in the post-exercise window of 0-90mins, ensured that they had optimal recovery and were well fuelled to complete such an enduring event.

On our journey to Donegal we stopped off in a lovely restaurant called the Yeats Tavern, just north of Sligo. When we went to pay, the meal had already been taken care of by the generous Adrian Murphy, James's dad. They were also in the restaurant and had spotted us dining there too.

DAY 20
DONEGAL

WEDNESDAY 21 JULY
340.6 miles (548.14 km) to go

Ballybofey
Gerry   4 hours 3 minutes
Ken   4 hours 3 minutes

"THE ice bath is in here," smirked Mark Connolly. "Let's see how tough you midland boys are." We were in Finn Valley Athletic club, the home of athletics in this part of Ireland. I climbed into the tub immediately, by now well accustomed to such temperatures. As I did, Mark threw in yet another large bag of ice. His smile widened.

"I'll give you three minutes tops," he said. He was right. I was out in two. It was mind-numbingly cold.

Twenty minutes earlier we had finished our run. As already mentioned, a huge proportion of runners who joined us were debutants. For most they were there to support the charities we had chosen. For some it may have been the uniqueness of the event or maybe it was the fact that many of the counties were seeing marathons events for the first time. Many had a direct or an indirect link to Ken and I. That is why Nigel Hogan as well as Freddie and Paula Murray appeared. They were all friends from home who were holidaying close by.

In Donegal, on the wettest day of the 32, two of Ken's aunts also braved the conditions and completed half-marathons. It was absurdly wet. The start line was 200 metres from race headquarters and even before we reached it, we were soaked. We had been very fortunate up to then, but Donegal was pay-back time.

Our race HQ was also the headquarters of Finn Valley Athletic Club located on the outskirts of Ballybofey. The manager of the Irish senior athletics team, Patsy McGonagle was our contact in Donegal. He was abroad on athletics duties, but before leaving he had prepared a nice flat route. Mark Connolly, a talented runner from these parts was our guide. We were also very grateful to the 15 or so local volunteers who waited for hours to marshal traffic and hand out water and bananas to the runners who braved the elements. One of that day's runners was an American lady living in Donegal who had spotted our challenge on the internet and had not only signed up, she had also posted regular messages of support on Facebook. Her name was Jessica LaTendresse.

By now I had become used to running without Ken by my side. The last time we had done so was almost two weeks previously. That was in Waterford on Day-7. He had borne his injuries with great courage and patience, his only objective being to finish each day. I was at pains to tell people that his getting injured was the luck of the draw. It could just as easily have been me. Ken was a super athlete, much faster than I, and I knew deep down he really would love to have been running beside me.

At mile five I got a shock. It came in the form of a hand resting on my left shoulder. The noise of the traffic and the pounding rain had disguised the approach. I had presumed that Ken would be slower than I, but I was wrong.

KEN: *As I neared Gerry, I tapped him on the shoulder. He got a great surprise and we were both thrilled that we were once again running shoulder to shoulder. Given the size of this challenge and the mental focus needed to get through it all, I have rarely let myself get either too low or too excited over the last three weeks. This control disappeared momentarily though once I caught up with Gerry. I was genuinely thrilled to be running alongside him again.*

There were three more people as happy as me to see him back at my side. Ken himself, his dad and his mum. Celine smiled all day long when she heard we were running together.

Ironically at mile 15, I was the one struggling to keep up. Niall Murphy, our crew member, had joined us for the second loop and had a strong pace going. I think he wanted to get out of the rain! I was really working to stay with Niall and Ken and did not fancy being left alone. For a mile or so, I had to dig deep to stay within touching distance of the lads. Despite the inclement conditions, with three miles to go we were at sub 4 hour pace. We decided to back off a little and cruise home through the last few miles, finishing in 4:03. Another day filled with great memories.

LOGISTICS

In many ways each day was like Groundhog Day. Long before Ken and I opened our eyes each morning, our team were busy preparing the logistics of the day ahead. Every day we had different people running with us. This all required a massive amount of organisation.

At seven am each morning Brendan, Freddie, Joe, Pat and Niall would meet and begin the assembly of the start/finish line gantry and position the mile markers and directional arrows out on the course. We were mindful of not putting out the markers the night before as we had been advised that they might disappear. The one night we took a chance... they did. Thankfully a second set was in the van as back-up.

The evening before each run, Niall, Freddie and Brendan would drive over the course to give it the green light. Niall and Brendan were seasoned runners so they observed each course from two perspectives - a runner's eye and a safety eye.

On four occasions we had to make last minute changes. We favoured multiple loop courses which at first glance might not seem advisable. Anyone who ran with us agreed that it worked very well. Two, four or six loops was the order every day. It made so much sense from a logistical point of view and it ensured that no one was ever left in isolation.

Registration usually began at 8.30 am. Each day was an amazing sight for Ken and I as we appeared usually around nine or so to meet and greet the wonderful people who made the effort to come and support us. We looked forward to this part of every day. Until now many of these people were names on spreadsheets that we had reviewed at weekly meetings over the previous six months. To meet everyone finally was great.

By 9.30am volunteer marshals were briefed on our route and by 9.45am, they would leave to take up their positions. At approximately 9.50am, Ken and I officially welcomed everyone and acknowledged our gratitude to the local route co-ordinator, the local volunteers, the local sponsors where appropriate and importantly those people who were there to run with us.

By 10am each morning we were almost ready for off. Mervyn Rundle was in charge of ensuring that all time commitments were met each day. A man who adhered to scheduling with military precision he was always tipping his watch as 10am approached. The reality was that such was the huge crowd of well-wishers every morning, we almost never started on time. The only day of the 32 that Mervyn was absent we made an extra effort to start at ten. Pat Whaley rang him at 9.58 so that he could hear the starter's whistle. We all got pleasure out of that early start and we didn't let him forget it. The one day he was absent we had started 'early'.

DAY 21
DERRY

THURSDAY 22 JULY
314.4 miles (505.55 km) to go

Derry
Gerry	4 hours 39 minutes
Ken	4 hours 39 minutes

ANTHONY TOHILL blew the starters whistle at 10:13am on a very sunny Thursday morning. A giant of a man, Tohill won an All Ireland football medal with Derry in 1993. He seemed genuinely in awe of what Ken and I were doing and such was his interest, he returned later to see us finish.

Maybe it was inevitable after three successively faster runs that I would have a tough day at the office in Derry. I found the last nine miles very hard. Ken was a little stronger than I was but was still feeling the pain for the last two miles of the 26.2.

The day had started beautifully. We had set up adjacent to the river Foyle, nestled in between the Waterside and the Bogside of Derry. This city and its surrounding walls date back to the late 17th century and looked resplendent in the late July sun. It felt hot which was not ideal for marathon running.

Both UTV and Downtown Radio had heard we were in town and requested interviews before the start. For the first half of the run both Ken and I enjoyed the company of Fiona McCann, a lady originally from Derry but now living in Donegal. We left Fiona at the half way mark as she crossed the line of her first ever race, a great moment not just for her but for her entire family as they all gathered, flowers in hand to celebrate her success.

Onwards we soldiered for the second half but I soon felt some aching in the lower part of my legs. Perhaps it was the six loops, but that would be the mental side of this challenge. It could have been the three fast runs of previous days catching up on me. Each mile felt like five but finally the GPS watch climbed into the twenties. I found every mile a chore where I had to grind myself mentally to put one foot in front of the other. It was hot and the surface was all concrete and tar. I was having my hardest day by far. I always knew I would finish but it was very hard. I had to revert to the '2.30pm hypnotist technique' where I would remind myself that no matter what happened, 2.30pm would eventually arrive and I would be close to finishing. I also reminded myself of the words of the old man I had met at Foster Avenue in the Dublin City Marathon.

"Just put one foot in front of the other and you will reach the finish."

The sight of my nephews Andrew and Mark and my niece Lucy who were there yet again to cheer us on, helped me through this tough day as well. Another example of wonderful support came from Olivia Munnelly, Enda's sister. The charity needed something delivered from Mullingar and Olivia kindly volunteered for what would be an eight hour return car journey.

With six miles to go, Ken and I were joined by Jessica, the same American lady who had ran with us in Donegal the previous day. She had heard on the radio that we had only one runner in our company in Derry, so she drove across the border, put on her running shoes and kept us company for the last ten kilometres or so. A lovely gesture.

As we climbed towards 24 miles Ken had to stop momentarily to stretch out his right ankle. As I watched him and the painful expression on his face, I forgot my own minor issues and gave myself a talking to. How insignificant was my pain compared to what my running companion had endured for too long.

Finally the finish line was in sight and we crossed it together in 4:39, both very relieved to have marathon number 21 behind us.

I mentioned earlier in the story that we had sought local expertise for our six marathons in the North. That came in the form of Colin Telford, Johnny Davis and Carly Ferguson.

Colin was a former professional footballer. On his 14th birthday, the 14th January 1988, he had signed for Manchester United no less. Manchester City and Rangers had also expressed an interest but he chose the 'Red Devils'.

Over the following three years or so Colin travelled back and forth from his home rising through the ranks of the underage United teams. By 16, he was living full-time in Manchester and had graduated to the reserves but a bad injury meant he would only manage 10 games in two years, thus scuppering his early career. One day Alex Ferguson called him into his office and suggested that given the fact that he had not gained much match experience because of his injury, he might want to consider moving back a step and move to another club. Colin took Ferguson's advice and joined a Scottish club, Raith Rovers. The year was 1991.

Johnny Davis also had a highly impressive sporting CV. He was a two-time fencing olympian having represented Great Britain in Los Angeles in 1984 and again four years later in Seoul. Carly Ferguson co-ordinated our logistics and the runners for the six counties. Her warm personality and hard work late into each evening ensured our stay in Northern Ireland went like clockwork.

Earlier in the year when planning the logistics of the event, Colin had recommended that we offer runners in Northern Ireland a 'relay' option. It had worked exceptionally well in the Belfast Marathon and Colin felt it would work for us. In addition, he felt that if we gave people the option to fundraise for a second charity of their choice it would boost numbers considerably. We listened to his advice and it worked.

Colin had organised the Derry relay on the same routing as we had run earlier in the day. The relay event took place in the evening when over 120 runners left their workplaces and headed to the start line.

Awareness of the 32 Marathon Challenge for autism and for cancer was by now increasing steadily and as a result people were still registering to run with us. When we started three weeks before, 28 people had registered for our penultimate run in Leitrim and 108 for the final marathon in our home county of Westmeath. Freddie told us the up-to-date figures were that Leitrim now had 58 and our final run in Mullingar had 145 now signed up. Much more to look forward to over the final 11 marathons.

Later that evening, I received a text from Anthony Tohill.

"What you two are doing is amazing. I wish I could have run with ye. Keep her lit."

DAY 22
TYRONE

FRIDAY 23 JULY
288.2 miles (463.81 km) to go

Newtownstewart
Gerry   4 hours 1 minute
Ken   4 hours 21 minutes

KEN and I have been fortunate to have run in some memorable locations over the years: our route in Tyrone was in the really special category. For this we must thank Lord Abercorne who gave us permission to run within Baronscourt Estate, a stunning setting just outside Newtownstewart. It offered a magical wonderland full of neverending trails. It will live long in my memory.

After the gruelling effort of the previous day, both Ken and I started off nervously, unsure how our bodies would adapt to the 22nd consecutive day of running this distance. For the first five miles we were joined by one of Tyrone's much loved and best known sons, Peter Canavan. It was obvious by observing how our local runners enjoyed running with this man just how high in esteem this two-time All Ireland football winner is held. He was scarcely out of breath as we bade farewell to him at the six-mile mark.

I ran a 2:05 for the first 13 miles, steady but not too fast. I felt really comfortable. The first half was run in the company of Johnny Davis, our new crew member. Johnny had just turned 50 but looked 10 years younger. He and I enjoyed a discussion about sport and we threw ideas back and forth of other challenges that could be taken on.

At the half way point I actually got a great surge of energy and had to really hold myself back when I noticed I had increased the pace to 7.30 minute miles. This was over 90 seconds faster per mile than my regular pace. On that third loop I found myself alone for a period of about four miles. I ran four consecutive miles at that pace. It was taking nothing out of me. In fact I felt I could have run each mile in six minutes or less.

The run had one long drag on each loop, nearly a mile in distance, but the stunning countryside kept me engaged throughout. Eventually I crossed the line in 4:01, my quickest of all the marathons. I ran the final miles with Gloria Donaghey, a member of Finn Valley Athletic Club in Donegal, the HQ for our run just a few days earlier.

Ever mindful of his previous problems, Ken decided to conserve his energy as he edged towards full fitness. He was confident he was making significant strides in that direction and felt that he had plenty left in the tank. One short physio stop to stretch out his ankle and he was soon on the move again, crossing the line in 4:21.

A special mention to quite a few. Firstly to Adrian Murphy, a Tyrone man living in Mullingar who realised five miles into his half marathon that he went to school with Martin O'Neill, the guy running beside him. Also to Teresa McGinn, our Kilkenny physio who hails from here. Despite their age, her sons Jack and Liam and their cousin Michael ran over six miles with Ken. Great lads who proudly displayed their Kilkenny roots by way of their county jerseys. Also to the O'Brien family from Mullingar who arrived unannounced to offer us their support. Finally to Sean McGlinchey and Daphne Scott who walked 13.1 miles and were before they left, proudly displaying their 32 Marathon Challenge Medals.

In my diary that evening, my comments were: "Twenty-six miles now seems like the norm. It takes little out of me, the equivalent mentally of running about five miles. We are so focused on our goal and never have a problem getting psyched up. I feel monumentally strong."

I am amazed to hear my voice from the audio diary I kept from this time. It floods my mind with great memories of what my body was going through. "I live for moments like this," I told Gloria about a mile-and-a-half from the finish. I was on a high. She did not have to reply. Her smile said it all. We were both thoroughly enjoying that pure feeling that running can give you.

My third lap had offered me a clear mind and a sense of physical sharpness where I felt I could have run any single mile as fast as I wished. But I knew I had to respect the challenge and the bigger picture.

This was about so much more than Ken and I accomplishing our goal of completing 32 consecutive marathons. Awareness of autism, fundraising and facilitating another 400 people still to realise their goal of 2010 by running a half or a full marathon continued to be our primary objectives. If we were to fully succeed, all boxes would have to be ticked.

An inspiring day in an equally inspiring location.

DAY 23

ANTRIM

SATURDAY 24 JULY
262 miles (421.64 km) to go

Belfast
Gerry   4 hours 9 minutes
Ken   4 hours 26 minutes

IN the early 90s I was a fan of the Gerry Kelly UTV television show on Friday nights. He delivered a mix of diverse and interesting personalities. Little did I imagine that one day he would be interviewing me. He had rung as was pre-arranged on mile 19 of the run, when we were somewhere on a tow path between Belfast and Lisburn. He now hosts a BBC radio show on Saturdays and the interview would be done alone as my running partner was two miles behind me and had 'forgotten' to bring his phone.

I finished off the five minute interview by telling Gerry that we had been fortunate to meet one of Northern Ireland's most famous sports stars earlier that day, Dame Mary Peters.

The former Olympic gold medallist in the pentathlon from the 1972 Munich Games, was so humble about her own achievements when Ken and I met her. She was a close friend of Johnny Davis and readily agreed to start our Antrim marathon.

As we spoke to her and an audience of about 60 people, I made a comment saying how honoured we were to meet her.

She interrupted: "You're honoured to meet me?" "I am honoured to meet both of you."

What's more, she really meant it.

My diary reminded me that I woke up "a little tired and feeling a small bit lethargic" that Saturday morning. The banks of the River Lagan in Shaw's Bridge provided us with a nice flat route. We were chuffed to be joined by so many runners, especially those who were taking on the distance for the first time.

A particular mention to our crew member Colin Telford and Lisa Barwise – it was great to see the delight on their faces crossing the line after 26.2 miles. Our Antrim leg was Colin's debut marathon. He told us that running a marathon had been an ambition of his for years but he had never had the motivation to train. We were delighted that he had found his inspiration by been a part of our event. He was a crew member, a fund-raiser and now on 24th July in Belfast a marathon runner. He had also organised a relay between his football team so at the half-way point we were flanked by 30 or so guys as they set off on a five mile race. Colin's partner Leigh Courtney and a large team of employees/runners from Diageo also turned up in support.

I felt great for the first 13 miles but as soon as I turned for the second loop, I felt the energy drain from my body. It was vacuumed out of me in an instant. The remainder would be a long hard slog.

In my diary I noted: *"Yesterday, at the half-way mark, I felt a shot of energy enter my body. Today at 13 miles, it was yanked back out again. My right upper quad started to play up. I was always going to finish, but it was one of my toughest days. Despite my pre-challenge expectations, I am no longer convinced that I will do at least one sub-four-hour marathon during this challenge. I eventually finished in 4:09, with the last three miles a huge struggle. Ken managed a 4:26, thankfully he is now consistently hovering around these times. It won't be long before we are running together again."*

KEN: *"Knowing how tough it can be to cover the distance while carrying an injury makes us all the more grateful to be finishing each of these days in good health and without niggles. Although there are only nine days left, we are still too far from home to take our health and fitness for granted. We know that tomorrow could throw up a new hurdle for either of us. It remains a mindset of one day at a time."*

As soon as we were finished with the smoothie, physio and ice baths, we were whisked away by Carly to do an interview with BBC Radio Ulster. We bantered with the two presenters on air, Joel and Michael, before they asked us to take part in their magnetic darts competition. Apparently they asked all studio guests to throw six darts in aid of a charity cause and that day was the final day. Never ones to back down, Ken and I had a go – the lads even gave us three practice throws – with two of Ken's darts falling off the board. It looked like we would have no chance of beating the top score of 214. Quite a target to beat.

By some miracle, after Ken's first throw landed on double-5, his last two darts landed on the treble 20. He later commented: "If I took a thousand shots, I'd never repeat that."

With his total, the pressure was really on me. Darts is not my forte and I was actually hoping he would throw a small number allowing me to throw for fun. Now however, all 'ears' were on me as we were on 'live' radio.

I was slightly nervous as I began to throw the first of my darts. My first shot missed the board completely. My second however, gave us hope. It was a treble 14. I cannot take any credit because I was aiming for the treble 20.

Joel and Michael insisted I stop at this point so that they could calculate what I needed to score if we were to beat 214. This made me even more nervous.

They worked out I needed 42 or more which would require quite a throw. Nothing to do but go for treble 20 again. I decided to use the 'close your eyes and hope for the best technique.'

The dart left my trembling fingers and headed for the board like a loaded missile. Where would it land?

Joel, Michael, Ken and his brother Barry all held their breaths. The production team pressed their noses against the studio glass-partition. Thousands of listeners waited for news.

The dart landed on treble 15 giving us a total of 217. Winners by three. BBC Radio Ulster Magnetic Champion Darts players. All five of us jumped and hugged in celebration. I wonder if we trained hard for six months how good we'd be.

DAY 24
DOWN

SUNDAY 25 JULY
235.8 miles (379.48 km) to go

Downpatrick
Gerry   3 hours 51 minutes
Ken   3 hours 51 minutes

KEN and I both had a good feeling about this leg. Over breakfast we discussed the possibility of being able to improve on our fastest time to date. Not that it was hugely important to us but we are a little competitive I guess. We agreed that now that we were 'both' enjoying good health and strength, over the coming days we might try to go sub four hours for one of the marathons. With our average times falling over the previous ten days or so, we felt it might be a possibility.

Our strategy involved being patient over the first 13 miles and then reviewing where we stood time-wise. The quarter marathon split of 6.55 miles in Downpatrick read 1:02, within touching distance of a-sub-four-hour time. At the 13.1 mark it read 1:58; our fastest split to date. This was consistent with how strong we both felt.

At the start line shortly before ten on a cloudy Sunday morning we had been sent off by Gerry Kelly, my interviewer of just 22 hours previously. He was full of admiration for the challenge and told us off-air of his great friendship with one Mullingar's favourite sons, the late singer Joe Dolan. He was also involved with an autism charity in Northern Ireland so he was delighted to help us out.

Downpatrick was the location and the route was pieced together by East Down Athletic Club. The volunteers and marshals who cheered us at every turn were out in huge numbers and it gave both Ken and I a great lift. East Down was home to Joe Quinn, a legendary running coach and marathon/ultra marathon runner himself. Joe had left no stone unturned in providing us with a route that was very pleasant not just underfoot but also to the eye. He later made the journey to Mullingar for our final marathon and it was great to run with such a modest gentleman.

On our third lap of four, Ken and I chatted briefly and reviewed our position. Both of us felt strong as the distance climbed towards the 20-mile point. With six to go we decided that we would in fact push on, confident of reaching our goal.

The miles flew by as we were in the company of Liam Keenan who was running his first marathon in 27 years. Having him by our side for the entire distance provided a welcome distraction as we shared life stories. Also running with us for the second half were our brothers-in-law Pat Clarke and Enda Finnerty. At the beginning of lap three, Ken's sister Alaine joined us for 100 metres or so. You will recall Alaine who was five months pregnant had visited us in Cork.

For the duration we were flanked on all sides by three members of the PSNI on mountain bikes. One of them would later remark that this event was his most enjoyable day ever in the police force. A lovely compliment for us to hear.

With two miles to go we knew we were well on target and barring injury we would achieve our first sub-four-hour marathon of the challenge. The last mile was fantastic and we crossed the line in 3:51, our fastest time by 10 minutes. Another highlight came a short time later from a lady who displayed a 'never give up' attitude. Her name was Kim Surgenor and despite a severe battle with cramp, she crossed the line beaming in 4:45. I was later to learn that Kim completed a second marathon later in 2010 finishing the Dublin City Marathon in 3:49.

DAY 25

ARMAGH

MONDAY 26 JULY
209.6 miles (337.31 km) to go

Portadown
Gerry   3 hours 24 minutes
Ken   4 hours 18 minutes

FIFTEEN years, two weeks and one day, that is how long I have been running. Over that time I have had some ups and some downs, many highs and the odd low (injury) thrown in. Never before however have I felt a day where I ran like I did in Armagh. A cloudy dull Monday morning on the day when we would run our 24th consecutive marathon was not a day when I would have expected such an occurrence. I knew I was getting stronger. My marathon experience in Armagh would give me definitive evidence to back up my theory.

It all started quietly. Over a 20-minute discussion in a hotel in Armagh, Ken and I chatted about how we were feeling. He said he was a little tired and would be happier to ease off the pedal somewhat. He had gone through some incredibly tough miles over the preceding three weeks. The Down marathon was a highlight for both of us, but particularly for him. You can understand why, when you consider the depths from where he had come. On days eight and nine he could barely walk. A few days later he was on the road to recovery only for the injury demons to strike again in Offaly. The Down run was one of the many experiences that made all the days of training, preparation and sacrifice over 12 months worthwhile.

Over our months of training we had sometimes spoken about whether we'd be able to have a real go at one of the marathons, just to see what time we'd be able to do. This was not though, something we took lightly as we were both acutely aware of how many miles were left before we would cross the finish line for the last time on day 32. To run a fast marathon now would mean the synergy of a number of factors: legs and body feeling fresh, suitable course, agreeable weather and focus of mind. Never once in the plan however was this a goal, an ambition or a prerequisite. If everything came together and it happened that would be great, if not it wouldn't matter.

The routing in Armagh was flat along a river bank, out and back twice over two loops. It had no traffic to navigate save the first and last mile each time where we had to run through the main street of Portadown. Joining us from the start was a new friend, Tomas McCormack, who was running his fourth marathon with us. What was startling about this statistic was that our first marathon in Longford was his first 'ever' marathon. During a brief chat after that run he told us of his plans to run three more with us. Given his lack of experience we initially thought he was mad. For the first 6.55 miles of the Armagh run Tomas and I ran side by side. The pace was strong and by mile five it was obvious by his breathing that he would need to ease off on the pace we were doing. He had done a personal best just a week before so after such efforts it was hardly a surprise he was feeling it. At the turnaround he signalled for me to go on, that he was going to drop his pace ever so slightly to ensure he finished.

For the return part of the first loop Johnny Davis joined me on his bike. He later told me he could see that I was running effortlessly. Coming back through Portadown I felt an injection of energy into my body which made me feel stronger and stronger. I knew immediately that it was going to be a good running day.

I was going for it.

I asked Johnny to radio ahead to ensure a bottle of water was at the turnaround. As I turned at the traffic cone, Noeleen was there bottle in hand. Noeleen had taken a week's leave to ensure she could be with us for the final leg of our journey. Apparently her boss had no hesitation in granting it as she said that all Noeleen talked about in work was the 32 Marathons non-stop every day. I snatched the bottle from her grasp, a signal of my intention to continue at a fast pace. A runner herself, she understood.

In my company for the second loop was Jacinta on a mountain bike and Niall Murphy our ever loyal crew member. Whenever we were short of company Niall stepped in to run six miles, a half marathon or some days like Wexford and Offaly, a full 26.2 miles. Realising I was now running alone he grabbed his running shoes and tore after me, catching me about 500 metres into mile 14. He confessed that he had run a hard eight miles the night before as part of his own training and was unsure about sustaining the pace I was on.

As we were on a looped river bank routing I had the opportunity to meet Ken on three occasions during the run. He was in the company of two runners, Eamon Sheehan and Laurence Fitzsimmons, who had run a few marathons before but not for a few years. It was only when a friend who had an boy with autism told him about this event a few months ago that Laurence decided to get back into training and raise some much needed funds for Autism Northern Ireland.

Eamon had a direct family link to autism, so he too was running for a reason close to his heart. We had met him for the first time the previous Friday in Tyrone when he and his partner helped out with marshalling. He told us then that he was more of a 10k/half marathon runner and was quite nervous about tackling the full 26.2 miles. He needn't have worried though, as he cruised through the first 18 or so miles. From there on, things did start to get a little interesting though as he had to contend with a sore blister on his foot. The pain seemed to get quite bad over the following mile or two but he didn't let it affect his spirit or his resolve to finish. From mile 22 on he really started to find it tough going. The top of his shoe had started to turn blood red whilst the rest of his legs seemed to be battling for attention. His gutsy determination didn't subside once and made Ken think twice about the sore calf that he had felt for the last few miles. It was only fitting that his family joined him on the final 400 metres jog to the line.

A finishing time of 4:18hrs for Ken and Eamon. Lawrence had finished just ahead of them.

Grabbing the bottle at the 13-mile point from Noeleen, I had glanced quickly at my watch. It revealed a time that surprised me. I was feeling very strong and was still very much running with ease, but a split of just over 1:46 was not something I was expecting. This was more than 11 minutes quicker than the previous day. I was a little taken aback but was certain that it was not taking its toll given the relative comfort I felt.

As an indication of how strong I was feeling, Niall, Jacinta and I chatted continuously for the following 10 miles or so bringing us up to the 23-mile mark. To get to this point was effortless. Thankfully I was able to live in the moment as I narrated my feelings to Jacinta over mile 24. By now given his run the night before, Niall had decided to drop off the pace. I had moved from what I felt was 3rd to 4th gear at the beginning of this mile. This shift in pace was again very straightforward. By now I was experiencing the pure joy of effortless running, the strongest day of my running life.

In my notes that evening I said... *"Never before have I felt this strong. The entire run as I got faster and faster was effortless. It seemed I was never even breathing harder that if I were out for a walk. What an incredible level of fitness I am feeling."*

I had long before realised that I would beat the previous day's marathon of 3:51. At mile 24 a quick glance made me realise a sub-3:30 was on the cards. I made a note to check my watch when I had one mile to go. If I was close and needed something resembling a last mile of seven minutes or so, then I might push it a fraction. It was not a priority however, as at all times I was conscious of the bigger picture.

As my GPS read 25.2, exactly one mile from home, I reviewed my position. It read 3:18:01. I was stunned. I had not known my pace but I knew nothing would stop a sub 3:30 now, in fact I would smash it. Colin met me at the turn off the canal to ensure a clear passage up the main street. He was on a mountain bike so I was surrounded, he leading the way and Jacinta to the rear. He later told me that he got goose bumps on his arm from being a part of this moment as he realised immediately the zone I was in. Quite a compliment coming from a man who once wore a Manchester United shirt on his back.

As I crossed the line I stopped the watch and even before examining it, I asked one of our photographers Tony to take a picture of it for posterity. It read 3:24:53. This meant a negative split where I managed to run the second 13.1 miles considerably faster than the first.

Later Ken would comment on the website: *"It really is amazing that the body can be capable of that this far into our challenge."*

What a day.

DAY 26
FERMANAGH

TUESDAY 27 JULY
183.4 miles (295.15 km) to go

Enniskillen
Gerry   4 hours 7 minutes
Ken   4 hours 7 minutes

"I FIND it hard not to get excited about being on the home straight, even though we have so much running left to do. Despite that, though, I feel the finish line is now in sight and, barring accident or injury, we are both going to make it. We are looking forward to the next few days and hope we can get through each day without incident."

These were Ken's comments on the online diary. Fermanagh would see our journey through Northern Ireland come to a close, leaving us with just six more marathons to be completed.

My second youngest niece Lucy Finnerty (4) made yet another appearance. Throughout the challenge many family members had made great efforts to support us as much as possible. Katherine and her children Rebecca and Gerry had visited us on more than eight occasions; Mary came with her children Mark, Andrew and the aforementioned Lucy, and in all would support us on 21 days by the time we returned to Mullingar.

Lucy, Mary's youngest child had something in common with Ken and I. Just one month shy of her fifth birthday, she was also challenging herself to new sporting ambitions. She had just learned to ride a bicycle unaided, no mean achievement at that age.

Our venue was Castle Archdale, about two miles outside Enniskillen. On arrival, Lucy spotted some similar-aged children in the distance, on their bikes that had stabilisers attached. Some company or perhaps some competition for later in the day. She turned to her mum who was busy unpacking the car and remarked very loudly and within earshot of the nearby children: "Mammy, can I get my bike with 'no' stabilisers out of the car?"

Competitive? She had made her point.

Every day we were privy to a new environment, a new routing and a new memory to be stored. Fermanagh was no exception. For two special ladies – both crew members – this was their day.

The previous autumn, Jacinta and Carly Ferguson had something in common. Neither of them had ever run in a race before, and I mean ever. In January both of them signed up to run a half marathon as part of our challenge. Carly had gone into vigorous training. Over February and March we exchanged emails to ensure her motivation continued. In April, she ran a half-marathon three months ahead of schedule. With that experience under her belt, she decided to stretch her ambition and changed her registration to a full marathon. Jacinta had by this time run her first ever half-marathon in Kilkenny, way back on Day-6. Over dinner the previous evening she disclosed that she would like to run another half-marathon.

As part of our Northern Ireland crew, we had spent a lot of time in Carly's company in the preceding five days. Each time we mentioned her upcoming run she went as white as a sheet. She was very nervous and it seemed she doubted her own ability to complete such a distance. Carly was even more nervous as ten o' clock approached. At the start line Jacinta, Carly and her sister Alison all lined up ready for the off. Alison had one marathon already to her name and had flown over from Scotland to lend support. In tow were Ken and I, and over 20 other runners.

Just a few short miles from Enniskillen, Castle Archdale – once home to an RAF Airbase – now houses a museum steeped with stories of soldiers who fought and died in World War II. Following a secret pact with the Irish government in that war, aircraft were allowed to take off from the airbase and travel over Irish airspace in Donegal.

The weather promised showers that thankfully never materialised. Our four-loop circuit was primarily run on a trail, offering some recovery for those aching lower leg muscles. The first few hours passed without incident. The course was lovely but as the miles climbed, Ken and I began to feel similar feelings of tiredness. As each mile passed we both became exhausted.

I was also wondering about Jacinta and whether she had successfully accomplished her goal when I spotted her.

"That can't be right," I thought to myself as she approached.

"What lap are you on?" I enquired, as she came into earshot.

"My third," she boasted proudly.

"What," I exclaimed. "Are you mad?"

This meant she was somewhere around mile 15 or so, over two miles beyond her declared intention of running a half-marathon. She just smiled and continued to 'put one foot in front of the other'. I shouldn't have been surprised. A real doer, she had been wonderful to me not just on this challenge but in the preceding 12 months when Ken and I worked to piece the logistics together. For the previous 24 days since we started, Jacinta had carried out a million jobs to help us. If she wasn't sorting our kit early morning, she was preparing the natural gels consisting of honey, sea salt and water, prior to departure. At the finish line every day she had the specially prepared smoothie and a raw vegetable juice for us as well as a welcoming smile of support. In between, Jacinta travelled countless miles on her mountain bike offering encouragement at every mile.

I was thrilled for her now but also concerned. Would she be able to finish? We chatted for a few moments but it was obvious she wished to run alone as we were on different pace settings. Niall, our ever-present guardian angel, was at her side. That was a great source of comfort as I knew he would carry her through any difficult mental or physical moments she might experience before the finish line.

A few minutes later I encountered Carly and Alison. Carly looked relatively comfortable. She still had a long way to go but the nerves seemed to have disappeared and she looked very determined. Perhaps the waiting had been harder. My mind was cast back to the 42 sleepless nights I had experienced prior to my first public speaking performance in 2005.

My thoughts on such an occurrence from earlier in the book were: *"Isn't it the case that the thought of doing something is very often far more stressful than the reality? The harder part can sometimes be changing your mindset or your limiting beliefs. Once your decision is made, the resulting action can actually sometimes be the easier element."*

By mile 20 Ken and I both felt spent. We racked our brains. Were the recent fast-paced marathons to blame? We discussed other possible reasons. Soon it became apparent. The previous day we both had missed our 4pm meal, missing a vital recovery ingredient. You would think we would know better. It had been such a busy afternoon in Armagh, we hadn't noticed. The journey to Fermanagh took two hours longer than planned as we had gotten lost. As a result we did not eat until almost 8pm. We were both very relieved to cross the finish line in 4hrs 07mins with another box ticked.

By the time I had finished physio, I got word that Jacinta had one mile to go. I walked out to meet her and waited about 500 metres from the finish line. The following minutes provided another very special memory on our journey. As Jacinta approached and despite the discomfort she was now in, she managed a smile. She was very sore but was determined to finish with a flourish. As she passed, I tried to pick up her pace but I couldn't. I had finished a little over an hour by then. My body was aching and refused to allow me to run anymore despite my best efforts to do so. I met up with Jacinta about 30 seconds after she had completed her first full marathon and hugged her warmly.

What a champion.

Twenty minutes later we had another victor. Eight months previously, just like Jacinta, Carly Ferguson had never run in an official event. There she was completing the challenge of running her first marathon. She too had a smile that quite rightly beamed with pride as she was greeted by family and friends.

DAY 27

MONAGHAN

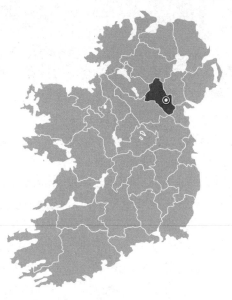

WEDNESDAY 28 JULY

157.2 miles (252.98 km) to go

Castleblayney
Gerry   3 hours 58 minutes
Ken   3 hours 58 minutes

MY Uncle Brian would have loved the camaraderie in Castleblayney, the location for our 26th marathon. Sadly he is no longer with us but his spirit was all around this part of Monaghan – Lough Muckno, Castleblayney to be precise. A gathering of my extended family took place as my parents, my auntie Phil and my cousins were out in full support. They brought a great atmosphere not to mention some delicious catering for the spectators and crew alike. It was great to see Phil, Ann Marie, Helen, Mickey and Padraig Sherry, a first cousin now living in London. He had agreed to act as our route coordinator.

Our 26th marathon promised much but delivered more. For starters, there was the sight of Barry Kerr, a Blayney man now with roots in Leitrim who kept going for a second 13-mile loop, despite having trained for a half-marathon. Two hours later he finished and savoured the applause from the large crowd who were waiting patiently for their loved ones to finish.

Every day we were witness to special moments. This was no exception. A lady called Tara Duffy (no relation) was scheduled to make her full marathon debut. Tara had personal reasons to be here. The day was warm but showery, a typical summer's day in

Ireland. Tara fought her way to the finish line with incredible bravery. With just 100 metres to go of the 26.2 miles she had to stop as she was limping with pain, her calf having tightened up.

The medics ran to assist her.

"Leave me alone," she screamed. "I'm fine, don't touch me." It was obvious though she was in significant distress. She gathered herself, stretched out her right calf muscle and rose to her feet once more. Moments later she crossed the line and within seconds embraced her young son who had waited patiently for hours, saying: "I did it for you, I did it for you."

Her son had autism and that was our principal charity. We were humbled.

Ken and I had a ball. For the first six miles or so we were royally entertained by Nudie Hughes, a former footballing giant from these parts. We knew we were in the presence of a popular man when Ken received a request via text for Nudie's autograph.

Our run was thoroughly enjoyable. Both of us felt significantly stronger than the day before as we were guided around the route by a guard called Frances Merrick. At mile 25 I was feeling the strain, when Ken uttered some unwelcome words: "If we push it, we might break four hours."

I scarcely needed this, but the opportunity was too good to pass. We pushed the final yards and just dipped below the mark, finishing in 3:58:50. A very satisfactory day's work.

By this time, we were astounded at the amount of awareness generated about the event. Our fifth weekend on the road had almost 250 runners waiting patiently to run. The following Monday (our final day) had 160 people registered, and the numbers were rising.

DAY 28

LOUTH

THURSDAY 29 JULY

131 miles (210.82 km) to go

Drogheda

Gerry   3 hours 57 minutes

Ken   3 hours 57 minutes

THE Boyne Valley Hotel on the outskirts of Drogheda was the starting point for our 27th marathon. What a super turnout – we had 30 people running with us and at least the same number again at the start line to cheer us on. We were delighted to see the parents, teachers and children from the local autism school – Abacus – turn out in force to see us off. Most of the children ran the first few hundred metres with us.

Over the previous 26 days we met some people who had travelled from afar to join us. Rob Costello, who ran a full marathon with us in Louth, arguably deserved the top prize. He flew all the way from Sydney to join us. Ok, he might have been best man for his brother's wedding the following Monday but that was surely a coincidence. Rob was an experienced ultra distance runner who helped and encouraged many other runners as we covered the four laps around Drogheda.

We had another first in Louth; our first canine half-marathon finisher. Chris Roddy from Dundalk ran the 13 miles with his Siberian husky Tyson. We couldn't but give Tyson a medal on his achievement. Chris's cousin, Keith Roddy, (a good friend of Ken's) joined us for his first ever half-marathon too. Keith's longest run before that was seven miles so adding the extra six was a real challenge for him. Or so we thought.

At the 13.1-mile point Keith was looking so comfortable that he decided to try the third lap with us. You can guess what happened at the turnaround point for the last lap. That's right. Although a little red-faced and with his concerned wife Fiona looking on, Keith kept going for the fourth and final lap. It's certainly not the way we would advise anyone to approach a marathon but Ken and I had been constantly amazed during the event at how people like Keith could double or even treble their longest ever run and complete a marathon with us. It had happened by now on so many occasions. My own brother Tom completed five half-marathons by the end of our journey, three of which were in the final seven days. Tomas McCormack would run four full marathons and Ken's cousin Simon Hutchinson, six, yes six marathons. Previous to this he hadn't run one. A new friend, Lucy Foley, would add to her already impressive CV by running two full marathons in less than two weeks and Michael Maguire, a seasoned campaigner, ran three.

Keith struggled a bit over the last few miles but his gutsy determination carried him to the finish. His time of 3:57 was a hell of a debut for a first marathon.

Ken and I felt reasonably good and kept a steady pace throughout the run. We enjoyed the company of the new people whom we met which always gave us a huge boost and distracted us from our daily task. In Louth, this included Ollie McHugh who completed his second marathon in as many days.

Louth was only the second time that we got to stay in the same location for two consecutive nights. It was great not to have to pack up and travel as soon as we finished our run. Jacinta Walsh, one of the main organisers of the run had also organised a BBQ at the hotel that evening, so we took full advantage and chilled out for a few hours.

Later in the evening we were presented with a wonderful memento, it was a picture of all the children who had run the first few metres with us. In the photo each of them held up a letter displaying a message which read "THANK YOU FROM ABACUS". A gift to be treasured.

MARATHON TIMES

You will recall after the Laois marathon I mentioned the average times I had completed each marathon over the first two weeks. In week one the average was 4:36, week two was 4:23. I know I am repeating myself when I say that my running partner was every bit as capable of these times as I was. In the Ironman Austria event he had finished almost an hour faster than I did. In this challenge he was unfortunate insofar as he had got injured and so his only focus became to finish each day in as little pain as possible. I had the fortune to run injury-free.

Week three (marathons 15-21) was faster again, on average by three minutes, coming in at 4:20. By week four (marathons 22-28), this had shortened once more by a sizeable 25 minutes. The average for my fourth block of seven marathons actually dipped below the four-hour mark, coming in at 3 hours and 55 minutes.

Ken's times also began to consistently drop from the beginning of week three onwards. Even taking into account an agonising 7:59 duration in Offaly, week three for him averaged 5:11. In week four (marathons 22-28), his average run was over an hour quicker at 4:08. When you recall the challenges he faced, this was exceptional. His final four marathons would also dip well below the four-hour barrier, averaging at three hours and 54 minutes.

For me, the final four days would be faster again, an average of 23 minutes quicker than week four. My final four marathons averaged just 3:32.

It would start with a very fast run in Meath.

DAY 29

MEATH

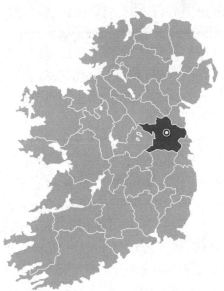

FRIDAY 30 JULY
104.8 miles (168.65 km) to go

Navan
Gerry   3 hours 17 minutes
Ken   3 hours 48 minutes

A FEW years ago, a close friend of mine travelled to support me and to witness an Ironman triathlon in the flesh. He was mesmerised by what he saw and rang his wife from the finish line.

"If I ever come home and tell you I am doing an Ironman triathlon," he told her, "do not under any circumstances let me do it."

Guess what? A few days before our Meath marathon, he did one.

Fresh from a Wednesday flight home from Zurich and with an Ironman medal now on his sporting CV was Paul O'Brien, our route co-ordinator. Paul had plotted a beautiful scenic route along the banks of the River Boyne, just outside Navan town. Bernard Flynn was here to see us off. Ahead of us was a four-loop circuit where I was joined for the first loop by the renowned former champion jockey and later horse trainer, Norman Williamson.

"Norman, I know nothing about horses," I confessed as we ran the opening mile. He laughed at the thought. As well as starting the race for us, he also ran the half-marathon distance and was scarcely out of breath crossing the line. A few other friends from home, James Carton, Justin Rice, Bernie Briody and Mary Taaffe also came and we were grateful for their support.

Ken had a good day, and was coming back strong from his injuries. He still held back a little though, respectful of previous concerns and the little matter of four more marathons still to be completed.

Three workmates of his who made the journey from Dublin cheered us on and ran a few miles with Ken. Karen Sweeney, Austin Garvey and Tammy McCarthy, a lady who continually posted words of encouragement on Facebook in the preceding 29 days all did their bit.

I had a super run. I had hoped to run one final fast marathon, if the legs would allow me. Our physio Noeleen had reprimanded me a few times, urging patience. How right she was. We started out quite leisurely as Norman and I chatted over the first five or six miles. I scarcely noticed that we were doing a good solid pace. Each week, as I have documented, my body had been getting stronger. Now with the same effort as a week ago I was travelling faster. I had a feeling of strength like never before where I simply felt I could have run forever.

At the half-way point, just like in Portadown four days before, I checked my time. It read 1:43, which was even quicker again. This confirmed my theory that with the same level of effort, I was getting faster.

For this run we found ourselves in a part of Ireland steeped in history. Given that we were at the height of the summer, heavy foliage camouflaged our River Boyne routing and the gravel trail we were navigating was barely two feet wide.

From miles 10 to 13 I ran alone with plenty of time to think. I had no desire when I woke up to run faster than 3:24. I simply wanted to run a solid marathon, perhaps 3:30 or thereabouts. I was trying as much as possible to enjoy the moment. My Mum had recommended before we started in Longford to enjoy being surrounded by nature. Her advice was in my thoughts in Navan and how much did I appreciate it on this run, where the landscape was unforgettable.

By mile 13, I knew a sub 3:30 was well on the cards but if I was to challenge the 3:24 time done in Armagh, I wanted to do it in the company of Jacinta. Monday had been such a special day primarily because she was beside me for the final 13 miles. Thankfully she arrived on her mountain bike on the third loop of four. With three miles remaining, I reviewed my position. The watch read 2:57. It meant that if I could manage the remaining distance at 8 minute mile pace, I would smash the 3:24 time.

With half a mile to go, we were joined by Paul O'Brien the organiser, on a mountain bike. I was running well within myself and I chatted comfortably with Jacinta and Paul for the remaining yards, he in front, and Jacinta behind. I was still well within my aerobic threshold. On reaching the 26.2 mile mark, I stopped the gps watch in order to freeze the time. I was chuffed by what I saw.

It read 3:17:44.

This was the fastest run not just of the 29 marathons but also a personal best, knocking five minutes off my previous fastest time. In terms of mental fulfilment, I would still rank the previous Monday's run in Armagh ahead of it but a personal best gave me a real sense of satisfaction.

My running partner had a fantastic day as well. The record books will show that he also ran his fastest of the 29 marathons, coming home in a very comfortable 3:48. Given the long roads he had travelled (Meath was our fifth Friday on the road), it was remarkable to see him returning to good form, despite the fact that he had not been able to take any rest days.

Roll on Cavan, more than 30 runners including one Ray D'Arcy at the start line.

DAY 30

CAVAN

SATURDAY 31 JULY
78.6 miles (126.49 km) to go

Cavan Town
Ken	3 hours 47 minutes
Gerry	3 hours 58 minutes

KEN: *"It's almost hard to believe that we have now run 30 marathons in 30 consecutive days. It's funny how the mind works but over the last 12 months or more, my mind has become very focused on completing 32 marathons in 32 days. Not 29, not 31, but 32. The one minor drawback of being in this mindset though is that I can sometimes find it difficult to appreciate what we've already accomplished. With only two marathons left we are finally beginning to relax a little as we allow ourselves to think that we are going to make it across the finish line in Mullingar on Monday.*

As always, our daily task has been made all the easier by the super support of fellow runners and a Saturday morning in Cavan was no exception. With over 35 people running it was impossible not to be carried along by their energy and enthusiasm. It was encouraging also to see familiar faces amongst the crowd; Johnny Donnelly from the Sawdoctors ran his second marathon with us and Ray D'Arcy also put on his runners and joined us for a half-marathon, although neither Gerry nor I could keep up with him.

We are deeply indebted to Ray for he took us under his wing in those months of our final preparation when we need the oxygen of publicity.

Time and time again he mentioned us on his morning radio show which helped create great awareness.

Brian Boyle co-ordinated the Cavan event. He had helped us piece together the challenge from the word go. Having relocated to London, Brian travelled back for the weekend to help us. A number of my relations also came along to run and lend their support. A special mention to my aunt, Pauline Hutchinson, who had worked tirelessly over the previous few months putting the Cavan event together and encouraging so many to come out and run.

Thankfully both Gerry and I continue to feel strong during our runs and we both remain free from major injury. Every day that we can complete another 26.2 miles is a good day. If we can do it without pain or injury it becomes a great one. Gerry was feeling the effects of his super run yesterday but still managed to cross the line looking comfortable in 3:58. I was also feeling ok and was happy to cross the line in 3:47 - a minute faster than yesterday. I have to admit that with a little over a mile to go I knew that I'd be very close to yesterday's time, so I ran a 7 minute last mile to make sure I'd be that little bit faster. I also wanted to see how my legs would hold up to a fast pace.

As I wrote a few days ago, both Gerry and I have talked about running a fast marathon during the course of this challenge. Gerry's big day was yesterday when he smashed his PB, running a 3:17. For the last week or more I've been planning to attempt one fast run in Leitrim tomorrow. Although I know I have the strength and stamina now to run a great time, unfortunately I don't think the niggles in the legs will allow it. Needless to say, it is more important for me to finish all 32 marathons, so although running a nice fast time would be personally satisfying, it must come second to the main objective.

Over the course of this diary, we have sometimes mentioned inspiring stories from the people we meet along the way. The source of today's is close to me as it comes from my cousins Simon and Ruth as well as Ruth's boyfriend Philip. Simon has now joined us every weekend – five in total - to run a marathon with us. Simon's longest run before his first marathon five weeks ago was five miles so to see him cross the finish line today put a huge smile on both our faces. But today he wasn't running for himself - Simon and Philip jogged the whole 26.2 miles with Ruth, keeping her company and encouraging her the whole way. It was hard not to get a lump in the throat when she crossed the line with tears of joy in her eyes, a little over seven hours after they started. What makes this tale even more uplifting is that two years ago Philip had a life threatening fall from scaffolding and spent more than five weeks on a life support machine.

DAY 31
LEITRIM

SUNDAY 1 AUGUST
52.4 miles (84.32 km) to go

Mohill
Ken   3 hours 54 minutes
Gerry   4 hours 2 minutes

9.00-17.00

JUST four weeks before we arrived, the Irish rugby captain Brian O'Driscoll, his new wife Amy Huberman and their guests had filled the car park of the location for our 31st marathon. Their wedding day was also the day of our second marathon. Lough Rynn Castle, an 18th century estate, once home to Lord Leitrim, formed the backdrop for our penultimate day on the road.

Over the course of researching this book, I discovered an interesting link relevant to the story of this book. Lord Leitrim was great friends with Lord Digby, who owned Sherbourne Castle, in Dorset, the setting for my second Ironman in 2008. Interestingly when Lord Leitrim was assassinated in 2nd April, 1878, a £10,000 reward was put up to find those responsible, £1,000 of which was donated by The Duke of Abercorne who had lived at Barons Court Estate, the setting for our 22nd marathon in County Tyrone.

In March 2010, nobody had signed up for Leitrim. Not a single runner. It stood out on our registration spreadsheet for all the wrong reasons. It concerned us, but such was the magnitude of our workload, we were unable to improve it to any great degree. Later however, we were fortunate to benefit from the efforts of locals James Martin, Mary Menton, Lisa Mulvey and Bernadette Glancy, all of whom played a part in ensuring we would have plenty of company and a memorable day in Leitrim.

We were shocked by the numbers that greeted us. Ninety five people had registered. It was our second highest turnout and helped to create a very special atmosphere. As Ken and I appeared shortly after 9am, we were greeted by the sight of the registration crowd, as they meandered through the historical hallways and out the front door of Lough Rynn Castle.

Over 120 people were present for our briefing including Ciaran Reidy, the general manager of Lough Rynn. He had been a great friend to our challenge by sponsoring our stay on 'two' occasions. Also there was one of Leitrim's most famous sons, the very welcoming, Charlie McGettigan. Charlie along with Paul Harrington had won the Eurovision song contest for Ireland in 1994 with the song 'Rock and Roll Kids'.

Many familiar faces were back for more, including some family members. My sister Katherine and Ken's brother, Barry, a vital member of our crew, both took part in the Leitrim run. Undeterred by having no training done and a couple of dodgy knees, Barry announced over breakfast that he was off to walk 26.2 miles. We watched in admiration as he left the room at 8am to ensure he would be home before the last runner would cross the line. This was in keeping with the efforts of hundreds more who made their own personal contribution to our challenge. Barry crossed the line in six and a half hours and Ken was at the finish line to congratulate him. Barry later confessed that the five minute walk to the physio was harder than the previous 26.2 miles. Another valued crew member, David Cahilan, despite having no training done, ran a half-marathon in support of the event.

I had retired to bed early the night before, feeling a little tired and in need of eight hours solid shut-eye. I woke up feeling great, eagerly anticipating the day ahead. After my exertions of running a 3:58 in Cavan, I had felt a tiny twinge in my right knee in the last few miles.

In Leitrim, it made itself known from the off. The pain was at all times relative but it was sore for the duration. By now both Ken and I felt that nothing could or would stop us from reaching our goal. It was after all, day 31. By midday, with 13 miles completed, the countdown was well and truly underway. Only 39 miles left.

Ken left me in his wake, a measure of his return to fitness. Like me though, he also found the going quite hard. His finishing time of 3:54 was completed with a small amount of discomfort. I was a little over eight minutes behind, crossing the line in 4:02. On closer examination Noeleen diagnosed the pain as a quad muscle issue leading into my knee. After 30 minutes of physio work, I jogged out the door, pain free once more.

The last 500 metres of our run was terrific as we were greeted by young sports stars, the boys and girls of the Gortletteragh GAA club, a tiny hamlet that we had ran through four times earlier. Organised by Madeline Doyle, partner of our crew member Brendan, they were all togged out in their club colours, it was a wonderful sight. Also running the final yards were the O'Brien children, friends from home, but originally from Leitrim and another son of close friends, young Paul McCool, an eight-year-old future sports star for sure.

At four pm today, I felt great. That however was about to change.

17.00-23.30

In retrospect, I should not have been surprised that my immune system was low. We had pushed ourselves beyond what many people had thought humanly possible for 31 days in a row, running over 800 miles in the process. A cold sore had appeared on my lip overnight, a tell tale sign that things were not 100 per cent within my immune system.

Minutes before our final car journey back to Mullingar, I started to feel unwell. Within a few miles I had to ask Jacinta to hastily pull over. Exiting the car, I was certain I was about to throw up, I was feeling very nauseous. All my life I have been very fortunate to remain pretty much illness free, something I am immensely grateful for. On the few occasions I have been sick, I have been a terrible patient.

For five minutes or more, I hunkered down in the ditch awaiting an avalanche. Nothing happened. Ken and Noeleen spotted our car as they passed and pulled over. They were concerned but I needed to be alone. I crossed over to the other side of the road for more privacy as I did not want a public performance. After 10 minutes of feeling terrible, I decided to take matters into my own hands literally, by forcing myself to empty the contents of my stomach.

Any previous stomach upsets had led to relief after such a strategy. Not on this occasion however, a first sign that this was more than a sick stomach. I felt there was more to come so I continued my intimate discussion with the flora and fauna at the side of the road. My girlfriend and close friends looked on from a distance and I appreciated their concern. Three evictions later, Noeleen suggested we continue our journey and go to an out-of-hours medical clinic in Mullingar, about 45 minutes away. I agreed.

In Longford we pulled over for a toilet stop. I ran in the front door with haste. Ironically the hotel was the Longford Arms, the setting for our first marathon, 31 days before. By the time I got back into the car I felt much better and my mood had perked up considerably. Onward towards home, with a quick stop midway for a cup of tea and a bar of chocolate. My stomach was empty and I was starving. I drank the tea and managed two squares of nourishment and was soon feeling 90 per cent back to normal, or so I thought.

Three miles from home, I rang Noeleen and asked her to cancel the medical appointment. She refused.

"Let's just go in and let them check you over," she insisted. "Ok," I agreed. Noeleen you see, can be very persuasive. Two miles from home, I spotted a sign welcoming "Gerry and Ken, Our Marathon Men" back to our hometown. That was two miles from home.

One mile later, I was asking Jacinta to increase our speed and get me to the clinic as quickly as possible. Out of nowhere the pain had returned, only this time it brought massive cramping, like a fist tightly squeezing my stomach. At the entrance to the business park where the clinic was located, I jumped out of the car again and headed to the undergrowth. Thirty seconds later I got back in and we continued.

Seconds later, I was out again for fear of emptying the contents of my stomach into the car's interior. I decided to walk the last few metres to the clinic where I was met by Jacinta, Ken and Noeleen.

Within minutes, I was sat on a chair nauseated and devoid of any emotional attachment for what the next 24 hours would bring. Running one more marathon was the furthest thing from my mind. I was on the eve of the greatest sporting achievement of my life but it was a million light years from my thoughts. My head was spinning and I could barely mouth any replies to the doctor's questioning. I am, as I said, a terrible patient. I left it to Jacinta to fill in the events of the previous few hours as best she could, to help the doctor offer a diagnosis.

Within 10 minutes I was lying on a bed with a needle stuck into my right arm. I could hear and see the repeating drip slowly inserting its contents into me. I would soon enjoy its benefits but for now, all I could think of was throwing up. I had been diagnosed with having gastroenteritis - thankfully nothing serious.

I drifted in and out of sleep over the following three hours. Jacinta stayed the entire time and I had a vague recollection of seeing my brother Tom and my cousin Padraig Sherry in the room at some point. I later found out my condition was the subject of much debate amongst our crew who worried that I might not make the final day. Keith Duffy from pop group Boyzone, the patron of the charity, had driven to Mullingar to thank Ken and I for our efforts, but I was unable to see him.

A little after 11pm, we left the clinic after thanking the medical staff profusely. I was exhausted but feeling considerably better. The doctor told me to eat nothing but dry bread and toast for the next 48 hours. Given the fact that there was the small matter of achieving my lifetime ambition in 11 hours' time by running one final marathon, I asked him was it ok to stretch to eating a banana or two during the next day's run. He nodded his approval. I fell asleep as soon as my head hit the pillow and slept soundly that night. Jacinta on the other hand did the worrying for both of us, long into the night.

DAY 32
WESTMEATH

MONDAY 2 AUGUST
26.2 miles (42.19 km) to go

Mullingar
Gerry   4 hours 8 minutes
Ken   4 hours 8 minutes

NO fear of sleeping in this morning, I was awake before seven. It was a day I had dreamt about for two years. I slowly got out of the bed monitoring my body for signs of recovery. I felt about 70 per cent better than the night before. The sickness had disappeared, the only remnants being a lack of energy and an empty stomach. I was starving but this was something I knew I would just have to deal with, doctor's orders.

On this day of all days, I wanted to be first out into the town park in Mullingar where our race headquarters was located. In excess of 200 people were busy registering and I knew most of them. The late surge in entries over the final two days brought our final tally of runners to over 1,100, almost 100 more than our original target.

I longed to be down at registration as I wanted so much to cherish every second of this day but I made an early morning promise to Jacinta that I would do the opposite, after she threatened to tie me to the chair. I would wait until the very last minute for fear of using up unnecessary energy. There was the small matter of one more marathon still to be run and I would have to do it running virtually on empty.

Ken arrived shortly before 8am and together we did a Newstalk radio interview. Ken did another pre-recorded interview for the RTE News at One after which we chatted briefly about the day ahead, both acknowledging we were looking forward to it immensely. I suggested he go down and do the meet and greet on his own and he duly headed off. I would not see him until the start line two hours later.

9.45

I stood on the podium in shock. Before me were about 400 people. What a turnout. My shock was not about that number, however. Just moments before, Kevin Whelan, the CEO of Irish Autism Action, had announced the final tally of funds raised by the event, €490,000. The final figure would actually reach €504,000.

It was way beyond our expectations. It was a combination of many contributors: Over 1,100 runners, company sponsorship as well as private donations from a number of parties who were spurred to action for one reason or another.

The final day itself was cloudy but warm, perhaps 19 degrees, and it was dry, a big bonus. I really had hoped and prayed for a final day that would offer perfect weather conditions. Thankfully it did.

It was very important for Ken and I to publicly recognise the enormous contribution of not just our crew but also the many people that had worked very hard behind the scenes. Most were present but not all. Those that were, we called onto the stage. Our crew which rotated constantly over the 32 days consisted of Jacinta O'Neill, Celine Whitelaw, Paddy Whitelaw, Barry Whitelaw, Freddie Grehan, Tony Guing, Sarah McInerney-Buckley, Colette Charles, Ashling Garry, Ann Reilly, Brendan Doyle, Brian Ivory, Niall Murphy, Pat Whaley, Joe Whelan, Darragh Thornton, Johnny Davis, Luke Hanley, David Cahilan, Colin Telford, Carly Ferguson, Ann and Ken Hickey, Mervyn Rundle Senior and Junior, Dr Alvaro Ramirez, Tony Kinlan, Stuart McChesney, Emily and Brenda Castles and Kevin and Peter Whelan. Without the contribution made by all of these people, our challenge would not have been the success it was. We owed them a lifetime of gratitude.

I recognised so many faces in the crowd. In front of us were our families, aunts, uncles, cousins and hundreds of friends. Over 40 people who had run with us over the previous 31 days were back again. Many of our route organisers were back also to lend yet another day of support. From my viewpoint, I spotted The Murphys and Horkans from Mayo, Brian Keegan from London, Gloria and Jessica from Donegal, Brian Keane from Kilkenny, Joe Quinn from Downpatrick and Finbarr Feely from Roscommon. Ken's cousin Simon was here to run his sixth marathon with us and Michael Maguire from Longford his third. There too was Daniel Magan who had run his first marathon in Longford on day one, and in Mullingar he would run his second. Did I mention he was only 16 years old?

Another lady who had run twice with us, Lucy Foley, also made the journey. Susan Duffy, my Dublin cousin, was running her second half-marathon. Norman Williamson returned with his wife Janet, who ran a full marathon with her sister Wendy. Louise McCartan and her husband Jim as well as Eamon, Rory and Tony our friends from Wicklow were also back for the final day. There were of course many other friends there, all of whom helped make it a truly memorable finishing experience. All of our title sponsors were represented and Brian Murnane the chairman of the Irish Autism Action opened proceedings, thanking them all.

I had about 25 friends who were all about to break their marathon duck and fulfil their goals. One friend in particular, Gerry Mulligan, had registered seven months earlier as an early 50th birthday present to himself. He would later cross the line having received some motivational assistance from another close friend John 'Thunder' Kane. John provided some help en route to Gerry when his spirits started to wane, joining him for seven miles fully clothed in jeans and shoes. Such amazing team spirit summed up a very memorable day.

So many other familiar faces were in the town park that morning. Just months before it had received an extensive makeover, and now it formed a fitting backdrop. There for us were Charmaine Kenny, the 2009 Rose of Tralee, a lady with proud Mullingar connections. Charmaine had run in Kildare and was now back to officially start proceedings. Also togged out again was Johnny Donnelly who was running his third marathon with us and Ryanair's CEO Michael O'Leary, who, true to his word, turned up, entertained everyone and then ran a 1:41:10 half-marathon.

It was such a family occasion for Ken and I. Indeed a close friend, Brian Ivory, together with Pat McDermott and my brother and sister Tom and Katherine had done immense work to ensure the final leg would be a success. The Midland Triathlon Club helped set up the marquee and the Mullingar's Lakeside Wheelers cycling club had organised all of the days marshals.

At 10:40am we set off, 40 minutes late, but nobody cared.

KEN: *I have many memories from this month that will last me a lifetime. One of these is the sight of all the runners who followed Gerry and I out of the town park today. Seeing so many people running because of this event, because they believed in the cause, or because they were in some way spurred on by what Gerry and I were trying to do has been hugely humbling.*

Over the last 18 months of planning we never could have imagined that we would have been supported by so many people throughout the country. As I often mentioned before our run each day, without the support of fellow runners, those 26.2 miles would seem a lot longer. Knowing that people have trained for months to be a part of this gave us a huge boost each morning. Even if runners weren't by our shoulder, the thought of a fellow runner or walker being on the course at the same time added to our determination to finish each day.

But the emotions didn't stop there. All month we have been witness to fantastic feats of achievement by fellow runners. To see the pride in people's faces as they crossed the line, despite the pain and tears, was a wonderful sight to behold. Runners and walkers of all ages, abilities and sizes exhibited huge determination each day in their quest to finish their first half or full marathon. Gerry and I feel privileged to have witnessed this.

If anyone disliked the route, I would have had to take personal responsibility. I had chosen the routing two years before. It was the first course I had thought about. Together with a friend, Murty Hanly who was our route co-ordinator for Mullingar, we tweaked and played around with my initial idea, to ensure all safety concerns were met.

I knew the route blindfolded. The first three miles along the banks of the Royal Canal were part of my own training territory. At the six mile point we entered the Belvedere Estate and Gardens. This is a beautiful old estate built in 1740 for Robert Rochford. When Sir Edmund Hillary conquered Mount Everest he sent two telegrams announcing his conquest to the world. One was to Buckingham Palace. The second was to the owner of Belvedere House, Charles Kenneth-Howard Bury, a renowned Everest explorer and close friend of Hillary's.

Our own expedition was now also nearing a close. Belvedere is somewhere I consider home. Not because I live there - I wish. Both Ken and I do live close by. In fact Ken's family home was just a few hundred metres from the main house itself. It is also a happy training ground for my local running club, the Mullingar Harriers, as well as the location for many a triathlon organised by the Midland Triathlon Club, a club of which I am a very proud member. Thus I know every inch of its routes and trails.

Murty and I had conspired to bring Belvedere into the routing. I was keen to showcase its stunning grounds to all our runners. Adding to the atmosphere that day was the fact that the long avenue leading to the main house had to be negotiated twice over a 10 minute period. This meant that as runners were entering the estate they were meeting fellow runners who were making their way back out again. It ensured a camaraderie and rapport between athletes, all enjoying the same experience, although some post race comments about the severity of the climb in Belvedere had me apologising to one or two.

Neither Ken nor I have memories of any mental or physical challenge on our final marathon. That is probably because we were working on high adrenalin. It was almost as if today was a 'cool down' run, albeit a long one at that.

My stomach had only been filled with two slices of dry toast.

Adrenalin and a few bananas would provide the remaining ingredients. I felt a sense of joy and pride for the efforts that everyone involved in this event had brought - the crew, the backroom team, the volunteers and all of the 1,100 runners, walkers and joggers.

Ken and I spent the day within 50 metres of each other at all times, keen to ensure we crossed the finish line together. We had soldiered and toiled at piecing this entire challenge together for a solid 12 months. Like every other day, we tried to talk to as many runners as possible keen to support them and to hear their story of why they were there. It was a little different on this final run because both Ken and I knew everyone.

The first 13 miles went by in a flash. Coming into the town park at the end of the first lap, Ken dashed across the road. I looked on to see why.

KEN: *Just before entering the park for the last 100 metres of lap one I heard my father calling me over to the roadside. And there, sitting on a chair outside her house and surrounded by family, was my 87-year-old granny. Having not seen her in a month, it was a joy to see her looking well and smiling as I robbed a quick hug. Trotting into the park just after this, I discovered one thing. Although I consider myself a bit of a multi-tasker there is a set of activities that I can't do at the same time; run and cry. For if I could, I would have been a bumbling mess right then. Thankfully running had to take precedence.*

We turned in a little over two hours. I am not certain, because we hardly cared. Now we had only one final loop of 13 miles remaining. A number of people joined us at this point to run the second half. The second half was a bit of a blur and it seemed to pass in an instant. We spent the following two hours or so chatting to family and friends, swapping stories and enjoying being back on our old training routes and savouring the last few miles.

As we neared the park we passed a friend, Trish Finnerty. I was surprised to see her as she had only signed up for a half-marathon and we were nearing the four hour mark. Trish was a very good runner but was more a five or 10 km specialist. That night she sent Ken and I a text.

"Lads, I said I would never ever run a marathon, but you two inspired me. Thanks for that."

With about 500 metres to go, we entered the town park and were joined by about 15 children. Among them were nieces Rebecca, Caoimhe and Lucy as well as nephews, Mark, Andrew, Gerry and Adam. Also there to greet us was young James Murphy and his brothers and sisters, whom we had last met in Sligo. Ken and I were thrilled to have them all there. Hopefully they would enjoy the finish as much as we would.

As we neared what we thought was the finish line, I spotted a couple of hundred people.

"Great," I thought, what a turnout. Ken and I momentarily stopped, thinking this was the finish.

Just then someone shouted from the crowd.

"Keep going!"

"Where to?" I thought to myself.

It was then that I took a look to my right and all I could see was an avenue of people either side of us. The distance to the end of the crowd looked perhaps 100 metres or so at first glance.

The further we ran the larger the crowd became. When that first 100 metres was negotiated there was a slight turn. Our visibility to wherever the finish line was actually located was blocked by the spectators closest to us. It was then I realised that the finish line had been moved to the main entrance of the town park, a further 100 metres. We had already passed the 26.2 mile mark metres earlier, but we didn't care.

We were stunned as an estimated 1,000 people cheered, screamed and yelled their support. What a truly humbling and joyous experience. Ninety seconds after we had thought we had finished, we still had 50 metres to negotiate. The noise was wonderfully deafening and we tried to savour as much as possible, the final steps of our 32 marathons, 838 miles journey.

Finally we finished, crossing the line in 4:08. For the next few minutes we enjoyed utter bedlam. Phones recorded, videos played, film crew taped and cameras clicked in huge numbers. Several photographers and journalists had come from all the main newspapers to capture the finish. Hastily arranged interviews with the three main broadsheets were carried out en route back to the start area where everyone was gathering.

Shortly after things had calmed down somewhat, Ken and I went to the marquee, keen to thank our fellow runners and physios for their support. As I entered, I surveyed all around me. It was like a scene from the US comedy show 'Mash'. Fifteen or so stretchers all filled with runners enjoying a well-earned, post-race massage. There I saw so many familiar faces including Katherine Surgenor, Gerry Mulligan, Derek Newcome, Trish Finnerty, Gerry Kiernan, Louise and Cliff Flynn, Andy Royle, Ian Cunningham, Michelle O'Halloran, Matt Glennon and JP O'Brien, to name but a few. Ken and I were still on the adrenalin rush, having no ill-effects thankfully from the run and we were keen to try to have a quick word to thank everyone. I also took the opportunity to eat a specially prepared bowl of potatoes and chicken broth. I was happy now to risk eating something more solid than a banana. I was starving.

That night a celebration attended by several hundred people was held in the Greville Arms Hotel. We felt truly grateful to everyone who turned up. It was too early perhaps for the feeling of accomplishment to sink in but it wasn't far away. I still wasn't feeling 100 per cent, so shortly before midnight Jacinta and I quietly slipped away. As we exited, Ken's father Paddy was giving a rendition of 'Old Man River' to a willing audience. A career in showbiz awaits, perhaps. I wonder would he have me on his crew?

The next morning our event made all of the national papers. It was a surreal experience to see our faces make front page news on both The Irish Times and The Irish Examiner.

Over breakfast we were informed by family members that RTE Radio One, 2FM, the Today FM Breakfast programme and the Ray D'Arcy Show had all mentioned our achievements. That morning we did an interview with a number of radio stations. A clearly delighted

Claire Byrne from the Breakfast Show on Newstalk rang us just before 8am to congratulate us.

"I'm delighted that Gerry and Ken are still standing," she told her listeners. "It looked at times as if you might not make it Ken, but you kept going through that injury you suffered. Can you tell us about that?"

Gosh! That brought back some memories. It reminded us from where we had come over three weeks before, down in Cork and Kerry. Too often we forget the hard work, the tough days, the extra efforts that we have to reach to achieve success with anything in life. Those days should perhaps be remembered and celebrated, for it's on such occasions that we define our character. They certainly made Ken realise just how strong an individual he was. His ability to triumph over the massive odds that were stacked against him was astonishing to witness and I use these pages to salute him. I could only hope I would have the same ability to overcome such odds.

The three goals Ken and I had written down at the very beginning of the challenge a year before, were firstly to run 32 marathons in 32 days, secondly to get over 1,000 people to run with us and thirdly to raise a hefty six-figure sum for charity. All goals had been reached and in some cases exceeded and so many people were responsible for that, not just Ken and I. In total over 2,500 people had played a part whether directly or indirectly.

That morning was spent chilling with the crew as well as family and friends. Slowly but surely as the day progressed the feeling of accomplishment started to kick in. If nothing else, it was the first day in almost five weeks that we did not have to run a marathon.

One day's rest might do no harm but the next day we both felt it important to get back running again. To stop now for any lengthy period might have a negative effect on our bodies. We simply could not stop, rather over the following month a gradual decrease in mileage would have to done.

It was a wonderful event and one we were both grateful to have the good fortune to start and to finish. As we said on day one:

"Every time we run, we feel blessed to have the health to do so."

We never forgot that.

ANOTHER DAY

MONDAY 25TH OCTOBER, 2010

LESS than three months later I was back at the scene of a former memorable life experience on Foster Avenue. I was at mile 21 of the 2010 Dublin City Marathon. Since we ran the last of the 32 marathons on 2nd August, life has settled back down now. I had run just one marathon since, the Longford marathon on the 19th August.

In the weeks after the challenge finished, I waited for some mental weakness to invade me. People told me it would come and I expected it to some degree. It would have been a natural reaction after what had been a roller-coaster adventure for 12 months or more. But the reality was it never came. Perhaps the physical fitness level I attained had filtered into my mental state. I am sure it did.

Every day since we finished I have talked about the marathons to someone. Thankfully it appears to have resonated and intrigued everyone I met. It came up in conversation every day and I loved talking about it. It did take a week or two to settle back into normal life, that much is true. The overriding feeling was one of quiet satisfaction as well as significant relief that we had pulled it off.

On reflection there was just one major moment during the 32 when I really began to feel a stark burden of extra responsibility. That was on day nine when we were travelling from Killarney to Limerick. Ken's injury woes were at their highest that day. We were all exhausted on that journey and it looked distinctly possible that Ken might not be able to continue. As we travelled in darkness towards the outskirts of Limerick, the rain poured onto the windscreen adding to my already fragile disposition.

Morale was plummeting. If Ken had to stop, all the pressure to continue would have been on my shoulders. That would have weighed very heavily. That's when I really felt it. Ken and I were in this together and there was some comfort in that for both of us. Thankfully it never happened. Now post-challenge we were experiencing feelings of relief that we had pulled it off. An opportunity and a time to reflect.

Writing this book has been rewarding because it has allowed me to record the experience in the tiniest of detail. I kept an audio diary every night. I am glad I did.

At the end of August I bumped into a close pal, JP O'Brien.

"You doing Dublin this year?" He was referring to the Dublin City Marathon.

"Dunno," I replied. I wasn't being evasive. I hadn't really thought much about it.

"A few of us are about to start ramping up our training next week," he explained. He told me their target time. "Any interest in joining us?"

"Sure," I agreed. I love having goals and the target time he mentioned, if I could achieve it, would provide a personal best. If nothing else, it would ensure my fitness continued. It would get me back training hard again. I had an easy four weeks or so but I felt like I knew my body was in good shape and it would be a shame not to at least maintain this.

We started training in the first week in September. My new running companions were old friends and had actually been training for several months. I had had a quiet month running perhaps four times a week, never more than five or six miles. The Longford marathon was an exception.

A week after we had run the final marathon, Ken was diagnosed with a stress fracture at the base of the left ankle. His physio Aidan Woods recommended a period of rest. As it transpired it would be February before Ken could safely return to running, however it was not all bad news. Mountain biking instead became his sporting passion over those winter months.

For six weeks we trained hard. Each week had a tempo and a speed session. It was completely different training than for the 32 marathons. That had no speed work in its strategy. This was different. I loved it. Matt Glennon was our running coach. He is hard as nails when focussed on a goal and is an animal for tough sessions. Glennon, a farmer and father of nine is thoroughly modest and unassuming but has great running knowledge in his brain. Coupled with that, he lives for running. We have much in common. Another friend, Mary Scully joined us for the sessions in preparation for her winter cross country race season.

Foster Avenue was a place I had paid homage to before. You will recall my encounter at this location on the Dublin Marathon route from 2007. There, an elderly man had reminded me to simply "put one foot in front of the other" to achieve any goal.

Now it's the 2010 Dublin City marathon and it's a little after midday. There were four of us in the group. Aidan Gorry, Mark Carroll, Matt Glennon and myself. Glennon was in charge. He was our pacemaker. He has done it all before. We were bang on schedule.

At the 21-mile mark, Aidan Gorry, who had run two marathons with Ken and I back in July, faltered a little. Our target finishing time was challenging to all of us. An average of 6:50 per mile or less was the benchmark. Gorry asked around the group for an energy gel as he needed food. Nobody had any but I informed him there was a food station just minutes away. This news perked up his six-foot frame which had started to weaken.

Aidan dropped off a little to take on the nourishment but there would be no room for sentiment now. Despite the close camaraderie, in reality, each man was on his own. We shouted encouragement to each other but ultimately any pain had to be borne alone, any reserves must be self-ignited. We were all on a mission. We have soldiered for over two-and-a-half hours. This was when the work began.

At the UCD flyover, Mark and Matt pulled ahead of me and opened a 50-metre gap but I didn't mind. We had only about four miles to run. Mark is about 10 years my junior and Glennon has a personal best that is way ahead of mine. I knew my pace was fine. I was on schedule. If I held this speed I would beat the target by over a minute.

As we hit 24 miles, Carroll started to fall back towards me and moments later I passed him, offering encouragement as we met. He was still in a good place mentally and was determined to dig as deep as was required. That much was still obvious.

As I approached Pearse Street I was still on target. It was a fantastic feeling. The reality was that I felt very strong. I had no pain, just strength. Yes, I was working but I was in a comfortable fourth gear. The engine was not overheating unlike my maiden experience a number of years before. Now it almost felt like cheating. I was savouring every metre, every second. I could up the pace a fraction if needed but that would have been silly. That might only bring injury. Isn't that what happened in 2008? A lesson learned. Unless a mad priest runs out from the crowd like in the Athens Olympics and knocked me over, I would achieve my goal.

With 300 yards to go, I spotted Dor and Jacinta on Nassau Street. They screamed encouragement. The crowds once again were five or six deep on both sides. It's just like the old days. Another amazing memory to store. How my cup overflowed that year.

Matt Glennon finished 11 seconds ahead of me and Mark Carroll 51 seconds behind. All of us have accomplished our goal. I hit my watch to freeze the time. I knew I had done it. The only question was by how much. I gazed down to savour the satisfaction.

2:58:04.

A new PB by almost 19 minutes and my first sub-three-hour marathon.

I joined my comrades in a celebratory embrace, all three of us. Moments later we were four, joined by an exhausted but exhilarated Aidan Gorry as he crossed the line in 2:59:37. Now that's cutting it fine. He too had dipped under the 180-minute barrier for 26.2 miles, beating it by just 23 seconds.

You will recall the Muhammad Ali quote I mentioned in an earlier chapter when I was training for the Double Ironman attempt.

'The fight is won or lost far away from witnesses - behind the lines, in the gym, and out there on the road, long before I dance under those lights." Ali would be proud of Aidan. He had danced under all the lights in training. He never missed a session; 2:59:37 was his reward.

JP, the original founder of this small grouping, suffered an injury midway, finishing in 3:25:20. He was fit enough but events conspired against him on this occasion. He will return to triumph this goal another day.

THE LIVING WORD

The past 16 years has been educating, exhilarating, challenging and hugely rewarding. I feel I am such a better person both physically and mentally. I remember when I qualified from a two-year course in UCD in 1999, I told someone that I was finished with learning. Gosh, that was naive. I had been learning every day to this, and I have been learning every day since.

Some people think I'm mad for doing what I do. I respect their opinion but I also disagree. It rocks my boat. It's not for everyone and that's fine. Different things for different people. Surely life is about two things, being happy in ourselves and helping others. Well, I now have a mind full of wonderful memories but I still have a lot of vacant space in my head so I intend doing much more in the future. Doctor Wayne W. Dyer has a saying in his book "10 Secrets For Success And Inner Peace." He says, *'Don't die with your music still in you.'*

I feel I am living my life actively and consciously. These are important words. For me running 32 Marathons was 'active living'. Whilst doing it, I tried to be always conscious of the fact that I was each day living my dream. That is how I try to live now. I am happy and have great clarity in my mind. I am lucky to be experiencing this. Life, I feel, is not next week. It is today. Why not live every day to its fullest? In my early twenties when I had no ambition and no exercise routine in my life, one day drifted into the next, as did the weeks, months and years. Not anymore. Now I am out *living*.

Sure, I have tough days, we all do. There is the odd day when running, or at least the thought of it, can be a chore. I don't think I ever came back from a workout, however, not feeling better than when I left. My business too has certainly tested me to the limits. It has changed dramatically and is completely unrecognisable from even two years ago. I realise though that I can admit that the business that I worked in for 65 to 70 hours a week to build up has disappeared and that was unfortunate. Thankfully, I have since managed to open new doors, one of which was where I have fulfilled a lifetime ambition of writing a book. I estimated recently that I have spent over 1,100 hours typing these words. It was actually a labour of love. There was the odd day when my brain was frazzled and was full of nothing. You might argue it was like that for the full 1,100 hours!

New opportunities have arrived at my doorstep. I have now embarked on a new career path. It has a few modules, all with one central theme. In some ways it has happened by accident and in others I have made it happen. I can now thankfully count myself as an author. I have gone back to college and am now qualified as a fitness instructor. Were my old business to have continued, perhaps I would never have got around to that.

Since the 32 Marathons I have been asked to address a multitude of groups including businesses, sports groups and secondary schools on goal-setting and the lessons we learned along the way. That requires that I speak in public. Thank goodness I moved out of that comfort zone all those years ago. Yes, it still scares me a little but it doesn't stop me doing it.

In the four months following the marathon challenge I estimate that I addressed over 3,000 people. Along with followers of our challenge, many people who attended our talks have told me they were inspired by our story and by watching the event unfold. Such kind words have encouraged me to develop our experiences into a seminar that can be easily adapted to any theme or audience, whether that is secondary school students, private companies or sports teams. The strategies, the planning, the vision and the sacrifices we made to achieve the goal of running 32 Marathons in as many days can be applied to achieve any goal.

If you have an idea that you subsequently decide has become a goal, then with the right belief and vision, a positive mindset and simply by formulating a plan, the rest usually just takes action. It really is that straightforward. To say it takes more is to begin to complicate matters. I think about this lesson every day now because every day I have goals. Some easy, some hard and some very challenging. The principle of how to achieve them never changes.

I am now combining this fitness and knowledge of the power of self-belief with a third approach, that of Life, Executive and Peak

Performance Coaching where I assist people in unlocking their own true potential whether in a business, academic or sporting environment. I am in the early stages but it is immensely rewarding and I am delighted to report I am building up a solid client base of individuals and companies.

To finish off, a final mention as I set sail towards the epilogue. To my parents, my greatest teachers and inspirers, Jacinta, my brother and sisters, to Ken, to all of our crew, to the 1,050 marshals and volunteers and to the 1,100 plus who ran, a big thank you. Directly or indirectly we were helped by approximately 2,500 people. A sincere thanks to one and all. The 32 Marathons demonstrated to me just how much we can all help and inspire each other.

EPILOGUE

SALTA is a city 777 miles north west of Buenos Aires, the capital of Argentina. Perhaps if I share a story about something that happened there, you will understand how it is that my mind works.

It was a mid-December day in 2006, high summer in Argentina with the temperature hovering in the mid-90s. An Irishman I know was on holidays there. Being Irish and having limited knowledge of this northern city, Michael felt it prudent to call into the travel agents located adjacent to his hotel.

"Ola Senor," he said walking in the door. "Michael," he said in an attempt at a local accent and pointing to himself.

"Como esta?" (How are you?)

That was the limit of his Spanish.

He was there to enquire about sights to see in the local area. The travel agent recommended a lake 42 miles outside of the city. It would offer a stunning landscape surrounded by a low range mountainous area, one well worth making the effort to visit. Even better, an opportunity to share a taxi with a Chilean family was right outside the door.

"Great," thought Michael. An opportunity not to be passed up.

Into the people carrier he climbed, introducing himself to the Chilean family as he did so. They were four in number, a husband and his wife, their son and daughter. They were on a pilgrimage to celebrate the life of the father's brother who had died a week previously. It was custom apparently in these parts for a family to go away and reminisce about a recently departed loved one in such fashion.

Ninety minutes later they arrived at the lake. It was huge, 25 miles wide and six miles across. On reaching their destination they spotted a large bridge which jutted across the neck of this vast expanse of water.

After the humid and cramped environment of the previous hour-and-a-half they were all keen to get some fresh air. As he stretched his legs, Michael noticed some activity at the edge of the bridge, perhaps 300 metres from where he stood. All five proceeded inquisitively. As they neared the commotion, they spotted the proprietor of the 'bungee jump facility'.

"He looked like Mick Jagger," Michael told his family weeks later.

"Long straggly hair, shadowing a rugged face."

Michael had never seen a bungee jump up close before and he was fascinated. Just as they reached the edge, a man in his early 20s was getting ready to plunge into the depths. Michael peered over the barrier and surmised that the lake was perhaps 200 feet or more below.

"Not for the faint-hearted," he thought to himself.

At the edge beside him were two other backpackers, both ladies in their 40s. He introduced himself and learned that one of them, Lauro, an Argentinean teacher was next in the queue to jump.

Michael went back to his Chilean friends and they informed him that Claudio, their son had decided that he too would take the plunge.

"To hell with it," thought Michael. "If they are jumping, then so am I."

The parents, the daughter and Lauro's fellow backpacker seemed delighted that they had not been talked into participating and they settled in to watch the spectacle unfold.

Lauro went first. Within seconds she disappeared over the edge and with that 17-year-old Claudio moved forward. After five minutes or so and once Lauro was safely in the boat, 200 feet below, Claudio edged his way towards the abyss. After what seemed like an eternity he jumped, screaming as he descended, his voice getting quieter as he travelled further away from the launch pad. His family looked on with a mixture of fear and pride.

Now it was Michael's turn. When he shared this story with his family back in Ireland weeks later, they were stunned.

"What possessed you?" they enquired.

"Ah sure, isn't life worth living? It was 200 feet of a drop but the water looked deep so I knew it would break my fall if the rope snapped."

Once safely strapped in, Michael listened to the Mick Jagger look-alike giving him a pep talk on what to do. The non-verbal demonstration would have to suffice. Neither spoke each other's language.

With that he started walking.

He would later narrate. "If I thought about it, I wouldn't have done it. I just walked forward and kept walking, until I was walking on air."

The Michael in this story is my dad, Michael Duffy.

On the day he did this bungee jump, he was 70 years old.

THE WRITE STUFF

THE days and weeks after we finished the 32 Marathons were filled with lovely comments, messages, letters and emails from a multitude. In addition we received thousands more along the way.

The power of words is immense. Ken and I derived great strength from them. To know that so many people were following our journey, and rooting for us to succeed, that so many were moved to help in a variety of ways as a result, was hugely inspiring to us. I have included just a small sample of the thousands of messages, letters, emails and texts we received. I hope you enjoy reading these as much as we appreciated receiving them.

Following you on the net all the way. You guys are great.
Eamonn Coghlan, former World 5,000 metre champion

Heh Duffy, heard the latest on your exploits. These are the days when all the training will prove invaluable. Just remember that everyone and I mean everyone is rooting for you. So hang in there and make us all proud, you b****** (unprintable). Now I'm off to get a breakfast roll.
Martin O'Donnell, a friend from home

Wishing you the best of luck and health etc over the coming weeks. You and Ken are an inspiration to us all. Talk to you after you have finished and recovered.
Lisa Treacy (aka Gloria Gaynor from the Karaoke Bar in Tokyo)

I'm gobsmacked, no words to describe what you are both doing.
Anne Kennedy (Wicklow runner)

Hi Gerry and Ken. You are both great ambassadors for Mullingar. Fantastic to get the updates on Facebook. See you on the 15th in my home county of Kildare.
Louise McCartan

Well done, you are both mighty men. Tommy Carr and myself are coming to see you run tomorrow.
Bernard Flynn, ex-Meath footballer.

Gerry, you and Ken are in my thoughts every day from 10am till 3. Keep strong and keep focusing on one day at a time. Your body is guided by your mind and your mind is the one with the strongest and the one with the greatest belief. I ran 40 km this week because of you. See you in Roscommon.
James Martin, a friend, a business mentor and a coach

Just read the blog. Superb! Noeleen should be canonised!
Andrew Fay, a friend from home, sent after Limerick Marathon

Just after reading about days nine and 10. Ken is some warrior. I am amazed at his ability to keep going. He is an inspiration to the world. Glad to see day 11 sees him back on form. What a legend.
Garret Murphy

Well done to ye both. 10 down, 22 to go! Ye must be made of Iron.
Deirdre Fallon

I'm sure you are both experiencing an amazing journey the last two weeks. A little note of sunshine for your journey. 'What sunshine is to flowers, smiles are to humanity.' You and Ken keep smiling. You have helped so many people. See you in Roscommon.
Breda Daly

Just reading your blog. Incredible what you guys are doing. Will definitely join you near the end, for a half marathon. Keep it up. Magnificent!
Noel Mason

It was a pleasure to be involved in such an historic event. Everyone who helped really enjoyed the day. You guys have a great crew with you. Regards to them all . It's hard for me to comprehend that you have another one done today.
Finbarr Feely, Route Co-Ordinator, Roscommon

Gerry, how was today? You guys are past the half way mark now. You both know you will achieve your goal. You have great people working with you. Enjoy every moment.
Alan Logue, Route Co-Ordinator in Clare

Thinking of ye this morning. Hope ye are well. Heard ye did a great time again today. Such admiration for you both. Great to catch up yesterday. Good luck tomorrow. Best wishes, Rachel McInerney.
Rachel's husband, Declan, ran his first ever marathon with us in Clare

Well Gerry, hope all went well today. It will be a remarkable achievement when you finish. If I can help in any way let me know.
Ross Munnelly, Laois county footballer

Fantastic. I am amazed more every day.
Michelle Sherwood (sent after Laois marathon)

Another amazing day. You guys are such an inspiration. I am so glad I am a part of this wonderful event. See you both in a few weeks in Mullingar.
Helen Moran

Well done, K and G. You guys are awesome and an inspiration. Proud to know you, proud to sponsor you and proud to support the IAA.
Stuart Kelly, Director of 'Just Mobile'

Well done, lads, did ye catch them yet? The lads that stole your sanity!
Fidelma Lennon

So many people behind ye lads. Hope you're ok Ken and start to get stronger once more. Rest up tonight and looking forward to tomorrow's update.
Tammy McCarthy (Sent on day 15 Offaly)

Keep in there Ken. It's a massive achievement to be able to do a marathon with an injury.
Ard Righ McCormaic (sent after Offaly marathon)

Ger, hope you are in bed asleep. Thinking of you both. You had a tough day today but put it behind you. Things will get better. We think the world of you. Just take it one day at a time. Love to Saint Jacinta!
My mum, sent the night we finished Offaly marathon

Did a half with ye in Galway yesterday. Didn't appreciate the extent of what you guys are doing. Congrats.
Declan Mulderry

I may have cursed you on the second lap but I am really grateful to be a part of this event. I never imagined it would be so tough. Makes it all the sweeter. A sporting highlight for me.
Jarlath Mahon, crew member from the Double Ironman event. Sent the night he ran his first marathon in Galway

I have everyone at work talking about you and wishing you well. They ask me every day how you are getting on so I give them an update. They all sponsored me so I am delighted to spread the word if it's helping the charities. I can't wait to run with you on Sunday in Mayo.
Lucy Foley (a participant)

Thinking of you every day. You are doing something incredible. Wish I could be there but Juliana is now the boss.
My brother Tom sent midway through our challenge. Juliana is his new baby daughter who was born two days before we started

Serious going today. Fair play, amazing stuff. Great to see Ken back strong again and alongside you. Pretty disappointed I won't be there on the last day. Will be following you online though. All the adjectives have been used, I'm just in awe.
Jamie Andrews my 17-year-old godson, (day of Donegal marathon)

Congratulations on finishing number 22 today. Every day I wake up and wonder how you keep going.
Brian Murnane, Chairman Irish Autism Action

Can't believe I made it through today. If you had told me a year ago that I would be running a marathon, I would have laughed at you. Tell Jacinta well done again from me. Good luck for the last six. See you Monday.
Carly Ferguson, Northern Ireland crew member who completed her first marathon on Day 25

Ken, a pleasure to run with you today and as for Gerry, you're having a laugh! Thanks for the big welcome. I know ye do it every day but it's very obvious you really appreciate the support of your fellow runners and there was a great feel about the today. Thanks to the physio who sorted out me old legs. Go on ye pair of good things!
Martin Moore (Day 29 Meath)

Bravo, bravo, enjoy your last few jogs. People here in Spain are talking about you and your incredible undertaking. We are proudly wearing our 32 Marathon t-shirts. Our thoughts are with you both this final weekend. Run well, run safe and then enjoy the party.
Amanda Andrews

After running my first marathon with ye yesterday, I now appreciate how tough one can be, but 29 consecutively and sub four hours... incredible!
Barry Gorham

The end is very near. Amazing, incredible accomplishment. Really hope for the best over the long weekend".
Terri Kruschkc, Lite FM Cork

On your final night before the end, I just want to say what you have done for autism in Ireland and runners alike is truly inspirational. It has given the country a great lift through the story of goodwill and also what is possible for any person in Ireland. Well done and fair play. Two great men with great hearts and humble to the end. Enjoy tomorrow men and sleep tight.
Johnny Donnelly, ex-drummer with the Sawdoctors, sent the night before the last marathon

Gerry, by doing a half-marathon, I now fully appreciate what it takes to complete a full one never mind 32 in a row! A great achievement for you and Ken, while also raising awareness of autism. If I drink any more water I think I'll drown!
Jude Lagan, one of the sponsors who also ran a half-marathon on the final day

We are all so proud of you. What an amazing feat you have accomplished, not just running 32 marathons in as many days, but the organisation of an event of this magnitude and the million and one details it required, takes some doing. Take a bow!
Ashling Kiernan

I was stopped at traffic lights when a runner passed the car and my son shouts. 'Is that Gerry?' Even three-year-olds are getting into this.
Sharon Foy

A lump came to my throat and my eyes welled up reading the 'Westmeath' blog. I think on days that I might not be feeling as good as others I will read that blog and feel automatically better, stronger, positive, hopeful, excited and proud. That's the gift I got from today.
Katherine Surgenor (Westmeath participant)

32 marathons in 32 days, 1,100 people with you, raise half a million in a recession and write a final blog that has tears streaming down my face.
Lucy Foley (Lucy ran two marathons with us)

Well done lads. Such an achievement. Tears in my eyes reading the final blog. Ran my first half marathon with you on Monday and it was such an honour. You don't realise how much you have done for people with autism.
Lisa Kiernan

Heh, congrats to you both and the team that helped you to do this. We embrace you from Argentina.
Nerina and Santiago Noonan

I've spent the last few years reading about special heroes who take on unbelievable tasks and their different motives for doing so and I have always aspired to be like those men. Not afraid, not backing down and not motivated by sponsor or glory. I never thought I would be in a position to play a part in one of these adventures until now. Thank you for being an inspiration. God Bless.
Stuart McChesney, our event photographer who was once told he would never walk again but is now an Ultra marathon runner

Congrats. What about 50 in the 50 states of America next year?!
Rory Connaughton (sent from Philadelphia)

Hey Gerry, a very big congrats to you and Ken. Fantastic stuff.
Richard Donovan. World record holder for running seven marathons in seven continents in just six days

Getting withdrawal symptoms' already and the gas thing is I didn't even run!
Emma McCabe-Byrne

I am en route from Spain to France and I just got my hands on a copy of the *Irish Independent*. Couldn't believe it when I saw your ugly mug on page 5. Huge congrats to you both.
Pearse Keller

Hi Gerry, I hope you and Ken are feeling well today. Enjoy your day off. I really enjoyed yesterday. Thanks a million.
Charmaine Kenny, 2009 Rose of Tralee

Loved every minute of the challenge. To think I could not run 800 metres a year ago and I have now signed up for the Dublin City Marathon next year. Thanks to you guys, I have found a new passion in my life and I'm loving it.
Linda Murray

I am just looking at your times for the marathons. You are an inspiration to many of us. Congrats to you both on a wonderful achievement.
Pauline Curley, Olympic marathon runner, Beijing 2008

It was a privilege and an honour to be able to support you. I send you my renewed congratulations and my unending admiration.
Michael O'Leary, CEO Ryanair

APPENDIX